Education and Analog Role-Playing Games

Education and Analog Role-Playing Games: TeachRPG – Tabletop Role-Playing Games in the Classroom, Volume II brings together a diverse group of educators and scholars who are using tabletop role-playing games (RPGs) in their classrooms to foster deeper engagement, build community, and support transformative learning. While educational games are increasingly available, many are created by designers without classroom experience or emphasize gamification through points and badges rather than the creation of immersive, gameful environments tied to real learning outcomes.

This volume fills a critical gap by centering the voices of practitioner-scholar educators who adapt RPGs to fit their unique disciplines, institutions, and student needs. Contributors share how these games enhance cognitive and affective learning, support marginalized students, and offer meaningful pedagogical opportunities for both instructors and learners. Striking a balance between practical strategies, empirical insight, and personal narrative, *Teach RPG* provides adaptable models for integrating analog RPGs into a wide range of classrooms. It moves beyond theory or anecdote to show how role-playing can be a rigorous, relational, and inclusive educational practice.

Susan Haarman, PhD, is Associate Director at Loyola University Chicago's Center for Engaged Learning, Teaching, and Scholarship. She facilitates the university's service-learning program and publishes on community-based learning. Her real love is her research on the capacity of tabletop role-playing games as formative tools for civic identity and imagination. She serves on the editorial board of the *International Journal of Role-Playing* and is also a professional improviser and a licensed therapist.

Education and Analog Role-Playing Games

TeachRPG – Tabletop Role-Playing Games in the Classroom, Volume II

Edited by
Susan Haarman

CRC Press
Taylor & Francis Group
Boca Raton London New York

CRC Press is an imprint of the
Taylor & Francis Group, an informa business

Designed cover image: Shutterstock

First edition published 2026
by CRC Press
2385 NW Executive Center Drive, Suite 320, Boca Raton FL 33431

and by CRC Press
4 Park Square, Milton Park, Abingdon, Oxon, OX14 4RN

CRC Press is an imprint of Taylor & Francis Group, LLC

ISBN: 9781041076162 (hbk)
ISBN: 9781041076148 (pbk)
ISBN: 9781003641384 (ebk)

DOI: 10.1201/9781003641384

Typeset in Minion
by codeMantra

Contents

Contributors

Justin Berry is an artist, educator, researcher, game designer, and writer whose work explores the intersection of virtual and real worlds with an emphasis on discovering individual agency in spaces constructed by others. He recently taught Tabletop Game Design at Quinnipiac University and was Core Faculty at the Yale Center for Collaborative Arts and Media from 2016 to 2022. He is now the Creative Producer and Project Director at the Yale Center for Immersive Technologies in Pediatrics. He was the principal investigator for the Blended Reality Project at the Yale Center for Collaborative Arts and Media for four years and chaired the 2019 IEEE Games, Entertainment, and Media conference. His recent talks include presenting on ways that tabletop role-playing games can help build communities at Games for Change in New York and Serious Play in Toronto.

Kristian A. Bjørkelo is an associate professor in journalism and communication at Nord University and Digital Culture at the University of Bergen. He was trained as a folklorist, and has researched internet culture and political extremism, before getting a PhD in games and transgressive aesthetics. He has 15 years of experience in teaching communication as a practical skill at the university level.

Aaron Brown served in the Air Force as a pilot and instructor for over 20 years before completing his Master of Science for Teaching degree at Le Moyne College in May 2024. He recently earned his New York State Teacher Certification in Childhood Education

(Grades 1–6) and Special Education. His goal is to use strategies based on popular culture, especially gaming, to help students with disabilities progress in academic and social emotional skills. He began a position as a Grade 5 classroom teacher in DeRuyter School District in fall 2024.

Maryanne Cullinan is a middle school teacher in NH, an RPG researcher, a PhD student at Lesley University, and a mom of four teens and tweens. She studies the use of RPGs as pedagogy in the middle school classroom, especially for non-traditional learners. Maryanne's most recent published article, "Surveying the Perspectives of Middle and High School Educators Who Use Role-playing Games as Pedagogy", can be found in the *International Journal of Role-Playing*, Issue 15. You can find more about her work at her website: www.culliopescauldron.com, and at www.tabletopedu.org.

Jennifer Genova teaches seventh grade (11- to 12-year olds) History and Social Studies at the Woodbury School in Salem, New Hampshire, USA. She received an MA in Teaching Secondary History from Brandeis University in 2009 and an MEd in teacher leadership from Brandeis University in 2021. Her research interests include using principles of game design to create engaging curriculum materials for K-12 teachers as well as empowering teachers to design, implement, and evaluate non-traditional curriculum materials.

Hanne Grasmo is a doctoral researcher in game culture studies at Tampere University, a larp designer, and a teacher at high school and university levels. Her PhD research centers around role-play and emotions. Her focus areas are role-play design, democracy, inclusion, and transformative play. Grasmo holds an MA in Sociology and has additional background in theater. Her research profile can be found at https://gameresearchlab.tuni.fi/researchers/

Lobna Hassan is an associate professor (tenure-track) of sociotechnical transitions in services at Lappeenranta-Lahti University of Technology,

Finland. Dr. Hassan's interests include game accessibility, gamification, and inclusion of people with disabilities. Her work and publications can be found at http://lobnahassan.com

Cathy Leogrande is a professor in the Teacher Education Department of the Purcell School of Professional Studies at Le Moyne College, a Jesuit college in Syracuse, New York. Her teaching, research, and publications address issues of race, class, gender, and disability in texts, media, and fandom. Her focus is on preparing novice and veteran K-12 teachers to creatively use digital texts, media, comics and graphic novels, film, gamification, and other aspects of popular culture to teach content to all students in inclusive classrooms.

Keely Mohon-Doyle, PhD, is assistant professor of English and Director of First-Year Writing at Austin Peay State University. She holds a PhD in English Composition and Rhetoric from Miami University. Her research explores how institutional policies, particularly in higher education, are enacted in public spaces in order to identify potential rhetorical disconnects and areas for productive revision.

Caleb Probst is a qualitative researcher and game designer whose work explores new ways to teach concepts related to equity and social justice. He holds a PhD from the University of Wisconsin–Madison. Before entering academia, he worked as a professional actor, an elementary school teacher, and as the education director for a Chicago-based nonprofit. Caleb is an adoptive parent of twins, and he loves peanut butter and jelly sandwiches.

William Stratton lives near Essex, Vermont, in a very old house with two young children and a woman who transcends age, to whom he devotes his love and life. He mostly writes in his "free" time, which consists of the few hours everyone else is asleep. At SUNY Plattsburgh, he teaches writing, and at Champlain College, he teaches whatever classes the college has a need for at any given moment. He served as editor at the *Saranac Review* and has so far published two full-length collections of poetry as well as a few dozen individual pieces here and there. His RPG history dates back to 1989 when he discovered, after wandering into a tiny bookstore in Lake Placid, NY, *The Player's Handbook*, AD&D 2nd edition. Since then, he's taken to convincing the powers that be in academia that RPGs are a useful tool, to various levels of success.

Ahu Yolaç is assistant professor of Game Design at Lawrence Technological University and a multidisciplinary designer, game studies researcher, game designer, and gamer. She looks at video games as multidisciplinary spaces and explores ways to create opportunities for collaboration in and through games among multiple disciplines, players, designers, and game enthusiasts. As a gamer herself, she plays board games, tabletop RPG games, and video games.

Introduction

Susan Haarman

Tabletop role-playing games (tabletop RPGs) are no longer fringe curiosities in education. In classrooms across disciplines and institutional contexts, instructors are increasingly drawing on RPGs not just to spark engagement, but to foster creativity, deepen collaboration, and model new forms of meaning-making. Whether guiding students through exploring masculinity or using dice mechanics to teach rhetorical strategy, educators are leveraging the structure and spontaneity of games to reshape their teaching practices and their classrooms. They offer another different way of knowing.

This volume is not about proving that games can educate. That conversation is well underway and a previous volume in this series examines the pedagogy and theory that analog RPGs (Haarman, 2025). Instead, this collection asks: What happens when we bring RPGs into the classroom with pedagogical intention and critical reflection? How do we adapt, assess, and sustain game-based learning in diverse educational settings? And perhaps most importantly: What kinds of classrooms, relationships, and identities are possible when we treat play not as a gimmick, but as a generative mode of learning?

This is not about badges, leaderboards, or reskinning a course in fantasy tropes. It is about designing experiences that invite risk, require interdependence, and allow students to shape their own learning in dynamic and often surprising ways. Analog RPGs are embodiments of ludic pedagogy when it is understood as a form of learning that is playful, relational, affective, and epistemically expansive (Haarman, 2025; Lauricella and Edmunds, 2022). Rooted in improvisation, shared storytelling, and ethical decision-making, analog RPGs offer students opportunities not just to

DOI: 10.1201/9781003641384-1

absorb content but to inhabit ideas, build worlds, and reflect on their place within them. In an age of standardized testing, institutional constraint, and increasing student disengagement, ludic pedagogy offers a powerful alternative: one that treats play not as escapism, but as a generative site of meaning-making.

At the heart of this approach is not just the content students encounter, but the way they encounter it. The structure of tabletop RPGs requires players to co-create narratives, navigate uncertainty through dialogue, and share interpretive and ethical responsibility for the unfolding world. In doing so, RPGs model an important form of learning: collaborative authorship. When students play RPGs in the classroom, they are not merely participating in imaginative play, they are enacting a mode of knowledge production that is shared, situated, and dialogic. They become not only learners, but co-authors of the educational experience.

COLLABORATIVE AUTHORSHIP IN RPGS AND CLASSROOMS

Our classroom can become true homes for collaborative authorship—that is, spaces not merely for the transmission of knowledge, but for co-creation, identity exploration, and radical imagination. Drawing from Dariel Quiogue's influential essay "Role-Playing Games as Collaborative Fiction" (1998), tabletop RPGs are not simply solitary storytelling devices, but as shared creative enterprises in which players and game masters share the roles of author, editor, and audience. In this framing, mechanics and narrative tools are not just features of a system. They are the switches through which participants co-author the plot, steering its direction in real time. The game, like a good classroom, becomes a living, negotiated text, responsive to its participants' ideas, identities, and decisions.

Composition studies scholars Lynn W. Ede and Andrea A. Lunsford critically interrogated traditional conceptions of authorship in their influential essay "Collaboration and Concepts of Authorship" (1990). Drawing on empirical research and rhetorical theory, they argue that the dominant Western notion of the solitary, originary author is both historically contingent and pedagogically limiting. Instead, they advocate for a model of collaborative authorship, in which writing is understood as a social, dialogic process shaped by shared responsibility, joint decision-making, and distributed authority among participants. Their work challenges the "romantic" ideal of the autonomous writer, showing that much of what we consider individual authorship is in fact scaffolded by interaction—with editors, peers, audiences, and cultural context. In classroom settings, this model reframes group writing not as a compromise or threat to originality, but as a generative encounter through which students negotiate meaning together. Collaborative authorship, in Ede and Lunsford's framework, is not a dilution of voice but a reconfiguration of authorship as co-construction, where knowledge and expression emerge from dialogue, consensus, and even productive disagreement. This perspective resonates powerfully with learning environments grounded in RPGs, where participants build narrative and epistemic meaning together through shared invention.

This perspective resonates powerfully with learning environments grounded in RPGs, where participants jointly construct both narrative and epistemic meaning. The structure of gameplay, which requires collaboration, improvisation, and perspective-taking, mirrors the dynamics found in dialogic learning. As both metaphor and method, collaborative authorship highlights the pedagogical strength of tabletop RPGs. Learners don't merely consume knowledge—they write themselves into it, collectively shaping meaning through play and inquiry (González González, Starosky, and Dias Pereira, 2013).

This co-creative approach directly echoes the liberatory pedagogy of Paulo Freire (1970), who criticized the traditional "banking" model of education and advocated instead for a problem-posing pedagogy rooted in questioning, reflection, and transformation. In RPGs, players interpret clues, make strategic decisions, and face moral dilemmas not because an instructor dictates these actions, but because they are co-creating the narrative world. Freire would view this as education with students rather than about them. It creates a dialogic space where consciousness and meaning emerge through mutual engagement. Similarly, foundational work by Plass, Homer, and Kinzer (2015) argues that the pedagogical impact of game-based learning depends on cognitive, affective, motivational, and sociocultural engagement which helps explain why collaborative storytelling in RPGs proves so powerful. By blending imaginative play with meaningful social negotiation, RPGs activate multiple dimensions of learning in ways that traditional didactic or authoritarian methods often cannot.

Extending the dialogic frame further, RPGs also manifest Mikhail M. Bakhtin's (1981) concept of heteroglossia and the dialogic imagination, in which multiple voices coexist, interact, and evolve to form richer, more nuanced discourse. When players negotiate character motivations, develop story arcs, and resolve conflicts, they engage in polyphony, or a chorus of perspectives that enrich the collective narrative. This mirrors the hallmark of dialogic classrooms, where knowledge emerges through equitable exchange and co-construction rather than unilateral didactic instruction. As scholars like Rupert Wegerif (2008) and Robin Alexander (2018) argue, dialogic education thrives when learners build on each other's ideas, testing and refining understanding through structured yet open discourse.

The collaborative authorship of tabletop RPGs embodies essential education frameworks and showcases how the games can facilitate the relationality that is a hallmark of ludic pedagogy. In such environments, instructors act as co-authors who design for emergence; dialogue becomes the core mechanism of learning; and students occupy roles that foster exploration, reflection, and agency. By weaving narrative co-creation with critical exchange, RPGs offer a compelling blueprint for learning as collaborative authorship, where every voice is integral and knowledge is collaboratively constructed through joint storytelling and sense-making.

This model of collaborative learning is intimately reflected in the work of educator-practitioners featured in this volume. When analog RPGs enter the classroom, they should not merely add a narrative overlay. They should reshape the learning environment. Instructors become facilitators who create scaffolds for choice and discovery, empowering students to explore identity and knowledge through the stories they author together. When we bring RPGs into the classroom, we are not merely layering stories atop content. We are inviting students to participate in a shared epistemic and narrative space: one that blurs the lines between fiction and inquiry, between learner and creator. Instructors take on the role of game master not to dictate the plot, but to structure possibilities and facilitate meaningful choices. This allows students to explore who they are and what they know through the stories they help build and participate in.

To honor the commitments of ludic pedagogy, particularly its grounding in lived experience and epistemic justice, this volume intentionally centers the voices of educators and practitioners alongside scholars. Unlike purely theoretical volumes that explore what games might do, this book centers the voices of practitioner-scholars, those academics and instructors who have used analog RPGs in real classrooms and can speak to both their pedagogical power and their practical challenges. Across the chapters, you'll find deeply grounded, diverse implementations with some authors adapting existing games and others building their own. Some use tabletop RPGs to teach technical writing or composition, while others use them to foster social inclusion, address disability, or critique cultural norms. What unites them is a shared commitment to treating games as serious pedagogical tools, not through simplistic gamification or novelty, but through thoughtful integration. In this way, the volume echoes the core ethos of role-playing itself: knowledge is not simply transmitted, but rather co-created, embodied, and shared in community.

CHAPTER OVERVIEWS

This opening section lays the foundation for understanding how tabletop RPGs can be meaningfully integrated into classroom environments, not as novelty or add-on, but as rigorously designed pedagogical tools. The chapters here offer both practical entry points for instructors new to RPGs and critical frameworks for those already experimenting with game-based learning. Together, they demonstrate that the power of RPGs lies not only in their capacity to engage students, but in how deliberately they are chosen, structured, and aligned with learning goals. Successful integration requires more than enthusiasm for games; it demands thoughtful design, intentional facilitation, and an awareness of how game mechanics shape classroom dynamics (Morales-Carbajal and Chavez Lizama, 2024). Whether addressing curriculum standards, exploring systems thinking, or interrogating the ideological underpinnings of game rules themselves, these chapters affirm that the educational use of RPGs must be as reflective and intentional as any other mode of teaching (Sousa et al., 2023).

In "Educational RPGs: A Practitioner's Guide to Bringing the Gaming Table into the Classroom," Maryanne Cullinan and Jennifer Genova offer an accessible primer for instructors unfamiliar with RPGs. Drawing on their work in K–12 teacher education, they introduce a flexible model that aligns game design with state standards and student learning goals. The chapter is rich in practical advice and sample scenarios, providing a useful entry point for instructors navigating curriculum mandates while seeking to expand active learning strategies.

Ahu Yolaç's "Tabletop Role-Playing Games in the Classroom: A Systems Thinking Approach for Quick Implementation and Meaningful Learning Outcomes" presents a robust framework for educators who wish to use RPGs to explore complex systems like environmental justice, ethics, and sustainability. Grounded in systems thinking, Yolaç provides a step-by-step process for adapting existing RPGs to address critical social issues, including worksheets and examples. Notably, Yolaç emphasizes the pedagogical value of making visible the connections between individual choices and systemic outcomes—whether in fictional game worlds or real-world environmental crises.

Justin Berry's "Game Mechanics in the Classroom" chapter invites instructors to think critically about the affordances of specific RPG systems and how rules shape learning outcomes. Rather than offering a one-size-fits-all solution, Berry provides a vocabulary and framework for evaluating and choosing systems based on classroom needs. He argues that game mechanics should not be taken for granted, as they serve as ideological structures that influence the kinds of learning—and learners—that are centered. By mapping game mechanics to pedagogical priorities, Berry offers instructors tools to intentionally scaffold play for learning.

The book's second section explores the transformative potential of tabletop RPGs to foster inclusion, empathy, and belonging in the classroom—while also urging educators to engage critically with the games themselves. As educational spaces strive to become more accessible and affirming for all learners, RPGs offer a unique vehicle for building community, centering marginalized voices, and supporting diverse ways of knowing and being. These chapters show how the collaborative, improvisational nature of RPGs can disrupt exclusionary norms and cultivate environments where students feel seen, heard, and empowered. At the same time, the section cautions against assuming that a game's subject matter alone guarantees inclusive or ethical outcomes. Instead, it calls for careful attention to design, facilitation, and representation to ensure that the experiences we offer in the classroom truly support justice and accessibility.

In "Everybody Wins: Role-Playing Games with Students with Disabilities," Cathy Leogrande and Aaron Brown share insights from designing and running RPG-based learning experiences for students with disabilities. They offer concrete strategies for accessibility, including sensory accommodations, session pacing, and universal design. The authors emphasize that RPGs create space for collaborative success and communal joy, particularly powerful for students who are often marginalized in more traditional academic contexts.

Hanne Grasmo and Lobna Hassan's chapter, "Cripping Tabletop Role-Playing Games: A Critical Analysis of Disability and Inclusion in

Inspirisles and Beyond," offers a critical complement to Leogrande and Brown's practice-based work. Grasmo and Hassan analyze the disability representation and accessibility features of the RPG Inspirisles, which teaches British and American Sign Language. Their critical lens opens up a larger conversation of how RPGs can affirm or challenge normative assumptions about ability, embodiment, and communication. This chapter invites educators to consider not only who plays, but how play is shaped by design choices.

This section highlights how tabletop RPGs can be deliberately adapted to serve the specific pedagogical needs of distinct academic disciplines. RPGs offer a flexible framework that can be purposefully aligned with disciplinary content and learning objectives. The chapters that follow focus particularly on writing instruction, demonstrating how game-based approaches can reinforce rhetorical awareness, narrative construction, and multimodal literacy. By designing and playing games, students are not just participating in imaginative exercises, they are developing core competencies essential to their fields, from genre analysis to audience consideration to the ethical dimensions of storytelling. These examples show how RPGs can act as discipline-specific tools that make academic concepts tangible, relevant, and memorable.

In "At the Crossroads of Composition, Creative Writing, and Technical Writing: A Proposal for Teaching TTRPG Design in Higher Education," Keely Mohon-Doyle explores RPG design as a site for multimodal composition. She argues that the work of creating a role-playing game—world-building, rules writing, and scenario scripting—requires students to integrate rhetorical awareness, genre analysis, and audience consideration. RPG design, in this framework, becomes a capstone genre that unites creative expression and professional communication.

In his reflective and practice-based chapter, William Stratton explores how tabletop role-playing games (TTRPGs), particularly *Dungeons & Dragons*, can serve as powerful pedagogical tools for teaching fiction writing. Framing character development through the lens of narrative identity theory, Stratton demonstrates how systems of character creation—complete with stats, flaws, and backstory—encourage students to think critically and empathetically about what makes a character feel real. Through scaffolded classroom exercises such as self-character sheets and one-room adventures, students engage in both imaginative play and deep narrative construction, linking their own experiences with those of their characters. Stratton argues that this playful, systemic, and embodied approach to storytelling not only enhances students' understanding of character but also bridges the gap between abstract academic concepts and the lived realities of students' lives.

The final section of this volume turns toward one of the most ethically charged and pedagogically complex frontiers for analog RPGs: the exploration of difficult, often painful social realities. While RPGs are well known for their ability to foster creativity, empathy, and collaboration, using them to engage topics like trauma, violence, or systemic oppression raises serious questions. What are the risks of reenacting harm in a classroom setting? Who gets to tell whose story, and at what cost? Without careful design and facilitation, educational role-play can slip into reenactment rather than reflection, potentially retraumatizing participants or reproducing the very dynamics of harm it seeks to unpack. Yet the power of RPGs to stage meaningful moral inquiry and social complexity cannot be ignored. The chapters that follow take up this challenge, asking not whether we should use RPGs to explore hard topics, but how we can do so with care, nuance, and pedagogical intentionality. Together, they offer models for navigating these tensions, equipping educators with tools to make difficult learning both possible and just.

Caleb Probst's chapter introduces distributed role-play as an innovative game mechanic designed to reduce the emotional risk of teaching difficult social concepts through RPGs. Using *The Hook Up Game,* which tackles the complex topic of sexual consent as a case study, Probst explores how spreading the embodiment of a single character across multiple players can mitigate harm while preserving the pedagogical benefits of experiential learning. Drawing from research in constructionism and transformational play, he demonstrates how this mechanic creates emotional distance between player and character without sacrificing the intensity or relevance of the learning. This design offers a way to preserve the transformative, empathetic, and experiential potential of RPGs while providing necessary care and ethical scaffolding for students. Through qualitative analysis of post-game reflections, Probst shows that distributed role-play allows players to confront complex and often uncomfortable social realities, such as boundary violations and coercion, without forcing any one participant to fully bear the emotional consequences of role-playing harm. The chapter argues that this approach offers educators and designers a promising path for ethically and effectively addressing topics often considered too risky for classroom role-play.

Kristian A. Bjørkelo's chapter examines *Blood Feud*, a GM-less tabletop role-playing game designed to surface and interrogate the social mechanics of toxic masculinity. Through observations of both convention and classroom play sessions, Bjørkelo explores how the game's honor-based economy incentivizes domination, homophobia, and misogyny, creating what he calls "mechanics of toxicity." Situated within feminist pedagogy and drawing on theories of bleed, transgressive realism, and transformative play, the chapter demonstrates how *Blood Feud* enables players to critically reflect on the cultural scripts of masculinity. The chapter highlights how discomfort, humor, and catharsis within the safe structure of play can foster awareness, complicity, and potential reorientation toward more just understandings of gendered behavior. As such, *Blood Feud* is presented not just as a game about toxic masculinity, but as a powerful tool for reimagining how we teach and learn about it. Through examples drawn from classroom practice, this chapter shows how the flexible narrative structure of RPGs opens space for interrogation and transformation of hegemonic social roles.

The chapter "Distributed Role-Play" proposes an approach to character and storytelling that centers collective authorship. The author argues that by distributing narrative control among players, instructors can facilitate deeper collaborative learning and support emergent ethical reasoning. This approach is especially valuable in classrooms addressing social complexity, as it mirrors real-world negotiation and coalition-building.

CONCLUSION: CRITICAL PLAY, PRACTICAL PEDAGOGY

This volume contributes to a growing body of scholarship that sees RPGs not as entertainment intruding into education, but as a legitimate and valuable modality for learning that deepens pedagogy and learning. Across these chapters, readers will find a spectrum of implementation models, from short, self-contained classroom activities to multi-week game-based curricula. Importantly, these contributions do not shy away from the complexities of game-based pedagogy: they grapple with questions of accessibility, preparation time, institutional constraints, and student diversity. Yet they also reveal the transformational potential of inviting students to play, imagine, and co-create within the classroom.

In an era of standardized testing, political pressure on curricular content, and increased student disengagement, this volume insists that there is still room for imagination and play, especially when play becomes a vehicle for critical thought, inclusive community, and deep learning. This volume asks us to treat classrooms not only as sites of instruction, but of collaborative authorship. These are sacred epistemic spaces where students and educators can build new worlds, and perhaps, learn how to better inhabit this one. Educators and students, take up your dice. The classroom is ready.

REFERENCES

Alexander, Robin. 2018. "Developing Dialogic Teaching. Genesis, Process, Trial." *Research Papers in Education* 33(5): 561–98.

Bakhtin, Mikhail M. 1981. *The Dialogic Imagination: Four Essays*. Edited by Michael Holquist. Translated by Caryl Emerson and Michael Holquist. Austin. University of Texas Press.

Ede, Lynn W., and Andrea A. Lunsford. 1990. "Collaboration and Concepts of Authorship." *College Composition and Communication* 41(2): 188–208.

Freire, Paulo. 1970. *Pedagogy of the Oppressed*. New York: Herder and Herder.

González González, C. S., S. P. Starosky, and A. G. Dias Pereira. 2013. "Role-Playing Game as a Pedagogical Proposition for Story Co-Construction." In *Games and Learning Alliance: Second International Conference, GALA 2013, Paris, France, October 23–25, 2013, Proceedings*, edited by Alessandro De Gloria, 160–171. Lecture Notes in Computer Science 8605. Berlin: Springer. https://doi.org/10.1007/978-3-319-12157-4_15

Haarman, Susan, ed. 2026. Education and Analog Role-Playing Games: Theory and Pedagogy, Volume 1. 1st ed. New York: Routledge.

Lauricella, Sharon & Edmunds, T. Keith . 2022. "Ludic Pedagogy: Taking a Serious Look at Fun in the COVID-19 Classroom and Beyond." Educational Considerations, 48(1), n1.

Plass, Jan L., Bruce D. Homer, and Charles K. Kinzer. 2015. "Foundations of Game-Based Learning." *Educational Psychologist* 50(4): 258–283. https://doi.org/10.1080/00461520.2015.1122533

Morales-Carbajal, Ricardo, and Eduardo A. Chavez Lizama. 2024. "Role-Playing Games as an Educational Stimulation." *Analog Game Studies* 11(3). https://analoggamestudies.org/2024/10/role-playing-games-as-an-educational-stimulation/

Sousa, Carla, Sara Rye, Micael Sousa, Pedro Juan Torres, Claudilene Perim, Shivani Atul Mansuklal, and Firdaous Ennami. 2023. "Playing at the School Table: Systematic Literature Review of Board, Tabletop, and Other Analog Game-Based Learning Approaches." *Frontiers in Psychology* 14(June): 1160591. https://doi.org/10.3389/fpsyg.2023.1160591

Quiogue, Dariel. 1998. "Role-Playing Games as Collaborative Fiction." AegisWeb. Retrieved on August 22nd, 2025. https://www.oocities.org/aegisweb/9-Articles/91-CollFic.html

Wegerif, Rupert. 2008. "Dialogic or Dialectic? The Significance of Ontological Assumptions in Research on Educational Dialogue." *British Educational Research Journal* 34(3): 347–61.

PART I

Roll a Knowledge Check

How Tabletop RPGs Help Us Learn

CHAPTER 1

Educational RPGs

A Practitioner's Guide to Bringing the Gaming Table into the Classroom

Jennifer Genova and Maryanne Cullinan

INTRODUCTION

Hail and well met, travelers. There is no doubt that tabletop role-playing games (tabletop RPGs) are having a surge in popularity and cultural relevance in the United States and across the world. But, tabletop RPGs are more than just a popular diversion. This chapter is designed as an overview for the educator at the beginning of their tabletop RPGs-as-Curriculum adventure.

We will provide some of the research supporting the use of tabletop RPGs as learning tools, an overview of how tabletop RPGs offer unique solutions to common problems in classrooms, and a practical guide for interested parties to use as they begin their journey as tabletop RPG educators. This chapter is not a formalized study, but rather a practical introduction for teachers who want to bring games into their classrooms. We have included references to formal studies and academic research at the end of this chapter for further reading. So, come closer to the campfire, adventurer, and we will tell you the tale of how two middle school teachers transformed their classrooms into gaming spaces without sacrificing academic rigor or robust learning outcomes.

DOI: 10.1201/9781003641384-3

PART ONE

Lore Dump: Academic Research Supporting the Use of Tabletop RPGs as Learning Tools

An ever-increasing group of studies (Katō 2019; Orr et al. 2020; Pitt et al. 2023) point to the efficacy of using role-playing games to build social skills in various youth populations. However, we as author-practitioners have observed that tabletop RPGs can also be used as an effective form of pedagogy in a middle school classroom setting – not only for social-emotional development, but as a vehicle for academic content delivery. This includes academic content, skill building, and opportunity for students to access more complex ways of thinking than in a traditional teacher-centered classroom.

In the following chapter, we will outline foundational theory for how tabletop RPGs impact players' frames of thought, and how that additionally can impact the way students think about learning and collaboration in the classroom setting. Then, we will explore why using a role-playing game is a good fit for fulfilling the intrinsic needs of learners both on an individual basis and collectively as a class.

We are teachers who use this approach in our classroom with real pre-teens and teens to not only teach core academic content, but also social and executive functioning skills. We have had particular success in middle school social studies, literacy, unified arts, and after-school classes and programs. Students in this age group are often seen as being reluctant to take social or academic risks and hyper-focused on individual success and competition. We were seeking a new way of teaching that would support student collaboration and provide opportunities for productive struggle and problem solving.

As lifelong gamers ourselves, we understood that games of all types have a unique ability to motivate players to achieve specific goals. We saw our students trying difficult video game levels over and over, using different strategies and methods to make progress. We also saw how students naturally helped each other when they came upon a particularly difficult challenge, learning from each other's experience and sharing different tactics for playing the game. After consulting research into the kinds of thinking and behavior patterns that game players used to be successful, we determined that game-based learning would provide the learning opportunities we were seeking for our students. Through a combination of action research and trial and error, we learned a great deal about how to create tabletop RPG experiences that would support our desired skill outcomes.

The first half of this chapter will serve as a brief overview of what we learned from experts in the field about the kinds of learning that can be done with games. In the second half of the chapter, we will take a more practical approach to how we determine the academic goals and social needs of our students and utilize gameplay as learning in real classroom settings. Welcome to the adventure!

FINE'S FRAME THEORY

The foundational text about how RPG players think while they play was written by Gary Alan Fine in 1983, republished in 2002. This was at a time where aspects of the popular cultural imagination in the United States were running wild with the idea that tabletop RPG players might be satanic or somehow have lost their grip on reality by playing these games. Gary Alan Fine was a noted sociologist who studied niche communities, and not a role-player himself. *Shared Fantasy: Role Playing Games as Social Worlds* rejected the idea that players were not able to separate fantasy from reality. Instead, Fine (1983) proposed a complex three-frame system of thinking within the minds of role-players as they played a game together. This multi-framed way of thinking is crucial to how we think about RPGs in a classroom setting.

The Three Frames

Self/Social Frame

Fine's first frame is an acknowledgment that the game is played by human people – in our case, children. There are skill sets that must be utilized by the players to facilitate the event taking place, and each participant's inclusion in the event. These include time management, turn taking, group dynamics, understanding social norms of the group, body regulation, and attentional regulation. These are all things that students are being asked to do in a classroom setting at all times, with or without the complexities of a game.

Strategic/Game Frame

The second frame is the player as strategist within the context of the game rules. In the strategic frame, the participant is gaming the system—using the resources, rules, and items they have within the game to work toward the best outcome for participants individually and/or as a group. The in-frame behavior may include teamwork with other players, using combined resources to assist in the goal, or working against them. This strategic frame is the frame of planning, logical thinking, and resource management. It is also the frame of dice rolling and calculating moves based on the intersection of resources, dice roll outcomes, and character stats.

In-Fiction/Diegetic[1] Frame

The third frame Fine describes is the in-game fictional world of play, also known as the diegetic frame or magic circle, where participants role-play as characters within the agreed-upon fiction (expanded upon by Stenros 2014). The diegetic or in-fiction frame is where players make choices in character that may or may not be the choices they themselves would make in the social frame. Part of the impact of playing tabletop RPGs is that sometimes Fine's three frames interact in interesting or unexpected ways. This is called *bleed.*

Bleed

Central to the magic of tabletop RPGs is this concept of bleed, the idea that emotions experienced by the player impact the character they are playing and vice versa (Lankoski and Järvelä 2012; Hugaas 2024). This well-established phenomenon is critical in the tabletop RPG format because it allows players to experience empathy, perspective taking, and the sense of accomplishment that comes from a job well done, even if it is in a fictional setting.

Because of how Fine's three different frames interact, students might indicate that their character knows how to do something that they themselves do not know how to do in real life, like ride a horse or repair a vehicle. Or, a player might note that they can infer what is happening in a situation, but their character might not have the level of insight to do the same. A player might choose not to do something strategic because it is better for the story drama, or might choose to give a strategic advantage to another player because they are friends in real life. The emotional response to these choices is shown in the bleed that occurs. We have had players jumping for joy or in tears as they feel the thrill of victory or agony of defeat alongside their fictional selves. Grognard the Dwarf may have just come within a single hit point of death, but Anna, the player, thinks it is hilarious. After all, just because the characters are having a bad time, doesn't mean the players are!

The way that students interact with their fictional characters, and the bleed they feel at those characters' successes and failures give the gameplay an emotional immediacy that does not occur in a regular classroom setting or while playing a game of Uno. The fictional character gives the student both a sense of stake and involvement in the fiction and seeing the story through to its end. This is crucial to the increased engagement created in tabletop RPG scenarios.

DON'T TRUST A MIMIC: WHY RPGS OVER OTHER TYPES OF GAMES?

Often people misunderstand the use of RPGs in the classroom as *gamification*. We understand gamification to be the utilization of game elements such as points, badges, and teams to encourage game-like states in learners, such as increased participation and competition (Landers et al. 2015). As Landers et al. (2015) and Zaric et al. (2021) suggest, game elements alone should not be the basis of pedagogy, but first must endeavor to provide sound and quality instructional content. *Gamification* on its own misses some of the most important possibilities provided by game formats, especially deeper forms of engagement that do not occur simply because you added some new set dressings to the same old format of teaching.

For a gaming medium to be valuable as a new type of pedagogy, we must not rely on leaderboards or review Jeopardy for student engagement. Games are inherently interactive, but without more complex forms of engagement also present; the educator misses the true value and power of moving the instructional content to a game-based system. Interactivity on its own is not inherently high-level emotional, social, or cognitive engagement.

Frankly, school is already a crappy game for many students. It is inherently individualistic, with students only engaging with each other intellectually when said collaboration is demanded by the teacher or the assignment. Like many games, school has its own version of leaderboards and points – we just call them class rankings, honor rolls, and grades – and they create a system where students are in constant competition with each other for the top spot. Gamification by itself highlights these points-based system, and may or may not increase student participation. Importantly, it does not make a meaningful change to the way we consider *how* students can be successful in a classroom. It is more of the same, with new bells and whistles.

Comparatively, RPGs are complex ways of engaging with in-game content and with other players in a manner that is not typical in most traditional classrooms, and we believe is also different from what occurs in a *gamified* classroom. High-quality engagement is an in-depth psychological phenomenon that involves a behavioral, emotional, cognitive, and agentic connection to the content (Ryan and Deci 2000; Reeve 2009, 2012). This is not just about working harder because there are points to score or more items to collect. Students who play role-playing games are already thinking in three different ways simultaneously, as noted by Fine, so educators can co-opt these ways of thinking to impact both the amount and quality of student engagement with the academic content and with each other.

Fine's Frame Theory has been an important part of our previous research and dissertation work into whole-class tabletop RPGs as well. Cullinan (2024a), using interviews with teachers who used RPGs as pedagogy in their classrooms, suggested that one of the values of RPGs in the classroom is that they impact the way that students think about how to 'win' school, a shift in their understanding of Fine's Frame Two.

The collective fictional world of the RPG experience encourages these students to think of themselves as part of a team working toward a goal together. This shift causes them to think of their academic class as a cooperative game with the other students, versus a solo game or competitive game against the other students. In a tabletop RPG-based classroom, individual success in the class is narratively tied to the success of other students in their party. The adventuring party fails or succeeds together, and when negative things happen in fiction to characters the student knows, even if it is not their own character, it has an emotional impact. The strategy and the bleed come together to create a new way of considering what success might mean, and this impacts student relationships both in the game and outside of the fiction (Cullinan 2024a).

Given this shift, the collective fiction layer of RPGs (Fine's Frame Three) is key to their use as pedagogy. This is not just because a story is interactive and fun for a wide variety of students, but because this fictional frame changes the way that students think about themselves in relation to the other students in their class. Therefore, it is not just that the fiction is entertaining, but critical to the impact of RPGs as pedagogy. The third fictional layer of thinking is what causes students to shift in the way they interact with each other and engage with the curriculum content to forward their fictional goals within the game. After all of this, for students to be successful in a classroom that uses RPGs as learning tools, they must reframe their thinking from competition to collaboration and from functional interaction to intellectual engagement.

WHAT DOES HIGH-QUALITY ENGAGEMENT CONSIST OF? AND WHY DOES IT MATTER?

Motivation versus Engagement

If asked, we're certain most teachers would say that they want students to be engaged in their learning. But what engagement actually is, and why it matters, is a complex topic that takes a little digging to uncover. Engagement is the observable corollary to the unobservable phenomenon of motivation (Collie and Martin 2019; Martin 2009; Reeve 2012). We cannot see student motivation, as it is an internal phenomenon. So, we look to behaviors that indicate engagement as a substitute measure.

Engagement: The ICAP Framework

One way of looking at engagement is through the ICAP framework (Chi and Wylie 2014). This categorizes student behaviors into whether they demonstrate Interactive, Constructive, Active, or Passive learning when participating in learning activities. This framework suggests that passive learning is the least effective type of learning, followed by active learning and then constructive learning – with the best learning activities being interactive. This differentiation of engagement is characterized by students engaging in attentive behaviors (passive learning), manipulation of components (active learning), generative behaviors (constructive learning), and co-generative behaviors (interactive learning). In this model, generative and co-generative behaviors in students most effectively demonstrate deep engagement and learning.

Engagement: The Self- Determination Theory Framework

Ryan and Deci's Self-Determination Theory (2000) is another well-established theory that explains peoples' intrinsic motivational tendencies as they learn, grow, and connect with people around them. This development of internal motivation is greatly impacted by student feelings of autonomy (a feeling of psychological freedom), relatedness (connection to authority figures and peers), and feelings of competence (the ability to do what is being asked). Thus, we can encourage intrinsic student motivational growth by supporting these inherent tendencies. More simply put, students will be more likely to internalize an academic goal if they understand it, have the skills to succeed at it, and feel that performing that goal brings them more in line with people who like and respect them (Reeve 2012; Ryan and Deci 2000; Cullinan 2024b).

Student engagement is fostered when adults in the classroom support their students' intrinsic psychological needs, and a lack of support for these same needs is more likely to result in disengagement (Burke et al. 2020; Cullinan 2024b; Guay 2022; Van den Berghe et al. 2016). When autonomy, relatedness, and competence are supported, students show more intrinsic motivation and greater academic success regardless of age (Reeve 2009).

Self-Determination Theory states that classroom engagement can be further broken down into three parts: behavioral, emotional, and cognitive engagement (Ryan and Deci 2000).

Behavioral engagement is task compliance and getting the job done. Examples include, following established behavioral norms and routines, persistence and following task directions.

Emotional engagement is both the presence of pro-task emotional regulation and the absence of anti-engagement emotional conditions that would not allow for engagement, such as emotional extremes of sadness, anger, or delight. It is also the connection students have with their peers and teachers and how that impacts their ability to engage with learning.

Cognitive engagement is how students engage with the actual content being learned. It has to do with the needed planning, ability to put in effort to conceptualize new ideas and develop a schema for content.

Reeve (2012) and Reeve et al. (2020) additionally suggest that cognitive engagement can be further divided into cognitive engagement and agentic engagement.

Agentic Engagement is when students personalize learning, make connections with previous learning, and ask questions that help take their own and other peoples' understanding even further. It is when someone takes the content and really makes it their own.

TABLETOP RPGS PROVIDE POTENTIAL FOR MULTI-FACETED ENGAGEMENT IN A CLASSROOM SETTING

Tabletop RPGS as Engagement through a Self-Determination Theory Lens

Looking at engagement through an SDT lens, we can see that tabletop RPGs provide the possibility for all four kinds of engagement at once. Let us consider the following example from a middle school social studies class: students are instructed to design characters who would live at a Medieval Manor, and they have to use their understanding of the Feudal system to work together to ensure that their hapless Lord retains the King's favor while during a Royal Visit.

Right off the bat, students are incentivized to behaviorally engage, as their behavior will have a measurable impact on their group. This kind of task also lowers many barriers to emotional engagement as it doesn't immediately demand students perform the kinds of tasks that generate anxiety, such as long-form writing or class presentation, and gives students a group from which they can derive support through the task. Cognitive engagement and agentic engagement are central to student success in the task, as students are not simply asked to regurgitate their understanding of Feudal society, but rather use that understanding to create something unique to them and their group. Students are then asked to take an active role in the content by playing characters within parameters appropriate for that content, and the task is designed to allow students to achieve success in a variety of ways that speak to their individual strengths.

From a broad perspective, the creative fictional framework and self-direction inherent in playing a character within an RPG allow for students to have autonomy and relatedness at the same time, while the established rules and norms and the possibility for content differentiation allow for developing competence. Additionally, students' autonomy and competence are not endangered by the success of other people in the class. Instead, each collective success supports team members' additional success (Cullinan 2024a). This encourages relatedness as a strategy to forward the win condition of the game and the learning (Table 1.1).

TABLE 1.1 The four types of engagement and the aspects of tabletop RPGs that encourage each one

Type of Engagement	Tabletop RPG Aspect That Encourages This Engagement Type
Behavioral	Established game rules, initiative orders, stat blocks, etc. that make the behavioral expectations clear and provide a separation between what happens to characters in fiction versus what happens with players
Emotional	Fictional situations with immediacy and characters that can be invested in, developing team camaraderie
Cognitive	Creative problem solving, ongoing fictional narrative, potential for differentiation of academic content
Agentic	Creation of unique individual characters, problem solving without one correct answer, art and writing about the characters or fiction, remixing of academic content

Tabletop RPGS as Engagement through ICAP and Frame Theory Lenses

We can additionally see that by their nature, tabletop RPGs provide the possibility for players to show not only attention to and manipulation of content. They must additionally show generative and co-generative behaviors, demonstrating constructive and interactive engagement.

In Fine's Frame One, the in-person frame, collaborating with others demands that students apply attention and manipulation of their environmental factors and attention to norms of behavior that impact the play of everyone. Also, they must participate in the co-creation of the norms of behavior so that there is an agreed-upon way of play that allows everyone to participate and the logistics of the play to move forward.

In Frame Two, the strategic frame, students are demonstrating attention to the rules and manipulation of both real-life and in-game assets. They are also working to generate a personal strategy and co-generate a group strategy to work toward the win condition of the game.

For Frame Three, the in-fiction frame, collaborative storytelling is by definition a co-generative experience. In this fictional setting, players are both generating their own character's story, and also co-generating the story of the group.

THE PROVISION OF ALIBI

Additionally, pretend games serve as an 'alibi'. Since it is 'just pretending', making choices in play is less intimidating. So, using the cover of a game, players feel comfortable trying out new things (Stenros 2014). This allows engagement in a different way than outside the fiction, as anything a student does in character is not *really* them. This allows them to take more chances academically and socially. Even if the character is just a small shift from the student themselves, students are more likely to try new things, knowing if they fail it isn't 'really them'. We can all enjoy the challenges the character encounters in a way that our own are not as equally hilarious. When asking students to take academic or social-emotional risk in the classroom, providing an alibi within a shared low-stakes fiction reduces student anxiety and promotes a culture where failure is part of and not a detriment to the learning process.

PART TWO

Tabletop RPGs in Action in the Classroom

BUILDING AN ADVENTURE: DESIGNING 'THE CURSE OF THE CLOUDED TEMPLE'

Given the unique ability of role-playing games to provide an opportunity for students to deeply engage with a topic and be motivated to progress through an activity, it stands to reason that the next step is to use a role-playing game in a classroom to teach content. As with any significant instructional or curricular shift, this must be done with intention and careful consideration. Tabletop RPGs have immense potential to enhance and deepen student learning, but it must also be acknowledged that they are a significant departure from established school culture and norms. When teachers seek to implement or design tabletop RPGs for classroom use, they must be very clear in the content the game is to teach, establish reasonable and measurable skill goals, and consider the context of their individual classroom to determine student preparedness for a tabletop RPG experience. It is only after this point that teachers should consider the fiction or gameplay elements that will comprise the game itself. The form of the game must be decided by the function it is to serve within the classroom.

With this in mind, the authors of this chapter collaborated to design an introductory role-playing game for students in a seventh grade Social Studies classroom for a unit centered on World Religions. The specific content goals were for students to gain a basic understanding of the origin, core beliefs, cultural practices, key figures, and historic events associated with one of six different religions. The core skills to be addressed were determining main ideas from a variety of sources, corroborating evidence, drawing conclusions based on textual evidence, and crafting logical arguments with a clear claim, evidence, and reasoning. These students had very little tabletop RPG experience and had not played tabletop RPGs as part of their core curriculum before. They were randomly sorted into the class and had a range of reading levels from kindergarten to high school.

Using the Gaming the Systems Conceptual Matrix for Game Design

In order to design a game that effectively met both the curricular and skill goals of the unit, previously published research was consulted. Game elements were selected based on the 'Gaming the Systems Conceptual Matrix' (Cullinan and Genova 2023) to ensure that the instructional purpose of the game was kept at the center of the design process. Beyond the aforementioned curricular and academic skill goals, it was determined that the game also needed to promote collaboration as a social-emotional skill and sequencing as an executive functioning skill. Using the 'Conceptual Matrix', it was determined that the game had to have the following elements to meet the skill goals for the unit (Table 1.2):

TABLE 1.2 The three skill areas of tabletop RPGs, the specific goals of 'Curse of the Clouded Temple', and the gameplay aspects that encouraged those goals

Skill Area	Specific Goal(s)	Game Elements
Academic	Content-Specific Knowledge (World Religions in seventh grade) Reading Comprehension (using multiple sources to determine key information and main idea)	• Rules include expectations of use of content material, vocabulary, and concepts for character and/or plot advancement • Rules written in a format/reading level appropriate to the reading level of students. Puzzles, advancement, connected to demonstration of reading skills as appropriate to class reading level
Social-emotional	Collaboration	• Gameplay that specifically requires or encourages working together, low combat, and collaborative world building
Executive functioning	Sequencing	• Gameplay that involves timelines, generational storytelling, and first-then-next narrative. Rules that require students to go through steps in a procedure to advance

Consideration of the Students' Familiarity with Tabletop RPGs as an Aspect of Game Design

Selecting these specific skill goals and their analogous game elements created the foundation upon which student-friendly fiction could be developed. Once the skills and core game elements were decided, the contextual constraints of the lesson and classroom environment were considered. In this instance, students were engaging with the game as the first unit of the new school year. These students had not played any sort of role-playing game as core curriculum before and were largely inexperienced with tabletop RPGs and the typical mechanics of role-playing. While classroom norms to support students stepping outside of the comfort zone of typical classroom activities had been established, it was still early enough in the year that expecting players to fully dive into complex character creation would be inappropriate.

Taking all these things into consideration, the following parameters were determined to make sure that students had appropriate scaffolding and support as they played 'The Curse of the Clouded Temple':

- Students would be in groups of four.
- Each student would be responsible for analyzing evidence from one location for their piece of pitch made to the sorceress.
- Students 'character sheets' would include mostly fun narrative information and have a minimal impact on the gameplay as a whole.
- Students would have a workbook to accompany the game with specific prompts, rather than a blank adventurer's journal.

When considering these contextual constraints, it was decided that these students would need a game that resembled typical classroom learning activities and role-play opportunities that were structured and scaffolded to maximize effectiveness while minimizing confusion or discomfort. This illuminates a central tension in incorporating tabletop RPGs as curriculum into the classroom: In order to get the greatest impact on student learning, tabletop RPG activities must be adapted to the level of student experience with this format. Otherwise, the gameplay becomes a hindrance to deeper learning, as the cognitive load of the student is focused on navigating the game rather than engaging with the material presented within the game.

Creating the In-Game Fiction

After outlining all of the parameters, the fiction of the game world could finally take shape. Each piece of the gameplay was deliberately crafted to support the students to make progress toward the goals of the unit. To encourage collaboration, students were put into groups of four with specific roles/expectations for each group member with regard to the final pitch to the sorceress. To support reading comprehension, students were given an organizer with scaffolded questions and prompts to help them identify the key information needed to progress through the game. Finally, to support logical sequencing, students were given a series of sentence stems to sequence the information they gained in order from least to most specific.

The fiction gave students an impetus to complete the game experience beyond simply compliance. Student groups were brought into the fiction with a short narrative about being on a school whale watch field trip and having their boat get blown off course in a freak storm. Students awoke to find themselves and their group on a cursed island with a temple in the middle. Each of the residents on the island was struck by a curse that made it impossible for them to remember the religion of the temple at the center of the island. To confront the final boss for 'battle', they had to gather evidence from each of the five major locations on the island. At the end, students must work together to correctly identify the temple of the religion at the center of the island and disarm the evil that has befallen the place and caused the amnesia. If students are not successful, they must collectively select the kind of place they will inhabit on the island and what information about the religion that they will hold onto, in hopes that a future traveler can draw the appropriate conclusion.

It is important to note that the role-play demand on students for this game was quite low. Their 'characters' were middle school students who were shipwrecked on a mysterious island. This was intentional, as the students in the class had very little role-playing experience, and therefore, it was decided that requiring too much deep role-play in this first game experience could be detrimental to students achieving their learning goals.

THE SCRYING ORB: OBSERVING REAL GAMEPLAY AS EVIDENCE OF STUDENT LEARNING

Using ICAP Theory to Categorize Learning Behaviors

As with any curriculum, teacher reflection does not end with the design of the learning activity. Student behavior can be observed by staff during the activity to gauge their level of engagement, interest, and progress toward desired skill outcomes. Using the ICAP framework (Chi and Wylie 2014), observed student behaviors can be categorized as to whether they demonstrate Interactive, Constructive, Active, or Passive learning (Table 1.3).

As is evident from the chart above, the base expectations of the game itself precluded students from relying purely on passive learning. To approach the activity, students had to, at minimum, be 'Active' learners according to the ICAP framework. To progress through the activity, students had to at least be demonstrating Constructive or Interactive learning, as they could not complete the game without generating an organic claim and supporting it with a reasonable argument based on the sources provided by the non-player characters (NPCs) in the game. While students worked in their groups to make their way through The Curse of the Clouded Temple Game, they were constantly finding information within a text, discussing what they learned with their partners, and synthesizing their learning with what their group members also learned.

Using SDT Theory to Consider Student Engagement

Similarly to the ICAP lens, when looking through a Self-Determination Theory lens to identify student engagement during The Curse of the Clouded Temple game, students were seen demonstrating behaviors showing their autonomy, relatedness, and competence. Students could

TABLE 1.3 ICAP Theory behaviors in evidenced in the 'Curse of the Clouded Temple' gameplay

Type of Engagement	**Student Behavior**
Interactive	Critiquing claims and requesting justification, debate
Constructive	Making inferences based on text, generating claims based on evidence
Active	Copying directly from the text, copying ideas from a conversation, quoting the text directly
Passive	Attending to the task, listening to group members

make choices in game as to where they traveled within the fiction, allowing for autonomy. They worked together with other students both academically and within the same fictional world, encouraging relatedness. The game was designed for students to be able to utilize what they already knew about information gathering and argumentation to scaffold feelings of competence, even when students were unclear at first about the answer.

SDT would call the constructive and interactive learning described by ICAP as emotional, cognitive, and agentic engagement. Students became emotionally invested in the fiction of trying to leave the island. They became cognitively invested in solving the mystery of the island and were able to rework the facts as given to come up with their own conclusions and ideas about what might be happening, leading to more agentic engagement. Even when students struggled to find the correct answers, the students had the in-game strategic and fictional motivations to try again, with a knowledge that the answer was there, somewhere on the cursed island.

Redefining Failure to Refocus on Learning

Along with students demonstrating evidence of deep engagement, the student relationship to the concept of 'failure' or 'getting it wrong' was measurably different from that in traditional learning activities. Students who either rushed through the activity, trying to get 'the answer', or were reluctant to define their answer in hopes for increased teacher intervention, were stopped from progressing and had no choice but to go back to the game materials and try again unless they wanted to run a cursed coffee shop or cat cafe in the next iteration of the game. Instead of panicking or feeling dejected, students would laugh and go back to their groups to consider what evidence or information they may have missed. The stakes were so farcical that the threat of failure was not a threat to the students' self-esteem, but rather an opportunity to reflect on their process and iterate in order to be more successful in the next round (echoing Stenros' concept of alibi).

Through a careful observation and analysis of the behaviors exhibited by students as they played through The Curse of the Clouded Temple, it was obvious that the anxiety level in the class was quite low and that students overall were engaging positively with the material. As they moved through the game, students willingly revisited locations and checked each other's notes for anything they may have missed. This behavior was a stark contrast from more traditional class assessments, where students are often uninterested in revising, editing, or reviewing their work once they feel it is 'done'. The collaborative environment meant that students were always sharing their ideas with their group and giving or receiving feedback. It is clear from these observations that turning this lesson into a role-playing game provided students with many opportunities for deeper learning beyond a traditional classroom assignment. Not only did students embrace the possibility of failure and iteration, but they also viewed that opportunity as valuable or even fun. One student who was used to having a relatively easy time with the traditional rules of the game of school was absolutely thrown off by the game experience, as they had to be open to feedback and accept that they were not necessarily going to get it 'right' the first time, all on their own. It was a humbling experience for them to have to rely on the understanding and perspective of students with whom they typically considered themselves in competition.

QUEST OBJECTIVES: HOW TO GET THE TABLETOP RPG EXP YOU NEED

For teachers considering this shift in their instruction, it is important that the scope is kept reasonable and the process is done slowly. From concept to rollout, it took more than 30 hours to design The Curse of the Clouded Temple. While the ideation itself was not difficult, as the game was modeled after classic point-and-click adventure which were a large part of our early gaming experiences, it did take time to gather materials that would allow students to work collaboratively without too much direct instruction. Regardless of one's gaming experience or confidence in their instructional design, breaking and remaking the game of school takes time. If one is considering building curriculum materials around tabletop RPGs, teachers must be sure to consider the following:

1. Be clear in the goals of the learning experience. Consider academic, social-emotional, and executive functioning skills as coequal in importance to the learning experience.
2. Be mindful of the students who will play the game. Consider their ability level, social cohesion, role-play experience, neurodivergence, and communication style when designing learning games.

3. Design fiction that supports the learning without taking student attention too far off from their goals. The game world should enhance and support the learning and not detract from it.

4. Look for signs of deep engagement during the learning process. If students are able to engage with the material passively and still be successful, the experience must be revised.

5. Build failure into the game to promote student iteration and reflection. Decentralizing the teacher as the arbiter of learning increases student confidence and agency in the learning process.

The unique set of cognitive skills and frameworks that must be utilized by players of tabletop RPGs give an innovative way to help students become deeply engaged in their learning on a variety of levels. As we developed and implemented 'The Curse of the Clouded Temple', we saw students blossom in many ways that traditional classroom assessments often miss. By thoughtfully utilizing the best of what tabletop RPGs can offer to students, teachers can change their classroom culture, impact student communication skills and critical thinking, and deliver content and skill building in a novel way that has a lasting impact on student lives. To take a group of students who are used to competing for grades and seeing the class as a series of compliance activities, playing a game with friends presents a novel method of learning complex content and practicing important social skills.

To develop this kind of curriculum does take time and a willingness to reimagine the fundamental assumptions of school – for both students and teachers. Between the two authors of this chapter, there are dozens of games in any imaginable stage of development.

Fear not, Traveler! The road to tabletop RPGs in the classroom may seem steep and fraught, but the journey is worth the trouble!

NOTE

1 The term 'diegetic' refers to anything happening within an established fiction and able to be heard and understood by the characters. For example, in the Science Fiction classic TV show *The Twilight Zone*, the narration done at the end of each episode by series creator Rod Serling was not diegetic, as it was not part of the fiction as experienced by the characters; rather, it was intended to only be acknowledged and understood by the audience. In *The Sound of Music*, the song 'Doe, a Deer' is diegetic, as it is sung by the characters who are intended to understand it as a song instead of an internal monologue or something similar.

REFERENCES

Burke, K. M., S. K. Raley, K. A. Shogren, M. Hagiwara, C. Mumbardó-Adam, H. Uyanik, and S. Behrens. 2020. "A Meta-Analysis of Interventions to Promote Self-Determination for Students with Disabilities." *Remedial and Special Education* 41, no. 3 (May): 176–188.

Chi, Michelene T. H., and Ruth Wylie. 2014. "The ICAP Framework: Linking Cognitive Engagement to Active Learning Outcomes." *Educational Psychologist* 49, no. 4: 219–243.

Collie, Rebecca J., and Andrew J. Martin. "Motivation and Engagement in Learning." Oxford Research Encyclopedia of Education. 22 Nov. 2019; Accessed 14 Dec. 2025. https://oxfordre.com/education/view/10.1093/acrefore/9780190264093.001.0001/acrefore-9780190264093-e-891.

Cullinan, M. 2024a. "Surveying the Perspectives of Middle and High School Educators Who Use Role-Playing Games as Pedagogy." *International Journal of Role-Playing* 15: 127–141.

Cullinan, M. 2024b. "Wild Magic Farms: Increasing Student Engagement and Decreasing Academic Regression in Middle School Extended School Year Through Use of a Role-Playing Game." PhD diss., Lesley University. ProQuest (3150964638). https://ezproxyles.flo.org/login?url=https://www.proquest.com/dissertations-theses/em-wild-magic-farms-increasing-student-engagement/docview/3150964638/se-2.

Cullinan, M., and J. Genova. 2023. "Gaming the Systems: A Component Analysis Framework for the Classroom Use of RPGs." *International Journal of Role-Playing* 13: 7–17.

Fine, Gary Alan. 2002. *Shared Fantasy: Role-Playing Games as Social Worlds*. Chicago: University of Chicago Press.

Guay, F. 2022. "Applying Self-Determination Theory to Education: Regulations Types, Psychological Needs, and Autonomy Supporting Behaviors." *Canadian Journal of School Psychology* 37, no. 1: 75–92.

Hugaas, K. H. 2024. "Bleed and Identity: A Conceptual Model of Bleed and How Bleed-out from Role-Playing Games Can Affect a Player's Sense of Self." *International Journal of Role-Playing* 15: 9–35.

Katō, K. 2019. "Employing Tabletop Role-Playing Games (TRPGs) in Social Communication Support Measures for Children and Youth with Autism Spectrum Disorder (ASD) in Japan: A Hands-On Report on the Use of Leisure Activities." *RPG 学研究*, 23–28.

Landers, R. N., K. N. Bauer, R. C. Callahan, and M. B. Armstrong. 2015. "Psychological Theory and the Gamification of Learning." In *Gamification in Education and Business*, edited by Torsten Reiners, T. and Wood, L., 165–186. Cham, Switzerland: Springer International Publishing.

Lankoski, P., and S. Järvelä. 2012. "An Embodied Cognition Approach for Understanding Role-Playing." *International Journal of Role-Playing* 3: 18–32.

Martin, A. J. 2009. "Motivation and Engagement across the Academic Life Span." *Educational and Psychological Measurement* 69, no. 5: 794–824.

Orr, M., S. King, and M. McGonnell. 2020. "A Qualitative Exploration of the Perceived Social Benefits of Playing Table-Top Role-Playing Games." *International Journal of Role-Playing* 10: 70–83.

Pitt, C., K. Chen, J. Rubin, D. Gibson, and S. Bindman. 2023. "How Youth Can Build Social and Emotional Skills with Tabletop Role-Playing Games." *foundry10*. Accessed June 27, 2025. https://www.foundry10.org/resources/how-youth-can-build-social-and-emotional-skills-with-tabletop-role-playing-games.

Reeve, J. 2009. "Why Instructors Adopt a Controlling Motivating Style toward Students and How They Can Become More Autonomy Supportive." *Educational Psychologist* 44, no. 3: 159–175.

Reeve, J. 2012. "A Self-Determination Theory Perspective on Student Engagement." In *Handbook of Research on Student Engagement*, edited by Sandra L. Christenson, Amy L. Reschly, and Cathryn Wylie, 149–172. New York: Springer.

Reeve, J., Cheon, S. H., & Jang, H. 2020. How and why students make academic progress: Reconceptualizing the student engagement construct to increase its explanatory power. *Contemporary Educational Psychology*, 62, no. 1. https://doi.org/10.1016/j.cedpsych.2020.101899

Ryan, R. M., and E. L. Deci. 2000. "Intrinsic and Extrinsic Motivations: Classic Definitions and New Directions." *Contemporary Educational Psychology* 25, no. 1: 54–67.

Stenros, J. 2014. "In Defence of a Magic Circle: The Social, Mental and Cultural Boundaries of Play." *Transactions of the Digital Games Research Association* 1, no. 2: 147–185.

Van den Berghe, L., G. Cardon, I. Tallir, D. Kirk, and L. Haerens. 2016. "Dynamics of Need-Supportive and Need-Thwarting Teaching Behavior: The Bidirectional Relationship with Student Engagement and Disengagement in the Beginning of a Lesson." *Physical Education and Sport Pedagogy* 21, no. 6: 653–670.

Zaric, Nadja, Rene Roepke, Vlatko Lukarov, and Ulrik Schroeder. September 17, 2021. "Gamified Learning Theory: The Moderating Role of Learners' Learning Tendencies." *International Journal of Serious Games* 8, no. 3: 71–91. https://doi.org/10.17083/ijsg.v8i3.438.

CHAPTER 2

Tabletop Role-Playing Games in the Classroom

A Systems-Thinking Approach for Quick Implementation and Meaningful Learning Outcomes

Ahu Yolaç

INTRODUCTION

In this chapter, I present a pedagogical approach based on systems thinking to adapt existing tabletop role-playing games (tabletop RPGs) for classroom use. I specifically focus on aligning tabletop RPGs with learning outcomes and addressing critical classroom topics such as environmental justice, ethics, and sustainability.

While tabletop RPGs are excellent tools for teaching a variety of educational topics, not all are suited for classroom use. Challenges such as extensive preparation time, managing content, available class time, and other constraints can limit their applicability. Given these obstacles, many educators simply lack the time or resources to design and implement a tabletop RPG tailored to their classroom needs. To address this issue, I propose a systems-thinking framework to adapt existing tabletop RPGs for educational settings. This approach offers a step-by-step guide to efficiently transform an existing game system to achieve critical learning outcomes.

DOI: 10.1201/9781003641384-4

All games are complex systems, and educators can leverage this inherent "system-ness" of tabletop RPGs to foster meaningful learning experiences. Within this framework, systems thinking can be used to identify key game components, target learning outcomes, and the synergies between the two. This would help educators modify games effectively to meet their desired objectives. For example, within the scenario I share in this chapter, students might role-play as a trend-following consumer, an overproducing company, and a waste sorter in a *Dungeons and Dragons* (*D&D*)-style city. Through this speculative scenario, they can explore how overconsumption leads to environmental injustice, one of many systemic issues that can be addressed through adapted gameplay.

This chapter serves as a practical guide for educators who want to integrate tabletop RPGs into their classrooms but are uncertain how to do so due to constraints such as those previously outlined. Additionally, it contributes to the fields of game studies and education by exploring how tabletop RPGs can be used to address critical, meaningful and informal learning topics, including ethics, sustainability, and environmental justice. While the learning outcomes are not limited to these areas, they are used as examples in this chapter to demonstrate how this pedagogical method can be applied in the classroom.

I also provide a worksheet (along with a completed example) to guide educators in using systems thinking to adapt existing RPG scenarios for their classrooms. The implementation steps, which I explore in detail in this chapter, include:

1. Identifying the learning outcomes
2. Identifying the core system of the game
3. Finding efficiencies between the game system and learning outcomes
4. Identifying the timeline
5. Getting help from students for the world setting (collective brainstorming)
6. Altering the scenario based on efficiencies and timeline
7. Conducting the game session
8. Discussing the outcomes with the students

BACKGROUND

Tabletop RPGs are already used in a variety of contexts, including more traditionally structured classes. Their uses include but are not limited to history, science, math, language, literacy, therapy, and even anti-bullying programs. For example, Shoenberger (2024) reviews the use of tabletop RPGs in higher education and notes a variety of different approaches. Abbott et al. (2022), Bagès et al. (2021), and Kaylor (2017) provide evidence of tabletop RPGs being used for social-emotional learning, literacy, and bullying prevention. Hammer et al. (2024) and Bowman (2010) showcase tabletop RPGs as tools for experiential and active learning, supporting a range of subjects and skills.

For the implementation of tabletop RPGs, the age groups vary; they can be deployed in K-12 classrooms or higher education. However, as I highlighted previously, it is not always easy to use tabletop RPGs in the classroom. Selecting the correct games, planning how to moderate them, ensuring the gameplay fits within the constraints of a packed syllabus, and more challenges often fall on the teachers. Running a tabletop RPG in the classroom often requires significant preparation, including story and character development, rule mastery, and adaptation to the classroom context. The extra-cognitive load and the need for rule mastery can be barriers, especially for instructors who are not already hobbyists. Additionally, Shoenberger (2024) highlights that tabletop RPGs can increase instructor workload, which is another significant barrier for the already overworked teachers.

As a scholar who wholeheartedly supports the use of games in the classroom, particularly for critical, meaningful, informal learning outcomes that are harder to address within traditional frameworks, my goal with this chapter is to contribute to the resources available for educators who wish to implement these outcomes through games but do not know how or where to start.

Before moving on to the other sections, I would like to position this chapter and its intentions more precisely. The core learning outcomes I focus on are informal in nature. This informality stems not only from the use of the games, but also from the learning goals they support. These goals differ from traditional outcomes like solving algebra problems, memorizing historical dates, or recalling formulas. Instead, the pedagogical approach introduced here centers on critical learning outcomes, topics such as discrimination, environmental justice, ethics, sustainability, mental health and so on. In this sense, both the environment (tabletop

RPGs) and the learning outcomes reflect a more informal pedagogy. As an educator, I believe that these outcomes should be integral to traditional education, even though they require more planning than rote memorization or standardized testing.

Another important consideration is the role of Micro Tabletop Role-Playing Games (micro tabletop RPGs). These games and game sessions are already designed to be shorter and easier to engage with than traditional tabletop RPGs. For example, Zamboni et al.'s book *Roll for Learning: 51 Micro Tabletop Roleplaying Games to Use in the Classroom* (2024) is an excellent resource filled with short-form games deployable in diverse educational settings. However, the goal of this chapter is to help make longer tabletop RPGs playable in the classroom, what I call "micro-fying", by modifying longer games into shorter formats that align with class time and learning goals. Thus, this chapter functions as a toolkit for deploying an existing tabletop RPG effectively, including strategies for involving students in the worldbuilding process, rather than providing a list of games to choose from.

Finally, systems thinking is the backbone of how I propose to resolve these challenges as well as providing an accessible, easy-to-implement tool for those who might wish to benefit from tabletop RPGs in their classrooms. Systems thinking is a framework for understanding how parts of a system interact to produce outcomes, often in ways that are nonlinear, complex, or unintended (Meadows 2008; Sellers 2017; Stroh 2015). Rather than focusing on isolated components, systems thinking emphasizes relationships, feedback loops, and patterns of behavior over time. It involves understanding a whole through its interconnected components that function both independently and interdependently. Many scholars and practitioners discuss the value of systems thinking as a tool for addressing complex, societal problems as well as how we engage with these as individuals and communities. For instance, Benson and Perullo (2017), Cababa (2023), and Jones and Van Ael (2022) consider systems thinking's benefits from a design perspective where they focus on how systems are understood, impacted and intervened. Naturally, this understanding of systems brings care and intentional practices regarding societal systems. In some ways, systems thinking eliminates individualistic thinking and allows people to engage with the larger, complex societal contexts. I would argue that systems thinking is itself a critical learning outcome since it allows a shift of perspective from individual to collective while it replaces lack of care with empathy. This is especially important in today's society where people are getting more and more disconnected with communities which is at odds with the fact that everyday actions do not occur in isolation but impact our collective wellbeing.

Therefore, including systems thinking in education and pedagogical practices is particularly important for illustrating how each student, as a member of society, is connected to larger-scale societal, economic, ecological, etc. systems that operate in the world. This lens enables students to see how individual actions relate to these broader structures and fosters critical thinking around causality and consequence (Arnold and Wade 2015). Teaching with systems is a necessity to raise new generations who understand their own agency and use it for positive impact. This implementation can be in a variety of levels and across topics, and can be modeled through a range of assignments. As a game design educator, I often teach my students how individual game elements influence the larger game system. For example, if a student designs a mechanic, I encourage them to think about what that mechanic asks players to perform during gameplay. One example I frequently use is the concept of collectibles and ownership. Collectibles are common elements in many games, yet designers and players often overlook their deeper implications. Introducing consequences for collecting items from dungeons, sacred areas, or temples can serve as a powerful tool to challenge students' assumptions about ownership, cultural respect, and entitlement. Similarly, I believe it is crucial to examine the assumptions inherent in gameplay, and to reflect on the broader implications of these assumptions, especially when adapting an existing game and its system for educational purposes.

With that, in terms of the way systems thinking is implemented, the tabletop RPG space is one of the few areas where the concept of system-ness in games does not need to be justified, as different games and rule sets are already commonly referred to as *systems* within the tabletop RPG community. Within this space, there is a wide variety of such systems, some more popular than others. These include, but are not limited to, *D&D*, *Pathfinder*, *Call of Cthulhu*, and *Vampire: The Masquerade*. It is also common for game masters and designers to create their own systems. Systemic understanding is essential for running and participating in tabletop RPGs as well as making sense of a game scenario and its elements.

In this sense, particularly in the context of tabletop RPGs, systems thinking is already an embedded and powerful tool: players interact with complex mechanics, take on roles with differing incentives, and observe how their decisions ripple across the game world. This makes tabletop RPGs excellent spaces for discussing societal and systemic issues by merging their existing system-ness with the systems behind topics and issues targeted by educators. Therefore, this chapter applies systems thinking as both a theoretical foundation and a practical method for adapting existing tabletop RPGs for classroom use.

HOW DO TABLETOP RPGS PRODUCE CRITICAL LEARNING OUTCOMES THROUGH SYSTEMS THINKING?

As I highlighted earlier, it has been established by a variety of scholars (Abbott et al. 2022; Bagès et al. 2021; Burns 2014; Kaylor 2017) that tabletop RPGs are an excellent way to engage students in critical thinking about diverse issues. They encourage players to empathize with characters who may have different perspectives, lived experiences, and life goals than the players themselves. This also provides space for active, experiential learning, where role-play becomes a pedagogical tool (Yolaç and Crum 2024; Hammer et al. 2024; Weiner 2018; Daniau 2016; Bowman 2010). While role-playing is not a magical solution for understanding all diverse experiences, gameplay can significantly enhance players' understanding of societal systems and the agents within these structures. Sometimes, these playful interventions are grouped under the umbrella of gamification. As an educator and game studies researcher, the term *gamification* makes me hesitant, as those unfamiliar with the field might perceive it as merely a rebranding effort. For instance, if exams are renamed *boss fights* and learning modules are called *levels*, the full potential of how games can be used in the classroom remains unrealized. This is because while the new names signify play, the activities remain the same as the original delivery method. Therefore, the intention of this chapter is not to simply make classroom content sound more fun but to deploy actual gameplay as a meaningful pedagogical tool.

As hands-on experiences, tabletop RPGs create a safe and engaging space for players to experiment with different ideologies while observing the impacts of specific actions. For instance, in a game where players influence a fictional society, different groups can observe the systemic implications of their actions within the context of the game. As I highlighted in the previous sections, this observation of systems is central to the approach I suggest for implementing tabletop RPGs in classrooms.

Usually, discussing societal systems and their agents does not evoke a large-scale, systemic understanding in students, who are often too young to conceptualize systems on an abstract level. Tabletop RPGs exemplify these concepts on a smaller, more manageable scale, making it easier for students to understand their own impact as well as the roles of others within these systems. As the core example of this chapter is environmental justice, the systemic connection between overconsumption and unsustainable practices that disproportionately affect developing countries can be the exemplary focus. Students may not initially grasp how buying unnecessary items and discarding them out of boredom contributes to global issues. However, through an RPG that includes perspectives from consumers, policymakers, and underrepresented groups in developing countries, students can explore how overconsumption connects to environmental injustice. The game might trace the journey of discarded items to landfills in other parts of the world, illustrating the health and economic hazards these practices impose on affected communities.

In this hypothetical scenario, students can better understand their role as consumers and the broader implications of their actions. Although this experience does not equate to living in a developing country facing such challenges, role-playing as someone navigating these systemic issues provides students with a more immersive and impactful learning experience. This method fosters a deeper understanding of the interconnectedness of systems and the roles individuals and groups play within them. By thinking of games as systems themselves, educators can identify and adapt these systems to achieve critical learning outcomes tailored to specific classroom contexts. This systems-based approach offers a powerful way to help students connect abstract concepts to tangible, experiential learning opportunities.

IMPLEMENTATION IN THE CLASSROOM

Building on the previous sections, we can now explore practical ways to leverage systems and systems thinking to adapt existing tabletop RPGs for classroom use. The following are suggested steps for adapting a tabletop RPG for educational settings. At the end of the chapter, I have included worksheets for both instructors and players. To illustrate these suggestions, I continue to use environmental justice as a critical learning outcome. This theme is applied consistently in the next section and in the completed worksheets provided as examples. However, as noted earlier, critical learning outcomes are not limited to environmental justice, and the worksheet can be applied to a wide range of educational objectives.

It is also important to emphasize that these are suggestions rather than prescriptions. As a scholar and educator who strives to create tools that are adaptable and versatile, I intend for this chapter to serve as an open invitation for educators to modify and adjust these strategies to best meet their specific teaching goals.

Identifying the Learning Outcomes

Identifying the learning outcomes is the most important aspect of this process. This is because, depending on the intended learning outcomes, the structure of the game session and the overall system can change drastically. I suggest identifying one main learning outcome along with a few supporting ones that are as specific as possible. If the learning outcomes are too numerous, the intended goals can become nebulous and difficult for players or students to grasp during a shorter play session, which is typical within classroom timelines.

To exemplify this, I will continue with my hypothetical scenario of teaching about environmental justice. For instance, within this topic, a potential learning outcome could be *Understanding Environmental Justice Issues Guided by Consumption Practices.* While this sounds specific, it actually remains a broad topic. To make it more manageable, we can focus on one of several possible scenarios that illustrate the issue—such as using the journey of a consumer product as the focal point of the learning outcome.

Identifying the Core System of the Game

As the second step, it is crucial to identify the core system of the game. This includes the core mechanics, gameplay rules, and how players interact with the game world and with each other.

Core mechanics define how actions are resolved whenever an outcome is uncertain, such as rolling a die or drawing a card to determine whether something results in success or failure. These mechanics influence the types of characters that can exist in the game and determine how player progress is tracked, potentially leading to new abilities or leveling up for the characters they portray.

Gameplay rules determine when and to what extent players have active agency in the game. Many games include distinct rules for various contexts, such as systems for engaging in combat or participating in negotiations, each implementing character abilities differently. For example, in *D&D*, there is a turn-based combat system in which players take turns and have a limited number of actions. However, outside of these combat events, such as when exploring a new town, shopping, or engaging with non-player characters, players take actions more discursively and in whatever order they choose.

Additionally, other systems exist to balance magic and special abilities in relation to the character's species, level, and class. Gameplay rules establish the structure of these distinct subsystems and determine how they interact with one another.

Some games also include rules governing the game economy, which define what equipment is available to players and how much inventory they can carry. This includes describing what players can do with specific items, how they acquire and trade these items, and more. For example, in some tabletop RPGs, players may possess weapons or materials that allow them to cast spells. In this way, the game economy becomes another essential component of the core system, shaping how players experience, participate in, and navigate the game world.

In most tabletop RPGs, these systems are highly complex. It often takes players a significant amount of time to develop an in-depth understanding of the core mechanics. Games like *D&D* and *Call of Cthulhu* have extensive rulebooks and guides to help players grasp these systems. This complexity is one of the main challenges of integrating tabletop RPGs into classroom settings. Unless all students are seasoned tabletop RPG players familiar with a variety of systems, it is nearly impossible to teach all the rules, create characters, and play a scenario within the time constraints of a class session.

For this reason, the first and most critical step in adapting a tabletop RPG for classroom use is to significantly reduce this complexity. To achieve this, I suggest preparing a toolkit that includes simplified character types and a few ready-made scenarios for students to play. This approach is discussed in more detail in the following sections and is exemplified through the instructor worksheet provided at the end of the chapter.

Finding Efficiencies between the Game System and Learning Outcomes

Finding efficiencies is crucial to conducting a gameplay experience that is genuinely beneficial for students. By efficiencies, I specifically refer to opportunities where the game system itself can be leveraged to structure learning outcomes in a systemic way—namely, when a single game element serves multiple learning goals. This is also the stage where the system-ness of the game is most effectively leveraged to address a systemic issue. For example, if implementing a specific rule leads to students understanding and experiencing multiple points in a systemic issue, that can be a strategic pedagogical decision. At this point, educators can decide which elements of the core system are essential to achieving the learning outcomes and which can be removed.

In the example used here—exploring the journey of consumer items and consumption practices in the context of environmental justice—combat mechanics are not essential, while mechanics for navigating conversations are. If the instructor is using *D&D*, for instance, skills such as persuasion, deception, and insight are part of the system that governs social interactions and can be used to engage with various agents within the scenario, resulting in multiple moments of learning.

Another important consideration is that the game does not need to be balanced. In fact, this imbalance might itself reflect the desired learning outcome. For example, in the environmental justice game, consumers and companies could be given more advantages, mirroring the inequities present in real-life systems.

Finally, it can be highly engaging to remain true to the typical setting of the tabletop RPG system being adapted for classroom use. For instance, the environmental justice issue could be reimagined within a *D&D*-like setting. The consumer might live in Baldur's Gate (a city in the *D&D* universe), the company could be represented as a wealthy merchant hoarding wealth, and the developing country citizens might be depicted as people living in the remote forests surrounding the city. Similarly, if the tabletop RPG system is *Cyberpunk*, the setting and characters could take on a futuristic tone, with consumed items represented as body enhancements and waste depicted as discarded body modifications. I find that using such speculative worlds adds an extra layer of interest to the role-playing and worldbuilding experience.

Identifying the Timeline and the Number of Students

The classroom structure is another important consideration. In most tabletop RPGs, players engage with a story that is largely predetermined. While the outcomes may vary based on player decisions, the overall story arc is typically prepared in advance by the moderator. As a result, the story length and the degree of player agency may need to be adjusted depending on how much time the instructor has for running the game. For instance, the gameplay experience can differ significantly between a fifty-minute session and a two-hour session.

Additionally, if the game is being implemented in a larger class, students can be divided into groups, allowing them to act as collectives rather than as individual characters. This method works especially well for more discussion-based topics, as the facilitator can check in with each group individually without needing to guide the entire conversation in real time. Therefore, these structural decisions should be made during the preparation phase.

Getting Help from Students for the World Setting (Collective Brainstorming)

Collective worldbuilding is a core step for involving students in the process and helping them understand both the systems and agents specific to a critical learning outcome. The brainstorming process should identify the main elements of the world, such as the systems, story, characters, and goals. As I previously mentioned, it is a good tactic to come prepared with a mostly defined world setting while allowing students to make smaller decisions, as this helps increase their investment in the experience. Alternatively, it is also possible to rely entirely on this step for worldbuilding, though it is important to note that this approach will require more time.

At this stage, depending on how the class is divided, the agents (i.e., characters and entities affecting the system) can be matched to the number of players or groups. For example, if the class is divided into groups of three, there can be three types of roles. While this can be done as a class discussion, these roles can also be identified through a systems diagram which simply marks the connections between different agents. Building this map of relations can be another class activity to engage the students. In the case of the environmental justice game, for example, the roles might include consumers, companies, and developing country citizens. If the instructor wishes to expand the scenario further, they could add roles such as policymakers, individuals responsible for transporting goods, factory owners, and so on. The depth of the system and its agents should be determined by the available time, the intended learning outcomes, and the classroom structure.

If students are newer to tabletop RPGs or the classroom includes varying comfort levels with performance-based play, the educator can simplify or pre-load certain narrative elements, such as offering pre-written character motivations or scenario prompts. On the other hand, more advanced or experienced groups can be prompted to co-create complexity during the session. For example, students might develop character goals based on their reading of a systems diagram or previous class content, creating a richer integration between systems learning and worldbuilding.

The most important aspect is ensuring that each character has a role in the system, a goal, a hindrance, and something that gives them an advantage. For example, using the *D&D* system, some characters might have a bonus or penalty applied to their dice rolls for specific actions depending on their roles.

Altering the Scenario Based on Efficiencies and Timeline

This step is closely tied to classroom dynamics and the goals established in the earlier stages. It can be facilitated during the brainstorming session or finalized shortly afterward. At this point, educators draw on the information gathered during previous steps, such as class size, available time, learning objectives, and key game mechanics, to fine-tune the scenario. This step serves as the final stage before launching the game session, where the instructor uses their preparation, student input, and classroom constraints to produce a scenario best suited to their goals. The aim is to ensure that the final gameplay structure not only fits within logistical limitations but also effectively supports the identified learning outcomes through an engaging and exciting scenario that keeps students invested.

Ultimately, in this last stage before running the game session, the educator acts as both designer and facilitator, curating the appropriate level of scenario complexity and shaping the balance between open-ended play and structured guidance. This helps ensure that the scenario is neither too shallow to provoke insight nor too elaborate to fit within the instructional framework.

Conducting the Game Session

Before starting the game, each student should complete their worksheets to ensure there is a shared understanding of the goals, how their character functions, and how they will engage with the game. While the worksheets can be filled out during the brainstorming session, they must be completed before the game session begins.

For this systems-based method, I offer a few suggestions for classroom management, particularly since one of the main challenges of implementing tabletop RPGs is that most require a game master or an equivalent role to run the game. First, this role can be directly replicated. The session can be conducted as a single large tabletop RPG session with the instructor acting as the game master. If the game is used in a large classroom setting, students can be divided into groups that decide on the next steps collectively. For example, one group might represent consumers, another companies, and so on. Second, the class can be divided into multiple smaller groups, each running its own parallel game session. Following the current example, each group would include roles such as consumers, different companies, merchants, and so on. In this setup, the instructor serves as a central facilitator rather than a traditional game master. The instructor introduces shared prompts, challenges, or dilemmas to all groups and provides a set amount of time for each to collaboratively develop a response based on how their gameplay unfolds. This process can be repeated multiple times with different prompts and scenarios, as long as they align with the overall narrative and learning goals. This more modular structure enables comparative discussion and analysis, particularly when group outcomes vary. To add a sense of closure and motivation, the instructor may designate a winning group, such as the one that most effectively meets its objectives or demonstrates the strongest engagement with the learning outcomes.

Finally, it is important to use safety tools during gameplay. One such helpful and accessible tool is John Stavropoulos's X-Card. As Stavropoulos (2022, 2) explains:

> The X-Card is an optional tool…that allows anyone in your game (including you) to edit out any content anyone is uncomfortable with as you play. Since most RPGs are improvisational and we won't know what will happen till it happens, it's possible the game will go in a direction people don't want. An X-Card is a simple tool to fix problems as they arise.

Because critical learning outcomes may touch on sensitive issues, it is essential to inform students about the structure and themes of the session in advance. Moreover, students should be explicitly told that they may pause or stop at any time, or choose not to participate at all. This ensures that students feel safe when engaging with fictional scenarios and complex social issues during gameplay.

Discussing the Outcomes with the Students

While playing tabletop RPGs in the classroom is an effective teaching tool, unpacking the play experience is equally important. Discussing the outcomes, what occurred during the game, and what students learned from their experience is a crucial step. Below are some suggested discussion points to reinforce and assess critical learning outcomes:

- Understanding of the system the game addresses
- Exploration of the different perspectives gained from playing various characters
- Discussion of the implications for the real world
- Reflection on how this experience may have updated the players' perspectives regarding the targeted issue

In the example sheet at the end of this chapter, I have included sample questions that can be used to initiate and moderate these discussions. While this section emphasizes class discussion, these learning outcomes can be assessed in a variety of other ways depending on the group's level and the classroom context. Assessment tools may include student reflections, short story writing, systems mapping, researching analogous real-world issues, creating artwork based on the theme, and more.

As I emphasized at the beginning of this section, these steps are intended to be used as a flexible tool that can help instructors quickly, easily, and effectively implement tabletop RPGs into their classrooms. The steps can be changed, moved, and merged. New steps can be added, or they can serve as inspiration for entirely new processes. All these adaptations are more than welcome, as the goal of this chapter is to help, guide, encourage, and inspire. Ultimately, what matters most is not strict adherence to a particular structure, but the commitment to creating meaningful, critical, and engaging learning experiences.

CONCLUSION

To conclude this chapter, I would like to reiterate the importance of systems thinking as both a tool for engaging with critical issues and a method for leveraging game systems to integrate these topics into gameplay. Once again, I hope this chapter serves as an invitation for more educators to adopt tabletop RPGs in exploring topics that are often difficult to teach through traditional structures and settings.

Whatever skills and knowledge our students gain, they will eventually apply them in the real world, creating tangible impacts on society. Tabletop RPGs are excellent tools for simulating that impact and for showcasing perspectives, thinking strategies, communities, and cultures that students might not otherwise encounter. While I do not believe tabletop RPGs are a definitive solution to addressing all the complex systems and diverse experiences we navigate, they are invaluable for helping students begin to realize how much they may not yet know, and how much they are capable of influencing. Tabletop RPGs create a safe space for negotiating, experimenting with, and understanding these systems. This is why leveraging them as both fun and meaningful pedagogical tools is more important than ever, especially as we face systemic issues in various scales. As educators, we should strive to produce more tools, guides, and suggestions to support the education of the next generation: communities capable of making a remarkable impact on the world.

INSTRUCTOR WORKSHEET

1. **The tabletop RPG system (which tabletop RPG game the session is based on)**

2. **What is adapted (mechanics and core elements)**

3. **The length of the session**

4. **What can a player do in their turn?**

5. **Learning goals**

6. **The scenario**

7. **Roles and goals**

8. **One round (what can each player do in a round, how long is a round, etc.)**

9. **Discussion points**

INSTRUCTOR WORKSHEET FILLED EXAMPLE

1. **The tabletop RPG system (which tabletop RPG game the session is based on)**
   Dungeons and Dragons

2. **What is adapted (mechanics and core elements)**
   Simple conversations and skill checks using a 12-sided die. Turn-based system.

3. **The length of the session:** 45 minutes

4. **What can a player do in their turn?**
   The player can roll a 12-sided die to determine the outcome of their action. In this adaptation, players can sort items, deceive and persuade other players. In their turn, the players can also continue their role-play through conversation and interact with their in-game environment as their character.

5. **Learning goals**
   Environmental justice.

6. **The scenario**
   In this scenario, the players attempt to achieve their goals based on their assigned roles. According to the narrative, the consumer is trying to keep up with new trends but becomes overwhelmed by their purchases, leading them to regularly clean out their house. The company works to sell more products by creating new trends. Meanwhile, the developing country citizen focuses on sorting as much trash as possible to prevent hazardous gases from building up in their city.

   Since the game uses the *D&D* system, the events take place in Baldur's Gate, a major city in the world of *D&D*.

7. **Roles and goals**
   The consumer is a citizen of Baldur's Gate. He enjoys following the latest trends in the city and is particularly interested in unique gadgets. His recent purchases include items like a shoelace-tying machine, an automatic horse brusher (which turned out to be a bad idea), a flaming mustache curler, and invisible ink that he struggles to write with.

The company is a well-known merchant. She frequently sets up large stands to showcase all the new gadgets she creates. It is also known that she distributes her gadgets to the wealthiest citizens of the city for free. Rumor has it that she even pays them to publicly use her gadgets. Who cares if the automatic horse brusher doesn't work? The Countess has one, so it must be desirable!

The citizen is a woman who lives in the forest far from Baldur's Gate. She is part of a small community tasked with sorting the city's trash. She dreams of starting her own business making backpack baskets for travelers. However, due to the increasing demands of sorting, she can't find the time, as the growing piles of trash are making people sick. She knows she could earn more money with her own business, but she is stuck in the never-ending cycle of trash sorting.

8. **One round (what can each player do in a round, how long is a round)** In this adaptation, one round of gameplay represents one month. Each player takes one turn per month. All players roll their dice simultaneously, and the outcomes are then resolved one by one in the order determined by the moderator.

The Consumer

The consumer's goal is to become the most trend-savvy person in Baldur's Gate. They aim to reach a point where they have a +20 bonus for all their trend rolls.

1. *Roll for Trends*
   The consumer tries to follow trends each month. If the merchant rolls higher than 15 for their influence, the consumer gets a +1 bonus to their check. This bonus accumulates each month. For example, if they receive +1 in the first month and +1 in the second month, they will have +2 moving forward. However, if the merchant rolls 5 or under, the consumer receives a –1 penalty to their check.

   The consumer also buys interesting objects each month, purchasing half of the trends they discover. For example, if they roll 16 for trends, they purchase 8 items.

2. *Roll for Trash (starting after the first month)*
   The consumer has limited space, so they must get rid of some items they previously bought. The player rolls a d20 to determine how

many items they throw away. If the number rolled is higher than the number of items they own, they discard all their items.

The Merchant

The merchant's goal is to develop 40 trends in a month.

1. *Roll for Exposure*
   The merchant rolls to develop trends each month. First, they roll for exposure among the wealthiest citizens of Baldur's Gate. If they roll 10 or higher, they convince one influential person to be seen using one of their artifacts. If they roll a 20, this increases to two influential people. The exposure benefit rolls to the next month, making it gradually grow.
2. *Roll for Influence*
   The merchant rolls for influence each month. The number of influential people using their products is added to this roll. For example, if they roll a 10 and have 1 influential person using their products, their total influence roll becomes 11. The number of trends is related to influence, which is twice as their total influence. For example, if the merchant's total influence is 11, then they create 22 trends that month.

The Citizen

The citizen's goal is to have extra time after finishing sorting trash. If they accumulate a total of 50 days, they achieve their goal of starting their own business.

1. *Roll for Sorting*
   Each month, the citizen rolls to determine how many days they spend sorting trash. The consumer's roll for discarded items is added to this number. For example, if the citizen rolls 13 and the consumer gets rid of 10 items, the citizen works for 23 days. If the total exceeds 30, the remaining number rolls over to the next month and is added to the consumer's upcoming trash for that month.
2. *Roll for Negotiation*
   Each month, the citizen attempts to convince the merchant to reduce their production. To succeed, they must roll the same number or higher than the merchant's influence roll of the month. If

successful, the merchant's influence is halved for the following month.

9. **Discussion points**
    - How fair was the system?
    - What are some real-life parallels to the gameplay?
    - How did the players feel during the session?
    - How could each character be reimagined to balance the system?
    - What might be some real-life implications regarding the behaviors of different agents in similar systems?
    - What actions can we take as individuals to promote environmental justice?

PLAYER WORKSHEET

1. **Character name**

2. **Character role**

3. **The scenario**

4. **What can the player do in their turn?**

5. **Tracker (note any items, numbers, etc. you might need to keep tracking throughout the session)**

PLAYER WORKSHEET FILLED EXAMPLE (COMPANY/MERCHANT)

1. **Character name**
   Eileen Lock
2. **Character role**
   Eileen is a well-known merchant. She frequently sets up large stands to showcase all the new gadgets she creates. It is also known that she distributes her gadgets to the wealthiest citizens of the city for free. Rumor has it that she even pays them to publicly use her

gadgets. Who cares if the automatic horse brusher doesn't work? The Countess has one, so it must be desirable!

3. **The scenario**

   In this scenario, the players attempt to achieve their goals based on their assigned roles. According to the narrative, the consumer is trying to keep up with new trends but becomes overwhelmed by their purchases, leading them to regularly clean out their house. The company works to sell more products by creating new trends. Meanwhile, the developing country citizen focuses on sorting as much trash as possible to prevent hazardous gases from building up in their city.

   Since the game uses the *D&D* system, the events take place in Baldur's Gate, a major city in the world of *D&D*.

4. **What can the player do in their turn?**

   The merchant's goal is to develop 40 trends in a month.

   1. *Roll for Exposure*

      The merchant rolls to develop trends each month. First, they roll for exposure among the wealthiest citizens of Baldur's Gate. If they roll 10 or higher, they convince one influential person to be seen using one of their artifacts. If they roll a 20, this increases to two influential people. The exposure benefit rolls to the next month, making it gradually grow.

   2. *Roll for Influence*

      The merchant rolls for influence each month. The number of influential people using their products is added to this roll. For example, if they roll a 10 and have 1 influential person using their products, their total influence roll becomes 11. The number of trends is related to influence, which is twice as their total influence. For example, if the merchant's total influence is 11, then they create 22 trends that month.

5. **Tracker (note any items, numbers, etc. you might need to keep tracking throughout the session)**

REFERENCES

Abbott, Matthew S., Kimberly A. Stauss, and Allen F. Burnett. "Table-top role-playing games as a therapeutic intervention with adults to increase social connectedness." *Social Work with Groups* 45, no. 1 (2022): 16–31.

Arnold, Ross D., and Jon P. Wade. "A definition of systems thinking: A systems approach." *Procedia Computer Science* 44 (2015): 669–678.

Bagès, Céline, Natacha Hoareau, and Alain Guerrien. "Play to reduce bullying! Role-playing games are a useful tool for therapists and teachers." *Journal of Research in Childhood Education* 35, no. 4 (2021): 631–641.

Benson, Eric, and Yvette Perullo. *Design to Renourish: Sustainable Graphic Design in Practice*. CRC Press, 2017.

Bowman, Sarah Lynne. *The Functions of Role-Playing Games: How Participants Create Community, Solve Problems and Explore Identity*. McFarland, 2010.

Burns, Kevin. "The therapy game: Nordic larp, psychotherapy, and player safety." *The Wyrd Con Companion Book 2014*, edited by Sarah Lynne Bowman, 28–41, Wyrd Con, 2014.

Cababa, Sheryl. *Closing the Loop: Systems Thinking for Designers*. Rosenfeld Media, 2023.

Daniau, Stéphane. "The transformative potential of role-playing games—: From play skills to human skills." *Simulation & Gaming* 47, no. 4 (2016): 423–444.

Hammer, Jessica, AlexandraTo, Karen Schrier, Sarah Lynne Bowman, and Geoff Kaufman. "Learning and role-playing games." In *The Routledge Handbook of Role-Playing Game Studies*, edited by José Zagal and Sebastian Deterding, 299–316. Routledge, 2024.

Jones, Peter, and Kristel Van Ael. *Design Journeys through Complex Systems: Practice Tools for Systemic Design*. Bis Publishers, 2022.

Kaylor, Stefanie LB. "Dungeons and Dragons and literacy: the role tabletop role-playing games can play in developing teenagers' literacy skills and reading interests." Master's Thesis, University of Northern Iowa, 2017.

Meadows, Donella H. *Thinking in Systems: A Primer*. Chelsea Green Publishing, 2008.

Sellers, Michael. *Advanced Game Design: A Systems Approach*. Addison-Wesley Professional, 2017.

Shoenberger, Michael. "Tertiary learning usage of tabletop roleplaying games: Affordances and challenges." In *Revitalising Higher Education: Insights from Te Puna Aurei LearnFest 2022*, edited by Bowell, Tracy, Nicole Pepperell, Anthony Richardson, Maria-Teresa Corino, 80–86, Cardiff University Press, 2024.

Stavropoulos, John. *Safety Tools for Simulations and Role-Playing Games*. 2022. https://upload.wikimedia.org/wikipedia/commons/e/e0/X-Card_by_John_Stavropoulos.pdf

Stroh, David Peter. *Systems Thinking for Social Change: A Practical Guide to Solving Complex Problems, Avoiding Unintended Consequences, and Achieving Lasting Results*. Chelsea Green Publishing, 2015.

Weiner, Susan. "Case Studies as Tabletop RPGs." *International Journal of Role-Playing* 8 (2018): 21–25.

Yolaç, Ahu, and Lilian Crum. "The Council," In *Roll for Learning: 51 Micro Tabletop Role-Playing Games to Use in the Classroom*, edited by Zamboni, Camilla, Matthew Farber, and William Merchant., 495–504. Play Story Press, 2024.

Zamboni, Camilla, Matthew Farber, and William Merchant. *Roll for Learning: 51 Micro Tabletop Role-Playing Games to Use in the Classroom*. Play Story Press, 2024.

CHAPTER 3

The Impact of Role-Playing Game Mechanics on the Classroom Experience

Justin Berry

INTRODUCTION

The free play of children, hosting tea parties for their toys or pretending to make meals out of mud, is done without the express intention of learning; it is a way for them to imagine themselves in the role of an adult. They watch adults perform the motions of activities and move through those motions themselves in a context-free consequence. The next time they observe adults engaging in such activities, perhaps they compare it to their own efforts, thinking of new ways to play or seeing steps in the process that they forgot to include. Next time they play, they might try to decorate the mud with pebbles or stir a spoon around in their empty cup before pretending to take a sip. There are no tests, nor any formal curriculum, but they are, of course, learning about the world (Vygotsky 1978).

Formal education, the kind that we implement in classrooms, needs to convey explicit information that such unstructured play is not guaranteed to address (Piaget 1950). Educators structure the information that needs

DOI: 10.1201/9781003641384-5

to be conveyed and strategize about how best to convey it. The default method, if the task is approached in its most literal form, is simply to recite that information, perhaps provide some examples, and to test student retention of such information through exams or quizzes. This manner of rote delivery is equivalent to trying to shove food in someone's mouth by force; it may or may not address their nutritional needs, but it most certainly will not make them excited for mealtimes, or lead them to wonder at the subtleties of spice or flavor (Freire, Ramos, and Macedo 2014). Rote delivery fails to solve the most critical goal of an education, which is not to make students a repository for what is known, but to instill in them the capacity to discover and articulate the unknown. John Dewey's work on educational theory suggests that the best outcomes for students occur when they meaningfully connect with the material being conveyed and engage with it in a hands-on manner (Dewey 2024). By solving problems with other students and communicating ideas, while listening to and critiquing the ideas of their collaborators, students build a foundation of knowledge that is robust and adaptable. Ideas do not exist in discrete pieces, relevant only within a given context; they are tools suitable to many tasks. The play of the young child making mud cakes does more than provide a recipe; it gives them a relationship to cooking and to the observation of cooking that expands as they grow older (Gopnik, Meltzoff, and Kuhl 1999).

Connecting the play-based learning of the child to the rubric-driven classroom is a challenge that effective educators approach in many ways. This book is looking at a particular type of play, the kind that occurs in tabletop role-playing games (RPGs). Much like the child's tea party, RPGs allow players to practice social dynamics and do so from a perspective that often differs greatly from their own. Pretend play, the kind facilitated by these games, has impact on children's ability to solve problems, and there is a deficit of time devoted to such play in typical classroom environments (Bergen 2002). The goal of this chapter is to reflect on the challenges and opportunities that exist when bringing tabletop RPGs into the classroom to rectify that deficit.

If the default method of conveying detailed and specific information is to present that information by rote, the default method of incorporating tabletop RPGs into a classroom might be to use the most popular game, *Dungeons and Dragons* (*D&D*), and embed course material as a parcel delivered through the game's narrative (Sousa et al. 2023). A class teaching about Egyptian burial customs might have players explore a pyramid to uncover the weakness of a mummy that is attacking local villagers. This approach effectively combines the fun and interactive features of the game with the specific learning requirements of the classroom, but it does not leverage the full capacity of the medium.

Narrative is a powerful feature of tabletop gaming (Kumral and Meza 2024; Bowman 2024), but an over-reliance on the use of narrative to convey material does not utilize the medium's ability to consolidate social bonds and build creative confidence in players. Narrative over-reliance is not the product of laziness or a lack of intention: it is the predictable outcome when educators, with an expertise in education, try to incorporate something that they know has value to their class but that they may not know how to optimize. Here is a teacher describing their own process of deciding to integrate tabletop RPGs in their classroom, as quoted in (Cullinan 2024):

> A friend] had just gotten me into D&D and I was sitting there and I was like, man, this is [a] really cool game, I really enjoy. This [is] fun! I heard Dragon Talk and Greg Tito and Shelly Masanobu talking to some educators and I believe it was a psychologist who was talking about how he used D&D as a part of the RPG therapy experience. [Dragon Talk: Teaching with D&D, 6/11/18] I was just like - Oh. This is great. I could do this. This is awesome, I love it.
>
> *(Cullinan 2024)*

This is an educator who sees the promise and the opportunity for games in the classroom but who might not know the best ways to implement them. They understand how games can improve their classroom experience, but they may not intuitively know why or how; they might be familiar with the most popular examples of tabletop RPGs, but they may not be aware of how they compare to other options. This chapter is for them.

What I want to do here is provide a deeper awareness of how tabletop RPGs function so that educators can supplement narrative-driven approaches with strategies that also produce emergent outcomes. Studies have shown that tabletop RPGs have embedded benefits (Walsh and Linehan 2024), and so, if the only way that they supplement the subject matter is to make learning it more fun, then students will have fun learning and acquire some social and emotional skills along the way. Emergent learning does something different though, it provides students an opportunity to discover something on their own, with their own logic, so that the material is not merely remembered, but it is understood.

Emergence, in the context of game design, is when players predictably take on roles, or develop strategies, without ever being told or encouraged to do so. Summarized by Eric Zimmerman and Katie Salen in their book *Rules of Play*:

> Emergence in games results from the formal system of the game put to use by players. Bluffing in Poker, for example, is not explicitly stated in the rules of the game, but it is a pattern of player behavior that emerges from the game.
>
> *(Zimmerman 2003)*

We can see emergent outcomes in tabletop RPGs like *D&D* as well. Almost every gaming party starts off as a random group of people meeting each other (most classically in a tavern) and taking on small jobs for quick money. Then they save the world, conquer it, or destroy it. Why do groups of independent individuals, with conflicting goals and personalities, consistently take on such dramatic shared aspirations? More importantly, why will a group of students, even with nothing in common, connect over a collaborative narrative, developing a shared investment in the outcomes that they shape together?

THE CLASSROOM AS PART OF THE MAGIC CIRCLE

Games such as tabletop RPGs rely on creating what Johan Huizinga described as 'temporary worlds within the ordinary world, dedicated to the performance of an act apart' (Huizinga 1950), often referred to as the 'magic circle'. Students need varying amounts of time or activity to construct this magic circle so that they can enter a social contract where their actions take on special significance. The magic of the magic circle is not the mythological fantasy magic of the game; it is the seemingly miraculous quality of kinship and community that develops when a group of people collectively agree to suspend their disbelief. Leveling up in a game might only involve changing a few numbers on a character sheet, but for a group of players that are operating in the magic circle, it is a moment of expansion into new realms of possibility (Meshcheryakova and Hemmert 2024). Inside the magic circle the outcomes of a collaborative fantasy can have tangible consequences (Bowman and Baird 2022). Players in an RPG are not merely telling a story, or listening to one, they are experiencing a narrative through the lens of their character, the game mechanics, and their own experience and contributions (Fine 1983). This complex interrelationship between active authorship and passive reception evolves over time and thus reinforcing the magic circle is integral to the sustained implementation of a game. To understand the ways that different games impact the magic circle, educators first need to understand the specific opportunities and limitations inherent to their own classroom.

Classrooms come in many shapes and sizes, and the material that they convey is even more diverse. No single game or singular approach can solve the challenges that might arise, and so determining the right game, or the right approach, requires a clear understanding of the kind of challenges being faced. Without reducing the complexities of the classroom experience too much, I want to highlight a few notable features that we can use to create meaningful comparisons between games and game mechanics.

LEARNING GOALS

From outside the classroom, the goal of an education might seem to be something discreet and well defined, but as educators, we understand that learning goals have a great deal of nuance. A botany class may teach the difference between a pistil and a stamen, but it also teaches students to practice observation in nature and to see the interdependence of organisms in an ecosystem. In the same way, elementary school classrooms teach reading and writing and the foundations of math, but they also teach social skills and emotion regulation (Pyle, DeLuca, and Danniels 2017). Tabletop RPGs are effective at supplementing and framing the overt focus of a class by reframing that subject matter in a fun and social context (Sousa et al. 2023). Social and emotional learning (SEL) is important at all ages, even in higher education, and many games will reinforce these skills without special rules or custom mechanics (Walsh and Linehan 2024); the act of play in such games is designed to foster effective communication, collaboration, and community behavior (Orr, King, and McGonnell 2020). Other learning goals might require more intentional approaches to integration, where one game might offer excellent frameworks for teaching math skills, another might encourage players to use language precisely and concisely. Tabletop RPGs are a genre of game, and within that genre, there are important differences that shape the outcomes of play in fundamental ways. When we look at a few specific games we can see how their mechanics reinforce specific learning goals more effectively than others. The work of Maryanne Cullinan and Jennifer Genova can offer a more robust and diverse array of examples for this (Cullinan and Genova 2023), but I am going to limit myself mostly to the selection of examples below in later sections for more direct comparison:

- Sustained games that integrate SEL with classroom management
- Highly specific educational aims such as understanding the political, cultural, and social complexities of 17th-century France through the lens of Louis 14th's court
- General approaches to teaching math or physics
- Using gameplay and game mechanics to support creative applications in reading, writing, and language development

CLASS SIZE AND GRADE LEVEL

Most tabletop games are optimized for groups of 3–6 players, one of whom is often designated as the Dungeon Master (DM) or Gamemaster (GM) and is responsible for running the game and arbitrating results. Most classrooms, by contrast, have many more students than that. One consideration in incorporating games into the class is knowing the best ways to bridge that gap by creating small teams of players or by isolating mechanics of the game that allow more players to participate concurrently. A useful solution is to find ways to incorporate elements of the game into the broader context of the class so that students are reinforcing the magic circle even outside of active play. If students at one table craft a potion to solve a problem, and another group builds a machine, part of the following week's lesson might involve learning about Leonardo da Vinci as an engineer of machines and as a painter whose methods involved experimental combinations of paint and substrate. Doing so means that even if students are playing in smaller groups, their actions in that game have relevance to the entire class.

The complexity of games also impacts their appropriateness for different age ranges and, while one solution is to choose simpler games, Jeremy Campell, in *Grammatical Man*, says:

> Complexity is not just a matter of a system having a lot of parts which are related to one another in nonsimple ways. Instead, it turns out to be a special property in its own right, and it makes complex systems different in kind from simple ones, enabling them to do things and be things we might not have expected.
>
> *(Campbell 1982)*

Complexity in games can limit their audience but it can also be integral to their effectiveness. When using complex games such as *D&D*, educators might select elements to include or exclude depending on the size and level of their class and consideration is required to understand how the mechanics of those elements will interact with other aspects of the game. In managing complexity, and accommodating groups of different ages and sizes, a general approach is to prioritize mechanics that support one's needs and minimize those that do not reinforce them. A class experience focused on geometry might eliminate most elements of play exist outside of combat and even reduce features of combat that don't reference the principles covered. Perhaps combat takes place across a gorge and requires that everything occurs at range, or perhaps the only effective options are based on area of effect. If the game is used to convey the challenges of a nomadic lifestyle, tracking the weight and size of belongings might embody cultural artifacts of that lifestyle. In a game meant to convey regional politics or practice social interactions, a mechanic that has so much detail might prove distracting or irrelevant. If the mechanics you employ as part of the lesson have dependencies on other game mechanics, it is important to include those additional mechanics. Mechanics that support totally separate pillars of play and do not support the content or skills to be learned are the ones that can be safely removed or reduced.

ACCESSIBILITY NEEDS

Accessibility barriers in tabletop gaming take many forms and not all of them are intuitive (Sousa et al. 2022). Additionally, it can be difficult, if not impossible, to accommodate access across all barriers. There are some strategies that can support students and are advisable in all contexts, and others that might be more particular to a specific population of students. Ultimately, the best solution is not to try and take an exhaustive approach but to equip yourself with a wide selection of accessibility aids and safety tools and implement them as appropriate. Advocates such as Jennifer

Kretchmer (Kretchmer) and JayOnyx (JayOnyx), among others, have compiled useful repositories of accessibility resources online, while books such as Elsa Sjunneson's *Fate Accessibility Toolkit* (Sjunneson 2019) offer more consolidated information. Tabletop RPGs can offer access to many groups of students and, when used appropriately, can even provide neurodiverse students new ways to connect with peers socially and emotionally (Atherton et al. 2024). Used inappropriately, however, tabletop games can alienate players or exacerbate their anxiety, which is why safety tools are used to give players methods to moderate play or communicate their needs (Bowman and Baird 2022).

For almost all game contexts, and especially in a classroom, it is important to include safety tools. Safety tools can best be described as procedures or practices that let players establish boundaries and foster healthy social interactions. The value of safety tools is not that they inhibit player behavior, but that they provide players a way to perceive and to reinforce the magic circle. An out-of-play tool, Lines and Veils (Edwards), involves checking in with players, prior to play, to establish 'lines' that should not be crossed, such as sexual assault, and those that can be part of play but only discussed in a 'veiled' manner that excludes details, such as physical confrontations.

For educators, this helps communicate appropriate topics and language choice, but for students it also gives them a way to communicate their needs to the teacher and their peers. A student whose house recently burned down may struggle to participate in a physics lesson that focuses on predicting and controlling the path of a wildfire threatening a local village. An in-play tool, the X Card (Stavropoulos), allows students to communicate distress and pause play by tapping a card or token on the table. Often the power of having an X Card is not in its use, it is often not invoked at all, but rather in the way that it clearly communicates agency and safety to players so that they can relax and learn. Finding the right approach for a particular class requires some trial and error. Resources such as the tabletop RPG Safety Toolkit (Lauren Bryant-Monk) provide an array of options that can be explored and tested with a group, or even presented to students as a means to select their own methods.

GAMES IN THE CONTEXT OF THE CLASSROOM

There are new games being designed every day, and new philosophies of game design that consistently emerge to shape and inform such games. Any effort to fully document the range of possible games or design approaches would require more than a single book, but by looking at a few games in some detail, it is possible to establish some of the key variables that educators will need to balance in selecting or implementing a game in class. The most commonly used game, both in educational settings and in therapeutic ones, is *D&D* (Wizards of the Coast 2014a). While many of its features make it an excellent choice, its general complexity can make it a challenging one for those less experienced in playing the game. To provide some comparison to *D&D* in the classroom, I want to look at a game system, Fate (Leonard Balsera et al. 2013), which is designed to be modified and adapted to various settings, and a design paradigm, Powered by the Apocalypse (Baker 2023), that has been used to create a wide variety of games that share relevant features. By no means a complete survey, this narrow selection offers enough diversity that educators exploring other options should have enough context for making meaningful decisions. See the below table outlining some of the key features and differences.

Game Features	**Dungeons & Dragons**	**Fate**	**Powered by the Apocalypse**
Specific vs General Actions	Generic actions such as Attack, Use an Item, Move, Jump, and Cast Spell	Player-defined Aspects that are loosely interpreted	Game-defined Moves that are context specific and genre-inspired
Character Development	Characters begin as weak and scale in power and complexity systematically	Characters evolve laterally, through redefining Aspects	Minimal character change
Duration of Campaigns	Can support potentially interminable campaigns	Designed for short to long-term campaigns	Optimized for single sessions or short campaigns
Complexity of Play	Layered mechanics and distinct modes of play with multiple subsystems	Low complexity, but requires creative investment from players	Streamlined, with many player options pre-defined
Consequences and Injury	Abstract values for health that support more tactical modes of play	Mental and physical stress with consequences other than death	Variable in relation to game setting and genre

(Continued)

Game Features	Dungeons & Dragons	Fate	Powered by the Apocalypse
Results	Binary results that succeed fully or fail completely	Graduated steps for success and failure	Often include mechanics for exceptional success
Randomization	A single d20 with an equal chance of rolling any given number (swingy)	Fate Dice with pluses and minuses, though invoking skills can often prescribe success	A 2d6 system (generally) where results fall more predictably into the median range

Dungeons and Dragons (D&D)

Part of the appeal of *D&D* is in its complexity and its scope, making it suitable for an extremely wide range of use cases and contexts. Many supplements and tools exist created specifically for *D&D*, in the form of adventures, settings, and modifications to the rules. The same complexity that makes it so adaptable is also what can make it difficult to use in a classroom (Petousi et al. 2023). Students need time to learn its rules and understand the different forms of play, with combat and exploration and social interaction often relying on subsets of specialized mechanics. Complexity, as mentioned earlier, can have its own inherent features and outcomes, and so reducing the complexity of the game to accommodate the classroom should be done carefully.

The history of *D&D* is based on battlefield simulation and many social features of the game were incorporated later (Peterson 2022). The challenge this presents is that many character features and game mechanics revolve around combat, which has value in developing mastery and in STEM education (Sousa et al. 2023) but in many cases might not be relevant to the course subject matter. Similarly, the mechanics around the use of magic and spell casting are integrated in such a way that applying them to a realistic setting requires clever interpretation. Examples of this can be seen in some online shows that play *D&D* and record their sessions, such as in the early episodes of Deborah Ann Woll's actual play show Children of Éarte (Woll). The characters start off in the real world and describe their early 'magical' abilities in ways that appear plausible. Making systematic revisions to such embedded mechanics to make them feel realistic, without necessitating player ingenuity, requires game design experience to be done effectively.

D&D involves multiple players representing individual characters while another player acts as the Dungeon Master and takes on the role of any non-player characters (NPCs) while providing narrative context. To take actions, with any chance of failure, players roll a twenty-sided die (d20), adding modifiers from skills or abilities, to try and 'meet or beat' a target number determined by the Dungeon Master. As Players win combat or achieve milestones, they gain power incrementally by 'leveling up' and selecting new abilities or features. Outside of combat, players take actions and make choices discursively but, in the event of combat, players roll a d20 in order to determine their initiative. Initiative defines the order in which players and NPCs act until the end of combat. While in combat, player agency is defined by a set of specific action types (action, bonus action, reaction, and movement) that are available as a limited resource which is replenished when their next turn begins. These rules are outlined more expansively in two core rulebooks, the Dungeon Master's Guide (Coast 2014a) and the Player's Handbook (Wizards of the Coast 2014b).

Key Takeaways

- Supports long-term engagements with incremental character growth
- Combines socially focused play and tactical conflict simulation
- Has binary outcomes where actions often succeed or fail completely
- The core mechanic is 'swingy' and generates unpredictable outcomes
- Character generation is customized by selecting features from a list

Dynamics of Play and Impact on Classroom Use

The way that *D&D* supports long-term engagements and sustained play is by emergently increasing the narrative stakes and the complexity of play. This is achieved in the short term through alternating modes of play, with social, exploratory, and combat scenarios taking on distinct mechanical structures that can re-invest players that might otherwise lose interest. When a social encounter starts to become stagnant, a combat can be introduced to create tension or engagement; if a series of combats feels tedious or arbitrary, a mystery is introduced or an NPC encountered. In the long term, complexity increases through the mechanical growth of characters as they level up, acquiring features that provide new opportunities for each of the game's modalities.

A level one character might manage a combat by choosing to swing their sword or their axe, while a higher-level character might be using special maneuvers to push enemies into a spell effect created by another player. The limited opportunities for early play establish familiarity with core concepts so that players become fluent in their use and confident enough to explore the abilities that they acquire later. This scheduled scaling within the game can mirror the scaling of subject matter in the classroom. A geometry class might have players calculating whether a target is within an arrows range during the first week of class while later calculating the damage per square inch of the spell Fireball. The mathematical concepts in play are generally abstracted to make them more streamlined, but the excitement of students about the abilities that they acquire can be leveraged outside of play to contextualize course material.

The scaling of *D&D* is defined by its positive reinforcement, and *D&D* is mechanically driven to scale players into ever more powerful versions of themselves. The scaling of the game also pre-supposes the acquisition of items or equipment that improve player abilities or offer other features. Classroom management strategies can leverage this by using out-of-game achievements to provide access to such items or make acquiring them part of formative assessments. Because characters will always improve, the rate and manner of those improvements can be tied to coursework or other features of the curriculum. To receive special equipment, students might be required to write letters from their characters to an established NPC, coherently explaining recent events and persuasively articulating their request. The quality of the equipment received can be tied to the quality of their writing.

Challenges That Might Arise

Combat and magic are not central to every subject and yet they are integral to many of *D&D*'s emergent features. In the historical court of Louis 14th, players might desperately want to avoid any combat situation other than a duel. While a cannon firing might be reimagined as a fireball, other spells may require a great deal more creative interpretation, as previously mentioned with Children of Éarte. Colloquially, this kind of non-mechanical revision is known as re-flavoring, a way of retaining the mechanical properties of skills or abilities but adjusting the language that describes them to match a particular setting or theme. The spell Suggestion, which compels an NPC to take on a course of action, might be described as Blackmail, highlighting the way that social standing was weaponized in that era. This is a solution that requires a great deal of preparation and planning and highlights the impact that *D&D*'s complexity has on ease of use and adaptation.

The embedded scaling of *D&D* is so central to its structure that it means new players who do not play through those lower tiers of play will often struggle to keep up. In essence, this means that a classroom implementation of *D&D*, relative to other game choices, requires a long-term commitment and a systematic incorporation of its more advanced mechanics. If there is not the affordance to spend that amount of time at the table with students, educators will need to find ways to streamline gameplay or provide supplemental materials.

Combat is not required for *D&D* to function, but its relevance in the game's early development means that most player features are designed around it. Combat in the classroom is complicated because the overt violence, despite being fantastical, might not match with the classroom culture. Additionally, the duration of combat can vary as many players need to take turns and consult their character sheet to make decisions. If play is tightly constrained to a timetable, then leaving in the middle of a combat requires additional effort to mark locations and hit points and spell slots for both players and their foes. Simplifying the rules for expediency can be effective but also take away some of the qualities that make the activity valuable in the first place. This challenge is also impacted by having multiple tables playing concurrently, where the story or timeline becomes more difficult to synchronize.

FATE

Fate is a setting-agnostic system designed to create high stakes action and drama. Its design philosophy hinges often on strategies of co-creating mechanical game features with players. The open-endedness of the system and its narrative focus make it useful for a wide range of implementations. Additionally, the game comes in a full version, Fate Core, and a streamlined version, Fate Accelerated. Fate is less mechanically complex than *D&D*, but its reliance on player created material makes it more conceptually complex. In *D&D*, players are always growing stronger, but in Fate, players often evolve laterally, or even grow weaker through complications that inhibit their agency. In Fate, players are strong and capable, but the game also treats failure as a narrative opportunity, sometimes even combining both success and failure into a single outcome. Players have defined strengths, but they also have well-defined weaknesses.

Fate uses a special set of six-sided dice called Fate or Fudge dice that have plus (+) and minus (–) signs instead of numbers. When players want to perform an action with the potential for failure, they roll four dice and add up the number of plus signs, subtract the minus signs, and then add any modifiers they receive from skills or abilities. The final value is compared to a ladder of escalating adjectives (poor, average, good, great, etc.) and, depending on the difficulty of the action, they fail, succeed at a cost, succeed, or succeed wildly.

Characters can improve these outcomes by spending an in-game metacurrency called Fate Points and invoking an Aspect of their character. Aspects are composed by players, rather than selected from a list, and include short phrases such as 'I'm not clumsy, I just like to fall'. These Aspects are invoked to generate success, but they can also be used to compel players to fail in a manner that reinforces their character's narrative, often in exchange for Fate Points. Rather than abstract values to describe health and well-being, characters take on physical and mental stress which can impact their effectiveness and participation.

Key Takeaways

- Supports long-term and short-term engagements with emphasis on character change
- Focuses on character-driven narrative
- Failure and success are scalable and have varying degrees
- Players have in-game resources to make success predictable
- Character and world creation is collaborative and literary

Dynamics of Play and Impact for Classroom Use

Fate reinforces a commitment to characterization by allowing players to define and redefine their narrative identity in unique ways through Aspects. It is common for players of *D&D* to make their characters together but just as common for them to arrive at the table with a character sheet already filled out. Fate makes character and world creation an integral part of play, fully devoting the first session of play to the development of the magic circle by involving players in the creation of their characters and narratively collaborating to determine Aspects of both other players and the world as a whole. Players commit to their character because the character is their own narrative invention and they commit to other player's characters because they have helped draft some of their Aspects.

This process extends to the creation of the world, where players help describe and define custom phrases that indicate the Issues that are driving them to action or the Aspects of a given situation. This engagement from players is a co-creation strategy that mechanically invests players in the setting and story. In a classroom context, this is a way to embed course content dynamically. Characters portraying nobles in Louis 14th's court might be asked to define what central Issues France faced at that time, and to define Aspects for their characters relevant to the context, such as 'always knows the latest fashion' or 'friends in all the foreign courts'. To create such Aspects and Issues requires a personal relationship to the material; they must actively imagine how they could or would respond to such circumstance.

What makes Fate an effective learning tool is that students translate concepts into their own words in order to make use of them in game. Aspects and Issues are essentially succinct descriptions of complex ideas. If Louis 14th's court has the Aspect 'the latest fashion is Louis's latest whim', then a player cannot invoke that Aspect without considering how proximity to the King was often communicated through clothing or hairstyle. Aspects in Fate have both positive and negative connotations. Characters can be compelled by their Aspects to make bad decisions. For scenes or settings that have Aspects, there is room for nuanced interpretation and discussion. This is an opportunity for social-emotional learning because it values diverse perspectives and enables students to reflect on how a disability in one context might become a strength in another.

This process of composing Aspects in a literary fashion is a way to discuss the power and impact of language. Characters in the game have Aspects that represent their strengths and their weaknesses; characters in existing literature or media can be analyzed in a similar context. Indiana Jones might have the Aspect 'anything but snakes', while Huckleberry Finn might have the Aspect 'a road to walk on is better than a roof overhead'. Creating connections between the characters that they create and the ones that they learn about is a way to build authorial confidence and frame critical discourse. The same process allows students to take on the role of literary characters and see how the Aspects that describe them impact their relationship to events. Fate's flexible character creation system and world-building capacity make it useful for referencing specific historical or literary events.

Because Fate is optimized for narrative interactions its combat system is not as technical or distinct from play as in *D&D*. Combat scenarios do have a similar shift in turn order from the discursive to the procedural, but the flow of play is less impacted. This makes it easier in a classroom context where time is less flexible, as shorter sessions can be resolved more predictably and do not require a separate set of skills or mechanisms. It also means that certain benefits of tactical combat, such as practicing STEM skills by leveraging existing mechanics, requires a less direct approach. STEM lessons that become mechanically relevant to play can be incorporated as Aspects specific to a scene or a location. In order to take advantage of a scene's Aspects the students can be required to unlock them through experiment or calculation, perhaps even spending time between game sessions exploring those problems. Before students need to sneak into an ancient pyramid, they might be learning about its construction in class and, during that lesson, try to define the Aspects that would be present in such a location. Aspects such as '30 Degree Slope Into Darkness' or '2 Tons of Stone in the Way' can be opportunities for student to solve problems using concepts covered in class, whether that is creating enough friction to keep from sliding or having enough leverage to move a heavy weight.

Challenges That Might Arise

Fate's mechanical ambiguity is both a strength and a weakness in a classroom context. Students need to be capable of creative interpretation and invention or the system does not operate as it should. Students that are uncomfortable expressing creative ideas in front of their peers might benefit from practicing that skill and gaining confidence, but they will also require special attention and consideration. Other games tend to have existing structures that students can learn and master, because their options are finite; they can simply select an option from a list if they are uncertain of what to do. Fate requires consistent engagement and involvement and, while that is nominally a good thing, it is a challenge because maintaining that engagement requires consideration and effort.

Where *D&D* can be planned in advance and have all of its components prepackaged, Fate requires more active engagement from the facilitator. An educator that has less experience running games needs to practice in order to take advantage of Fate's flexibility. Not all of the game elements are co-created, and many can be planned in advance, but the cost of doing so in excess means losing out on some of Fate's main advantages, specifically the way that it reinforces the magic circle and student buy-in by giving them agency over the world and the means by which they interact with it. Proper preparation for Fate is a group activity that is more about setting the stage for improvisation than establishing timelines, stat blocks, or outcomes. Approached thoughtfully, this preparation can be done outside of play, during a traditional class lesson, in a way that reinforces the material being covered. An example of this would be to pause, after presenting information about a historical event, and asking the class how the aftermath of the event might become an Aspect of daily life for people of that era.

POWERED BY THE APOCALYPSE

Powered by the Apocalypse (PbtA) is not a single game or a basic game system; it is a set of conventions and approaches informed by a design philosophy. Inspired by the game *Apocalypse World* (Baker 2016) by D. Vincent Baker and Meguey Baker, games that are PbtA share similarities in their features and their structure. A player who is comfortable playing one game will have a strong sense of how to play another game that is built on the same foundations. The strength of PbtA games is that they are designed with a very tight narrative focus and playstyle. PbtA games tend to be extremely easy to start and play, with very little time devoted to character creation or the memorization of complex mechanics. While a single PbtA game might be less useful as a long-term engagement, a series of games can be tied to course material and their similarity in structure can allow educators to have students playing them quickly and without much advance preparation. Notable games that are PbtA are *Monsterhearts* (Alder 2017), *Masks* (Conway 2017), *Night Witches* (Morningstar 2015), *Avatar: Legends* (Brendan Conway (Lead) 2023), *Dungeon World* (Sage LaTorra 2013), *City of Mists* (Moshe 2019), and *Thirsty Sword Lesbians* (Walsh 2021).

Most PbtA games use a system where two six-sided dice (2d6) are rolled, and the result is modified by player abilities or skills. Results are not binary, with success or failure, but scaled in a way that represents varying degrees of success. Character attributes are world-specific and thematic rather than generic, using adjectives such as 'Dark' or 'Cool' in place of 'Strength' and 'Intelligence'. Players choose a single Playbook as part of character creation that provides all of the unique actions, or Moves, available to them beyond the Basic Moves accessible to all players. Character creation is extremely quick relative to other systems, and many player choices are focused on aesthetic rather than mechanical options. Not all games include secondary systems for conflict, with health and well-being generally being descriptive rather than numerically abstract.

The fundamental structure of a PbtA game is streamlined, and it is possible to create a custom game successfully without much prior experience designing games. The basic set of operations is as follows: create three to five words for Player Statistics that describe meaningful approaches to problems and are evocative of your world; create four to eight Basic Moves that everyone in the world can attempt; create Playbooks by selecting distinct personas or archetypes and describing two to four Moves unique to each of them. It goes without saying that this is a gross oversimplification, but fundamentally, it contains the core underpinnings of a PbtA game. Other features are largely optional and can be added as needed to accomplish specific learning goals or social outcomes. Every game that is PbtA makes choices about how closely they will adhere to the conventions described above, and therefore, it is important to review the rules before attempting to use them in class.

Key Takeaways

- Supports shorter and more contained experiences
- Wide variety of games that share many mechanical properties
- Less attachment by players to characters and outcomes
- Embodies specific genres and tropes
- Character options are defined by a preconfigured playbook

Dynamics of Play and Impact for Classroom Use

What makes PbtA games effective, and so popular among designers, is that their design is powerfully driven by writing and less reliant on specific mechanics. For shorter term games that do not need sophisticated mechanics to drive and sustain engagement, PbtA's structure allows a great deal of flexibility and freedom in design. Given the way that thematic language underpins almost every feature, PbtA games tend to be less adaptable to a variety of use cases, but their modular and interchangeable nature makes them flexible in combination with one another.

Selecting a suite of games, with similar enough mechanics, means that a class can more easily switch between worlds and genres of play. Once the basic mechanics are established, a one-page worksheet can outline all of the Moves and options that are not specific to a Playbook. While other systems can be slow and stressful to alternate, PbtA's structure allows educators to do so effectively and as part of a lesson. While a game such as *Monster of the Week* (Sands 2015), that is designed to be episodic, might function as an ongoing social activity, most games will culminate within two to four sessions of play. For a History course that looks at distinct historical periods, a different game might act as an introduction to each era, or as a way for students to experience specific aspects of an era. Shifting the setting of the game *Monsterhearts* from a high school to that of 17th-century France is a way to show how secrets and personal connections were relevant in a power structure that was so closely connected with a single individual and their motivations.

The preparation for running PbtA games is similar to Fate, in that it does not require the organization of stat blocks and specific modules to function. The narrative drive of the game will generally propel players toward a given outcome of their own volition, but that same narrative drive requires that the preferred outcome is embedded within the logic of the world. Essentially, preparation means crafting the right villains or obstacles for the right game. A close-minded and socially conservative conformist that players encounter in *Monsterhearts* will immediately be seen as aggressive. Preparation is not labor intensive but does require creativity and insight to be effective.

Pro-social PbtA games include *Wanderhome* (Dragon 2021), *Girl by Moonlight* (Gillis 2023), *Masks*, and others that are designed specifically for younger audiences. PbtA games mechanically reinforce genre conventions through their use of thematic language and so selecting an appropriate game starts with a look at the language choices for Moves or player statistics. In almost all games, there are Basic Moves that are available to all players and these serve as a bellwether for the tone of the game.

Masks has the Basic Move 'Provoke Someone', while *Monsterhearts* has a similar Move called 'Turn Someone On' and in Apocalypse World there is 'Seduce or Manipulate'. These Moves are invoked verbally by players and so seeing the language choices used in such descriptions provides a strong correlation to how a particular game frames player actions. In a class that emphasizes the value of honesty, it might not work out to have students consistently manipulate NPCs that they meet. In that same class, a character standing up to a bully can be interpreted as provoking them.

In a classroom setting where a particular game is desired for its theme, but a particular Move feels inappropriate, you can adjust the wording. 'Turn Someone On' from *Monsterhearts* has sexual connotations, but changing it to 'Excite Someone' can maintain the functionality while reducing some of the overt sexuality. The power of specific language in PbtA games means that they are easier to tweak than some other systems and that they are easier to evaluate for their relevance or appropriateness. It is also possible to work with the class to address the language around Moves and use it as an opportunity to discuss the implications of word choice, ask the class what they think the goal of a Move is and what might describe that goal in a way that feels class appropriate.

Challenges That Might Arise

PbtA games do not generally span for multiple years or hundreds of sessions, they tend to use advancement or character growth sparingly and resolve for narrative reasons rather than mechanical ones. In a game about solving mysteries, the game resolves when the mystery is solved. Because a character might only be played a few times before being retired, players have less need to ensure that all of the characters at the table get along or share the same beliefs. Bickering between characters that are going to travel together for years, and have each other's back in battle, might grow tiresome and be implausible; bickering among characters that have only just met and embody distinctly different perspectives is more realistic. This impacts the classroom because, while many games mechanically reinforce cohesion among players using pro-social mechanics, not all PbtA games do. In the game *Monsterhearts*, players are teenagers hiding dark secrets and teenagers can be mean to one another. PbtA games are often focused on producing the overarching themes of a genre and thus a specific character's narrative arc is subservient to that goal. Characters tend to be personalities rather than people, driven by the Playbook that defines them as much as the specific backstory that a player has imagined for them.

The game *Night Witches* has players portray the female Soviet pilots that fought in World War II, many of whom faced tremendous pressure and sexism from the institutions they served. Highlighting the tensions between such women could be an effective way to discuss those forces, but it also needs to be done responsibly, where students have effective ways to establish, and adjust, boundaries. Creating a safe space to express conflict, and manage its implications, is always important, but it is especially so in games that leverage stereotypes and tropes systematically. STEM learning is not something that PbtA games address inherently. They lean away from the complicated math of other systems. This does not mean that they cannot be used to teach science or math, but that they are more useful as a way to contextualize concepts rather than practice them.

Comparisons, Interactions, and Opportunities for Customization

There are many other game systems and formats that exist, but these three offer a useful set of reference points to discuss how different games drive emergent play. With every system, there are benefits and opportunities but in many case there are also drawbacks. A common solution is to blend the mechanics of various games in a way that combines the most important features.

The game features that can most easily translate from game to game are not the core mechanics that define success or failure, but the sub-mechanics that impact the odds of such success and failure or help contextualize those results.

Looking at a game to see how it modifies outcomes helps keep new or translated mechanics from disrupting the balance of the game. In *D&D*, for example, success is generally modified in one of three ways, by having Advantage or Disadvantage (rolling two d20s and keeping the highest or lowest roll), adding a proficiency bonus relative to the character's level, or a static bonus or penalty that adds or subtracts from the roll. If you want to bring a feature like Aspects into *D&D* you can use them to modify outcomes using those methods. A player with the Aspect 'can't say no to a dare' might have Advantage when goaded into an action but have Disadvantage when trying to avoid being goaded. Because Advantage and Disadvantage are existing game features, they don't disrupt the overall design of *D&D*. In *Monsterhearts*, players can acquire Strings on other characters, implying obligations or knowledge that they can use to influence those characters. Using Strings in a game of Fate can translate as a free invocation of an Aspect.

Other game features that can easily transfer are those that frame outcomes rather than determining them. Graduated results in Fate or PbtA games help communicate complex dynamics and provide SEL opportunities because they offer nuanced ways to interpret success and failure. In *D&D*, a roll that would normally be a failure, but that is close to the target range, can use the 'success at a cost' or 'failure with a boost' concepts from Fate. For younger players, it might make sense to move away from graduated success, keeping the outcome of actions simple to keep the game moving quickly.

You can borrow a co-creation strategy from Fate and have students participate in crafting the language around spells. *D&D* includes long lists of spells with intricate descriptions, but the mechanics that balance them within the game are often fairly straightforward. Before players can add a spell to their spell book they simply need to integrate the mechanics with their character and write a description for it, or give it a flavorful name. Instead of saying 'I cast Magic Missile', they might say, 'I summon my swarm of bees and invoke Honey Strike'. Conversely, this same approach might be challenging to use in a PbtA game, where the language for features is often tightly connected to the overall experience of play.

What is common to all of these examples is that they avoid altering the core mechanics of the game, they are simply changing the way that existing features are accessed or described. Changes to a game should be focused on targeted outcomes to avoid unnecessary complexity. PbtA games excel in shorter campaigns, but a particular game might be useful for the entire semester or year. In this case, the target outcome is to sustain engagement. A PbtA game can borrow from *D&D* and incorporate the scaling of abilities and more intentional character customization. Characters can start the game without a Playbook or access to Moves other than the basic ones, selecting a Move from a Playbook of their choice after each session or milestone. There is potential for complications and negative interactions of rules but achieving sustained engagement might be worth the risk.

Where game mechanics can create negatively emergent outcomes is when they have multiple dependencies and many moving parts. Combat in *D&D* is tactical for many reasons, not simply because it involves playing on a grid. You can use a grid for combat in Fate or PbtA and the result will still be less tactical than doing so in *D&D*. The abstractness of health in *D&D*, in the form of Hit Points, means that characters can easily get knocked unconscious and then be fully functional in seconds after drinking a healing potion. Attacks deal damage in numbers that can be multiplied and divided, but in Fate and PbtA games characters take on Stress or Harm and suffer consequences that cannot, and should not, be fixed within a few seconds after drinking a potion. Fate and PbtA focus on the narrative implications of combat; the outcome of a foolish strategy might be emotional trauma. *D&D* focuses on the combat itself, as an activity that is valuable for the pure pleasure of solving the puzzle that it presents.

The important thing is that tactical combat is a potential way to teach STEM-related concepts. The solution is not necessarily to bring in the mechanics for tactical combat; the solution is to incorporate STEM-related concepts into play. For a game of Fate that might mean using experiments or calculations to determine the kinds of Aspects that can be unlocked for a situation, or providing free invocations of an Aspect if students can figure out the equation that explains it. Characters that get into a fight in underground steam tunnels might be able to vent the steam and create advantages for themselves using an Aspect, but only if they can explain how and why the steam pressure builds up. In a game that is PbtA, a session might end with the characters all falling off of a bridge into water. How much Harm they take can be determined outside of play, by giving a lecture on the physical properties of fluids and then evaluating how well they can demonstrate those properties through an experiment. The value of leveraging game mechanics is that they can generate emergent outcomes, but that does not make them inherently superior to a narratively focused approach. The goal is to understand all of the options available so that you can make the right decision for your particular needs.

QUESTIONS TO CONSIDER IN SELECTING A GAME

- Will the game be systematically embedded in the class structure or is it isolated to a few sessions of play?
- How many students do I expect to be playing at the same time and what is my strategy if they need to be split into multiple groups?
- Do I want to tackle many subjects and themes with the game or do I want to use it specifically for a single topic, such as creative writing, historical perspective, SEL, or math?

- How much time will be setting aside for actually playing the game, and how much time will I need to set it up or clear it away?
- What are the social dynamics of my particular class and how will the structure of the game interact with those dynamics?
- Do I need specific assessment outcomes to derive from play or is the game meant to supplement or complement more traditional assessments?
- How accessible is a particular game and how does that impact the accessibility needs of my class?

CONCLUSION

The underlying mechanics of games have an impact on how students will interact with the narrative and with each other. The best results occur when the right game is chosen for a particular classroom setting and curriculum but, like a character in *D&D* that begins with few abilities and ultimately achieves world-altering power, you don't have to start with the best results. Being comfortable and confident with a game has a tremendous impact on your ability to use it effectively in the classroom or a clinical setting (Kilmer et al. 2023; Cook, Gremo, and Morgan 2017), and so if the only game you are familiar with is *D&D*, use it! *D&D* is a great game and has numerous ways to support a classroom: conveying complex ideas in a way that connects with students, helping them develop social and emotional skills, and making class fun and exciting.

Players in a tabletop RPG have tremendous freedom to take risks and try out new things, you have that same freedom. Having the right safety tools will keep games from having negative results and ensure that, no matter what game you are using, students can advocate for their needs. If you make a mistake and use a feature that creates distractions, work with your students to find a solution. Part of what they are learning by playing tabletop RPGs is how to collaborate in a way that focuses on the collective interest rather than just their own; this is part of that lesson.

Just as in Fate, failure is rarely absolute. Sometimes, when succeeding at a cost, the cost is simply trying something new next time. In my experience, every classroom is different and every student is unique; there will never be a solution that works without effort. Listening to students and learning co-creation strategies will ultimately drive toward the outcomes that you want. As one of the people playing the game, you will always need to keep learning and trying new things, testing game features and using new mechanics, but part of effective learning is having fun in the process!

REFERENCES

Alder, Avery. 2017. *Monsterhearts 2*. Buried without Ceremony.

Atherton, Gray, Rhys Hathaway, Ingela Visuri, and Liam Cross. 2024. "A critical hit: Dungeons and Dragons as a buff for autistic people." *Autism: The International Journal of Research and Practice*. https://doi.org/10.1177/13623613241275260.

Baker, Vincent. 2023."What Is PbtA." *Lumpley Games*. https://lumpley.games/2023/11/22/what-is-pbta/.

Baker, D. Vincent, and Meguey Baker. 2016. *Apocalypse World*. Lumpley Games.

Bergen, Doris. 2002. "The Role of Pretend Play in Children's Cognitive Development." *Early Childhood Research & Practice* 4 (1), 1–13. https://eric.ed.gov/?id=ED464763

Bowman, Sarah, and Josephine Baird. 2022. "Transformative Potential of Immersive Experiences within Role-Playing Communities." *Revista de Estudos Universitários - REU* 48: e022013. https://doi.org/10.22484/2177-5788.2022v48id5028.

Bowman, Sarah Lynne. 2024. "Finding the Self in Role-Playing Games: Weaving Myth, Narrative, and Identity." *Media Practice and Education* 25(2): 160–173. https://doi.org/10.1080/25741136.2024.2324085.

Carla Sousa, Sara Rye, Micael Sousa, Pedro Juan Torres, Claudilene Perim, Shivani Atul Mansuklal, and Firdaous Ennami. 2023. "Playing at the School Table: Systematic Literature Review of Board, Tabletop, and Other Analog Game-based Learning Approaches." *Front Psychol* 14: 1160591. https://doi.org/10.3389/fpsyg.2023.1160591.

Carla Sousa, Filipe Luz, Maria Fonseca, Pedro Neves, Phil Lopes, Vicky Maratou, Rizos Chaliampalias, Achilles Kameas, and Yama Abdullahi. 2022. *An Accessible and Inclusive Future for Tabletop Games and Learning: Paradigms and Approaches*.

Campbell, Jeremy. 1982. *Grammatical Man*. Simon and Schuster.

Conway, Brendan. 2017. *Masks*. Magpie Games.

Conway, Brendan (Lead), James Mendez Hodes, Yeonsoo Julian Kim, Sharang Biswas, Daniel Kwan, and Sen-Foong Lim. 2023. *Avatar Legends: The Roleplaying Game*. Magpie Games.

Cook, Mike P., Matthew Gremo, and Ryan Morgan. 2017. "We're Just Playing: The Influence of a Modified Tabletop Role-Playing Game on ELA Students' In-Class Reading." *Simulation & Gaming* 48(2): 199–218. https://doi.org/10.1177/1046878116684570.

Cullinan, Maryanne. 2024. "Surveying the Perspectives of Middle and High School Educators Who Use Role-playing Games as Pedagogy." *International Journal of Role-Playing*: 127–141. https://doi.org/10.33063/ijrp.vi15.335.

Cullinan, Maryanne, and Jennifer Genova. 2023. "Gaming the Systems: A Component Analysis Framework for the Classroom Use of RPGs." *International Journal of Role-Playing*: 7–17. https://doi.org/10.33063/ijrp.vi13.305.

Dewey, John. 2024. *Democracy and Education*. Edited by Nicholas Tampio. Columbia University Press.

Dragon, Jay. 2021. *Wanderhome*. Possum Creek Games.

Edwards, Ron. "Lines and Veils." https://rpg.stackexchange.com/questions/30906/.

Kilmer, Elizabeth D., Adam D. Davis, Jared N. Kilmer, and Adam R. Johns. 2023. *Therapeutically Applied Role-Playing Games: The Game to Grow Method*. Routledge.

Fine, Gary A. 1983. *Shared Fantasy: Role-Playing Games as Social Worlds*. University of Chicago Press.

Freire, Paulo, Myra Bergman Ramos, and Donald Macedo. 2014. *Pedagogy of the Pppressed*. Thirtieth anniversary edition. Bloomsbury.

Gillis, Andrew. 2023. *Girl by Moonlight*. Evil Hat Productions.

Gopnik, Alison, Andrew N. Meltzoff, and Patricia K. Kuhl. 1999. *The Scientist in the Crib: Minds, Brains, and How Children Learn. The Scientist in the Crib: Minds, Brains, and How Children Learn*. William Morrow & Co.

Huizinga, Johan. 1950. *Homo Ludens: A Study of the Play-Element in Culture*. The Beacon Press.

JayOnyx. "Accessibility Resources for Gaming." https://writingalchemy.net/podcast-2/unfamiliar-heroes/accessibility-resources-for-gaming/.

Kretchmer, Jennifer. "Accessibility in Gaming Resource Guide." https://docs.google.com/document/u/0/d/1ZFSXz-Yva1KZAsP7NblCdkoiQ6RcjxSV2gj98eXusJs/mobilebasic.

Kumral, Joy, and Luis Meza. 2024. "Character-Driven Narratives in D&D5E and Fate: Core System." *Transactions of the Digital Games Research Association* 6: 67–86. https://doi.org/10.26503/todigra.v6i3.2176.

Lauren Bryant-Monk, Kienna Shaw. "TTRPG Safety Toolkit." https://ttrpgsafetytoolkit.com/.

Leonard Balsera, Brian Engard, Jeremy Keller, Ryan Macklin, Mike Olson. 2013. *Fate Core System*. Evil Hat Productions.

Meshcheryakova, Anna O., and Fabian Hemmert. 2024. *Playing against the Rules: A New Perspective on the Potential of Games and Play as Convivial and Critical Tools for Imagining Futures*. Cambridge University Press.

Morningstar, Jason. 2015. *Night Witches*. Bully Pulpit Games.

Moshe, Amit. 2019. *City of Mists Player's Guide*. Son of Oak Game Studio, Modiphius Entertainment.

Orr, Matt, Sara King, and Melissa McGonnell. 2020. "A Qualitative Exploration of the Perceived Social Benefits of Playing Tabletop Role-playing Games." *International Journal of Role-Playing* (10): 70–83. https://doi.org/10.33063/ijrp.vi10.277

Peterson, Jon. 2022. *The Elusive Shift*. Edited by Raiford Guins Henry Lowood. *Game Histories*. The MIT Press.

Petousi, Dimitra, Akrivi Katifori, Maria Roussou, Yannis Ioannidis, and Pantelis Sakellariadis. 2023. "Historical Reality vs Anachronistic Fantasy: The History Educators' Perspective on Tabletop RPGs." *Proceedings of the 18th International Conference on the Foundations of Digital Games*, Lisbon, Portugal. https://doi.org/10.1145/3582437.3587197.

Piaget, Jean. 1950. *The Psychology of Intelligence*. First edition. Routledge.

Pyle, Angela, Christopher DeLuca, and Erica Danniels. 2017. "A Scoping Review of Research on Play-based Pedagogies in Kindergarten Education." *Review of Education* 5(3): 311–351. https://doi.org/https://doi.org/10.1002/rev3.3097.

Sage LaTorra, Adam Koebel. 2013. *Dungeon World*. RNDM Games.

Sands, Michael. 2015. *Monster of the Week*. Evil Hat Productions.

Sjunneson, Elsa. 2019. *Fate Accessibility Toolkit*. Evil Hat Productions.

Stavropoulos, John. "The X Card." https://tinyurl.com/x-card-rpg.

Vygotsky, L. S. 1978. *Mind in Society Development of Higher Psychological Processes*. Edited by Michael Cole, Vera Jolm-Steiner, Sylvia Scribner and Ellen Souberman. Harvard University Press.

Walsh, April Kit. 2021. *Thirsty Sword Lesbians*. Evil Hat Productions.

Walsh, Orla, and Conor Linehan. 2024. "Roll for Insight: Understanding How the Experience of Playing Dungeons & Dragons Impacts the Mental Health of an Average Player." *International Journal of Role-Playing*: 36–60. https://doi.org/10.33063/ijrp.vi15.321.

Wizards of the Coast. 2014a. *Dungeon Master's Guide*. Fifth edition. Dungeons and Dragons.

Wizards of the Coast. 2014b. *Player's Handbook*. Fifth edition. Dungeons and Dragons.

Woll, Deborah Ann, "Children of Éarte," in *Children of Éarte*, https://www.demiplane.com/childrenofearte.

Zimmerman, Eric, and Katie Salen Tekinbas. 2003. *Rules of Play: Game Design Fundamentals*. The MIT Press.

PART II

Playing Together

Creating Inclusive Community in the Classroom Through RPGs

CHAPTER 4

Everybody Wins

Role-Playing Games with Students with Disabilities

Cathy Leogrande and Aaron Brown

It is often difficult for teachers to find time and strategies to help students with disabilities develop academic and social skills. This can be more of a challenge in special class settings where there may not be many appropriate models for behaviors such as sharing, conversation and dealing with frustration. Role-playing games offer all students opportunities to learn and practice these skills in a low-risk and comfortable context, but this is especially promising for inclusive classrooms with students with disabilities. This chapter will describe the results of a pilot project using a teacher-adapted role-playing game in a special class with students with learning and behavioral struggles. In addition to improvement in social skills, benefits included increased skills in some academic areas, such as literacy and mathematics, improvement in so-called "soft skills" such as communication and problem-solving, and skills related to executive functioning. Future research could begin with specific goals in areas of cognitive, social-emotional and executive functioning, with clear and appropriate data collection for those goals.

DOI: 10.1201/9781003641384-7

PLAY AND GAMES IN EDUCATION

Play has been identified as an important component of children's cognitive development (Ahmad et al. 2016; Anderson et al. 2023; Lillard 2015; Lillard et al. 2010; Whitebread et al. 2009). Play is difficult to define and includes a wide spectrum of behaviors, generally with no purpose and no goal other than enjoyment. Pretend play in particular can improve cognitive and social skills such as symbolic thinking, language skills and reasoning (Lillard et al. 2013; Weisberg 2015). It has been linked to improvement and reinforcement of executive functioning skills such as working memory and recall, controlling emotions, internalizing language and complex problem-solving (Eberhart et al. 2023; Lockhart 2010). Pretend play has been shown to help children with disabilities learn and engage with their environment and improve interactions with others (Barton 2015). Play has benefits for individuals of all ages. Eberle (2014) states that "Play plainly offers a mix of physical, social, emotional and intellectual rewards at all stages of life (217)." Role-playing games have many of the same characteristics as pretend play and provide a structured opportunity for children and adults to hone communication and interpersonal skills in enjoyable situations.

The word "game" has come to mean many different things in the past decade. Salen Tekinbas and Zimmerman (2003) define a game as a system in which players engage in an artificial conflict, defined by rules, that results in a quantifiable outcome. In this case, there is a goal and that is to win. Baranowski and colleagues (2008) defined games as a physical or mental contest with a goal or objective, played according to a framework of rules that establishes what players can or cannot do inside the game world. Raph Koster, in his book *A Theory of Fun for Game Design* (2014), discusses at length how games are tied to learning as well as a feeling of fun. He grapples with various definitions by others, including Sid Meier's famous statement that games are a series of interesting decisions (Alexander 2012). Koster connects games, play and fun and states, "A good game is one that teaches everything it has to offer before the player stops playing. That's what games are in the end. Teachers. Fun is just another word for learning. Games teach you how aspects of reality work, how to understand yourself, how to understand the action of other and how to imagine" (46). He goes on to discuss what games teach us based on how the brain works. This is a good foundation for a discussion of games in education with a student population often forgotten in these discussions.

In recent years, studies have focused on various types of games and methods of adapting game components to education. Becker (2021) developed a chart that compares terms and use of games and game elements for learning on a variety of criteria. She makes a distinction between game-based learning (GBL) in which the game is the lesson from the learner's perspective, game-based pedagogy (GBP) in which the game is used as process for teaching by the teacher, and gamification in which gaming principles are used to enrich instruction (Willig et al. 2021). Research related to the use of games in education in all formats (video games, board games) has shown benefits and challenges of both traditional academic skills as well as social-emotional learning (Noda et al. 2019; Stancin and Hoic-Bozic 2020; Stancin et al. 2022). This project drew from this research but was based on the belief that tabletop role-playing games are different in many ways from board games and digital games and provide unique educational and social-emotional benefits because of their structure. Research that specifically speaks to the connection between role-playing games and educational settings is discussed later in this chapter.

FOUNDATIONS OF LEARNING FROM TABLETOP ROLE-PLAYING GAMES WITH STUDENTS WITH DISABILITIES

In studying possible theoretical foundations, the authors selected several theories as the basis for this pilot that related to effective learning practices. Tabletop role-playing games (tabletop RPGs) stand on a foundation of learning theories that demonstrate they are powerful learning activities, similar to the type of hands-on learning found in other pedagogical approaches, such as project-based learning and maker spaces (Steele 2023). A key aspect of role-playing games is interaction between players and the opportunity/need to learn from each other. The world is being built as they play so players are constantly adding to their existing knowledge and making meaning as the game progresses. The process, or journey through the scenario, is the way actual learning occurs. Playing the game is the "lesson," and the teacher must be ready to guide the learning as it proceeds.

John Dewey's ideas about education are an important foundation for this pilot study. Dewey is known for the concept of education as experience, learners doing things within a structured setting that helps them make meaning on their own (Dewey 1934). He saw learning as a social process that is at its best when learners are communicating with each other and making associations individually and as a group considering prior information. These connections help them revise and expand what they know. This idea of connected learning and generalization of knowledge is often difficult for students with disabilities. Building on the scientific method, Dewey posits that learners make meaning through inquiry, interacting with information, watching and reviewing the results, and then learning from the consequence. Consequences and results provide useful knowledge that assists in the specific setting but also reinforces processes for decision-making and transfer to other situations. By working together to make meaning and respond to the consequences that occur and the choices they provide for next steps, learners gain skills and habits to negotiate competing needs and concerns and consider next steps. Through this experiential process, learners begin to form habits of thinking, communicating and adjusting to each other that are necessary to live and work together in harmony (Haarman 2023). These ideas align with tabletop role-playing games. Scenarios are designed so that players are faced with choices of action in conjunction with other players. There are potential unforeseen obstacles based on rolls of the dice and gamemaster responses, so critical thinking is a continuous process. Group members must communicate at every step, discussing the results of previous actions and potential outcomes. The game group becomes a small community whose members learn to adjust their individual ideas and actions to work together toward a common goal. These skills are often lacking or poorly applied to real settings by students with disabilities. Role-playing games have experienced a resurgence since the pandemic, when they served as a way for individuals to connect online. The use of role-playing games as pedagogical tools for experiential learning that encourages participation, increases content retention, motivates and promotes teamwork has been documented with participants from various contexts and ages (Beidatsch and Broomhall 2010; Ruiz-Ezquerro 2021; Sousa et al. 2023). Gamemaster is the perfect role for a teacher in a special class or inclusive class to guide and shape learning of positive processes and habits.

Dewey's work further informed this project with his thoughts on the combination of playfulness and seriousness. In a section entitled, "Play and Work in the Curriculum," he explained that play is not merely a leisure activity but an essential means of learning and exploration (Dewey

1914). These two activities have become artificially separated in school when they should really be intertwined for effective teaching and learning:

> The task of the teacher is not simply to develop the right kind of orientation towards activities but to achieve an ideal balance between the inspiration and vision necessary to engage and animate students and provide them with the guidance essential to acquiring mastery over the means of executing that which they have been inspired to produce within a particular subject or academic discipline.
>
> *(Skillback 4–5)*

While this is a wonderful blueprint for any teacher in any classroom, this instructional blend has great potential in inclusive classrooms with students with disabilities. Many students with disabilities have negatively experienced school in the form Dewey bemoaned. These students have struggled and failed with the traditional model of instruction in which knowledge is imposed onto passive students who verify that learning has taken place by restating it often in its original form (Haarman 2023). Students with disabilities, especially those in special education placements, have been identified as needing additional supports and modified instruction due to their struggles and poor performance within this long-established context. Connecting play to curricula offers options for students with disabilities to reframe the work of learning and see the possibility of success where they have experienced struggle.

Plass et al. (2015) also connect playfulness and learning theory. They state, "Play becomes more abstract, symbolic and social as children mature through different developmental stages" (258). They cite how play allows children to hold multiple, sometimes conflicting representations of reality, something critical in cognitive development and learning. In addition, they point to learning theory beneath the motivational aspect of games. Vygotsky also pointed that play is a leading factor in children's development (Smolucha and Smolucha 2021). Children find play and games that are too easy are boring and those that are too difficult frustrating, in both cases leading to lack of desire to continue. Good games are those in which players can succeed but only with some struggle and feedback. Vygotsky saw play as symbolic and social, a good description of tabletop RPGs. Playing with an adult or peer who is more capable and provides guidance and models appropriate gameplay can help a child succeed at a level higher than his or her current ability. Students with disabilities may be more willing to accept "graceful failure" within a game rather than what they may perceive as a higher-stakes academic task. These students generally have a lived experiences of failing that hampers their willingness to attempt learning tasks, particularly in front of peers. Game environments are built on expected failure as a necessary step in learning and improving, so the embarrassment and perception of being inept are not heightened as they are in high-stakes classroom spaces and this failure can be productive (Grafwallner 2021; Kapur 2008; Kapur and Bielaczyc 2012). This can encourage different ways of thinking, risk-taking and willingness to attempt difficult tasks.

These authors created a simple model that describes the elements of a basic structure that virtually all games have: challenge, response and feedback. These elements form a learning loop when feedback constitutes a new challenge or prompts the player to provide a different response to the original challenge. Tabletop role-playing games foster this loop and do so via social engagement and group interaction guided by the gamemaster. Games with a more behaviorist design, like Kahoot or Jeopardy, limit choices and establish that there is a right or wrong answer and winners and losers. These games reduce the cognition required to play or win. However, these may be more comfortable for students with disabilities who are used to struggling and the often-negative effects of putting forth effort with poor results. Tabletop RPGs allow players to formulate their own challenges, use available tools to construct a response and provide feedback through peer interaction. In many cases, there are no wrong choices, merely choices with different results that help the game move forward. Students with disabilities often demonstrate a persistence despite repeated failure when playing games because the feedback is direct and immediate and allows them to progress toward success (Sinha and Kapur 2021). As Bowman (2010) suggests, educators must consider the relationship between challenge and reward as they select RPGs for use in pedagogical settings, especially with students with disabilities.

Cullinan and Genova (2023) describe a conceptual matrix directly related to RPGs. By merging the work done in game analysis and curriculum development, they designed a matrix to help educators consider which games provide students with the tools to meet desired learning goals. Like the discussion by the previous authors, they integrate existing research to formulate three categories of gaming elements: context, materials and structural. These combine to form the functional experience of the game. Educators can use this conceptual model to analyze games in terms of their prospective effectiveness at teaching, reinforcing and assessing specific academic, social-emotional or executive functioning skills. RPGs offer unique methods for supporting and developing multiple skills and transferring knowledge to new situations. Teachers need a roadmap such as this to evaluate and create RPGs for purposeful classroom use.

Westborg (2023) created a complimentary matrix based on game design elements to assist educators. She first considers the pre-game, mid-game and post-game phases of learning. She further examines the post-game reflection or debriefing as it relates to emotional, intellectual and educational processing. This stage, often informal, should be critical when using RPGs with students with disabilities. While all students generally require formal debriefing, students with disabilities may need greater assistance and specifically designed activities in order to reflect on their learning, no matter the focus or skills. Westborg's model allows educators to consider designable game components (framing and gameplay), intended purpose (leisure or educational), types of education (formal, informal and nonformal) and possible control over the learning process (high, medium and low). The resulting model provides educators a framework to intentionally select, modify or create RPGs that can help provide the right learning experience for different settings, student populations and educational goals. Tabletop role-playing games are an untapped tool for students with disabilities that can link content with low-stakes competition, provide a more collaborative, engaging classroom experience and build social skills and executive functioning in a safe space with peers, all areas of needed growth for struggling students.

DISABILITIES AND TABLETOP RPGS: REPRESENTATION AND ACCESSIBLE GAMING

Current conversations among and about tabletop RPGs relate to their use with people with disabilities. First, the games themselves have been criticized for lack of representation of characters who are outside the heteronormative traditional sphere. This criticism includes race, gender and sexual orientation, but also has shown the lack of characters with disabilities and the negative situations in which a character created with lesser abilities is demonized or the attribute negatively impacts their abilities within the game. Second, individuals with disabilities report accessibility problems in terms of gameplay options as well as community. This can be as simple as problems accessing the physical space in which the game is being played to problems with gameplay like lack of adapted dice or materials for players with vision or hearing loss. These two issues are briefly discussed here to ensure that educators consider all aspects of gameplay when planning for students with specific disabilities.

Gaming in general, including tabletop RPGs, has historically had problems with inclusivity in terms of representation. There are implicit problems related to disability representation, including lack of characters with any type of difference in ability, or overtly negative aspects, such as blindness or physical challenges being assessed at point deductions. Discussions began several years ago when gamers with disabilities like Elsa S. Henry (2015) began to speak out:

> Gaming is supposed to be fun. But when you start out with a character creation system which takes something that impacts your life as much as say, blindness does, and reduces it to a five-point flaw, it hurts. It hurts because it feels like erasure. I have never been able to see myself as a character in a game...I've never gotten to play a bad-ass blind and deaf character who swashbuckles, or who is a ghost, an angel or a vampire.
>
> *(Para. 11)*

More discussions and articles related to this issue have improved representation to some degree (Femia 2024; Jones 2018; Stokes 2017). Educators must consider the degree to which students with disabilities can create or use characters that resonate with their own identity, even within the fantasy focus of many tabletop RPGs.

Accessibility for all players has also been examined. Access to tabletop RPGs Kamm and Freudenthal (2024) state, "Access is not merely about accommodating individuals with different needs, it is about examining the structures, cultures, and material spaces that shape who gets to participate in the first place" (2e). With a more inclusive game design community and game mechanics systems like Fate (The Official Fate SRD n.d.) and Fudge (Grey Ghost Press n.d.), a wide range of tabletop RPGs can be designed for a broader range of players. Groups such as DOTS RPG Project (n.d.) created Braille dice and other tools for RPG accessibility. Accessible

Games (AbleGamersFoundation 2022) has courses, articles, tips and tools to help players and designers create accessible games. Greater emphasis on tabletop RPGs for younger children has created possibilities that may also be applicable for students with disabilities. The website TTRPGkids (Campbell 2024) has an extensive amount of simple and creative tabletop RPGs for all ages and abilities, using simple game mechanics (limited decision choices, fewer dice) and centered on stories and adventures that appeal to a younger audience. From videos (Roll 4 Initiative 2023) to blog posts (Kaminske 2018), there is current information related to easy adaptations that make tabletop RPG more accessible to all. Features such as lower reading requirements, fewer rules and more structured game play can also be used with students with disabilities if they are age appropriate. Educators must be aware of these issues when choosing and using tabletop RPGs. They must also be able to access the resources, which are not always easy to find. However, the amount and selection are varied and many specific games are available that may increase the potential for enjoyment and success by students with all types of disabilities.

HARRY POTTER MEETS DUNGEONS AND DRAGONS: AN EXPLORATORY TABLETOP RPG PROJECT

While this was not a formal research study, the structure followed was systematic to establish a baseline of initial conditions and findings in an exploratory context that can inform future research. The information below provided data that will be the basis for future action research. Both authors are experienced players in various commercial RPGs and were familiar with gameplay, character design and other components of the tabletop RPG. They discussed different ways to potentially integrate role-playing games into classrooms during several courses leading to student teaching placements. The following information provides descriptions of the decisions made and the results of this exploratory pilot project.

Context and Participants

The student teaching placement selected for this pilot was a fifth-grade special education classroom in a rural district. This was designated a 12:1:1 classroom as defined in state regulations (12 students with disabilities and Individual Education Plans, one teacher and one paraprofessional). However, the district had received a waiver (permission granted by the state education department to override a regulation due to extenuating circumstances), so there were 13 total students from third-, fourth- and fifth-grade levels. Prior to student teaching, the teacher candidate spent 50 clinical hours in the site with the students and host teacher over the preceding fall semester. During that time, the teacher candidate discussed the potential role-playing project with his host teacher and determined that this was a feasible activity for the seven-week student teaching placement. The project was designed as a small group activity with all five fifth-grade students (four males and one female) in the special class. All male students were identified as having learning disabilities. The female student was identified as having emotional disabilities. Reading levels ranged from the first grade to the fifth grade, and several students exhibited disruptive behaviors during the school day. As part of the daily classroom schedule, the host teacher included a period at the end of the school day prior to dismissal known as "WIN" time (What I Need). Students were allowed to choose material and activities that would help them progress in specific areas. This seemed to be a good way to incorporate the role-playing game as a fun and engaging activity that would support improvement but not be seen by students as a high-stakes academic assignment.

Planning and Playing the Game

Based on observations and social-emotional goals on the students' Individualized Education Programs (IEPs), the teacher candidate developed a role-playing game in the style *Dungeons & Dragons*. He decided not to use traditional *Dungeons & Dragons* characters and scenarios due to the limited time daily and across the seven-week placement. Teaching these students the more complex game play of a traditional Dungeon & Dragons campaign would be difficult. Students were reading *Harry Potter and the Sorcerer's Stone* (Rowling 1998) as a class and students enjoyed the text. The teacher candidate chose to use the Harry Potter world as the setting because students were familiar with the world and characters and could focus on game play. Using that familiar world and characters allowed students to move seamlessly from text to game scenario. The teacher candidate explored Harry Potter-themed games, including previous iterations of role-playing potential games described in detail (Chapman 2017) and the recently released single-player, immersive, open-world video game (Davies and Lewis 2023; Avalanche Games 2023), as well as free online RPGs (Brunell-Brutman 2019; Lacroix n.d., 2022). Given the diverse academic and social-emotional needs of the students and the brief time for learning and playing the game, the teacher created a scaled-down version of *Hogwarts: A Role-Playing Game*, one of the free published games (Brunell-Brutman 2019). The teacher candidate used ChatGPT (Open AI 2024) to assist in developing a scenario in which he took the role of Hagrid and was transported to this classroom to enlist the five students to help Harry Potter.

Game materials were developed and adapted so that these students with disabilities would be more likely to be successful at game play. The teacher candidate assisted each student individually to create a character sheet that enhanced their strengths and was adapted to present their learning challenges as possible helpful traits in the game. For example, a quiet student who was slow to participate was helped to see himself as thoughtful and someone who took the time to consider possible actions. Non-playable characters (NPCs) were included who helped maintain world-building. Familiarity with the Harry Potter world made gameplay easier; if Professor Snape or Draco Malfoy was an NPC who entered the story, students immediately understood that character's personality and probable actions. A version of a spell sheet limited potential magical choices and actions and eliminated more violent options (including actions like stabbing or killing). Instead, choices for possible actions for obstacles like defeating an enemy became humorous. For example, when fighting a troll, students used a spell to make his club grow and hit him on his own head or create a wedgie with his clothes. Students were provided brief directions with bullet points, as well as prompts. This helped ensure the scenario and required actions, decisions and options were clear.

Modifications were made in the initial planning as well as during the campaign. The AI-generated scenario was modified by the teacher to better adapt to individual student strengths as well as areas of needed growth. Students with lower reading abilities were able to read passages tailored to their level and students who read excepts aloud during the game with prosody earned bonus rolls of the die. When students were missing from the group, the teacher candidate created side quests that were engaging but did not interfere with or advance the main story. He also added a bonus die that could be earned as a reward for cooperative behavior or other positive interactions and behaviors, like complimenting a teammate. This allowed individual in-game rewards that could be used to help the group advance.

Limitations

Since this was a pilot descriptive study, data were collected in the form of anecdotal field notes after each session. These notes were analyzed to determine the development of future research questions and game play. Themes identified related to logistics, skills needed by the teacher as gamemaster and impact of disabilities on game play. The game was originally planned for several sessions each week. However, only six sessions were held, and the full group was only present for three. Absenteeism was a problem, as were competing instructional demands that made it difficult for all students to participate as planned. In the scenario, the main villain was responsible for making everyone in the Harry Potter world forget who Harry was and why he was famous. The group was unable to advance in the campaign to the point where they faced this "boss." This was an exploratory project designed to require these five players to use academic, interpersonal and social-emotional skills, and executive functioning while playing under the guidance of the teacher as gamemaster. This pilot was conducted to inform one teacher's future practice. As such, the findings are suggestions based on limited game play with a small sample.

USING TABLETOP RPGS WITH STUDENTS WITH DISABILITIES: SOME FINDINGS AND CONSIDERATIONS

This exploratory project examined a six-week tabletop role-playing game that used adapted *Dungeons & Dragons* style of play with a brief scenario based on a familiar text with a group of five fifth-grade students with disabilities. Tabletop RPGs can provide meaningful and motivating spaces for students with disabilities to learn and improve skills in cognitive, affective and social-emotional areas. Benefits and challenges identified here are possible points for decisions in selecting and creating tabletop RPGs with this target population. Specific applications may differ for each individual and group, but this pilot can enhance the planning process and adapt game play. Although there were no specific research questions for this pilot, there is still value in considering descriptions of events and teacher and student responses for future research and practice. These observations based on the limited pilot study provide a starting point for additional research and classroom practice.

Logistics and Classroom Demands

Challenges faced included those that were systematic based on larger factors and those that could be addressed within an individual classroom. Time and consistency were the biggest problems. Students were often absent, something that has been on the rise in many districts post-pandemic.

Absenteeism meant that some members of the group were unable to proceed with the scenario despite motivation and willingness, and the teacher had to ensure this did not become divisive in terms of the cooperative group once a student returned. Since all students were identified as having a disability, there were other service providers with whom they worked and sometimes schedules were changed due to factors such as snow days or assemblies. This meant that even though there was a well-planned uniform time period for game play, the group was not always able to have any or some of the necessary time to proceed with the game. Finding ways to ensure that students stayed motivated, did not give up in the face of interruptions and did not place blame on circumstances or individuals fell to the teacher.

There will always be circumstances that result in interrupted game play. This teacher candidate was constrained by this situation in that it was a brief placement and not his own classroom. Although it was conducted within the academic day, participation was voluntary and loosely structured. Moving forward, consideration must be given to the place of a similar project within the routines of the classroom and school. Alternatives include making it a regular part of academic instruction or moving game play to more of a club-like schedule. The gaming group could then include other students from outside the class; however, that may be problematic in terms of successful and cooperative gameplay. There is a needed balance between motivation that comes from a non-academic activity and the potential of a more traditional structured place within instructional time.

Individual Disabilities and the Role of Game Master

In this pilot project, there were no specific goals for individual students or the group.

Selection and adaptation of a tabletop role-playing game for students with disabilities require the educator to know student strengths and challenges and how the game can accommodate these. In this case, the game was designed as a beginning opportunity to practice basic academic skills (reading, speaking and listening) as well as social-emotional skills (cooperation, perseverance and conflict resolution). These were not clearly planned and the teacher candidate found it necessary to provide immediate and specific feedback and sometimes modifications to help students stay motivated and operationalize success within a cooperative situation. Students with disabilities must be willing to trust their own capability for success, trust the abilities and assistance of peers and trust the adult will make necessary changes to keep the group on track toward that success. Future projects with a clear focus on specific goals can maximize benefits and structure the game in ways that address these objectives.

Placement in a special class is indicative of students whose disabilities impact their learning and behaviors to such a degree that they cannot be successful in general classrooms.

The impact of individual student disabilities affected game play. All participants struggled in areas of English Language Arts, including reading, writing, speaking and listening. The game was dependent on text and verbal discussion, something that was difficult for most players. They were required to listen for important information versus tangential details, avoid getting sidetracked by other players or actions, weigh possibilities and make decisions in the face of problems. These were all extremely difficult skills for these students. Maintaining gameplay at a level in which all could participate and have moments to shine and contribute to success required many unanticipated adjustments during game play. The glow of the spotlight was something most of these students had not experienced, so even success was at times problematic because it was fleeting and brought new and different feelings. The game was not linear, which differed from the expectations of most of their school day. Students were unsure and hesitant with the power they had for choices (Amauger 2023). Making decisions by weighing options and anticipating consequences for each choice require executive functioning, something that is a struggle for most students with disabilities. When clear goals are set, teachers can analyze tasks and work toward these with smaller, more manageable steps.

One way this teacher candidate ensured success was through his skills as gamemaster. Motivation is often cited as a benefit of game play, but individuals are only motivated by situations in which they believe they have a chance for success, and that success lies within their power. The teacher candidate ensured that students were provided clear expectations both in actual game elements and in gameplay itself. Through continual clarification and sometimes adaptations, students felt safe and remained motivated. This game was unlike some academic games in which responses are clearly right or wrong, actions can be judged by other players and there are clear winners and losers. While that was positive, it was also a challenge to maintain that cooperative atmosphere. It took time and explanations to help students grasp that in this game, there was one group objective with trials along the way, and although players took turns and made individual decisions, the goal was for all students to reach the objective successfully as a group. The larger concept of cooperation became operationalized as a set of skills, including turn taking, patience, listening and withholding judgment. Some students wanted more of a leadership role and had a difficult time remaining engaged as other players weighed options and made decisions. Risk-taking was also difficult without clear-cut knowledge of the result and impact. These students were keenly aware that in their school experience, taking risks when you are unsure is not generally a good thing. Students sometimes slipped back into traditional interactions. For example, when one player chose a certain course of action, others might interject critical, even derogatory responses (such as "That was dumb, why would you do that?"). The teacher found himself required on occasion to gently redirect, model and teach students how to share the attention and encourage each other. The teacher continually kept the expectations clear: the focus was on working together to solve problems in a non-judgmental way.

Considering different perspectives in a respectful way was a function of character development and challenging for these students. The ability to create a character on their own was daunting, something other teachers have also experienced and described (Lazrow 2022c; Roman 2018b). The teacher helped students manage this by limiting choices and reminding students of the need for their characters to complement each other's skill set so the group would be stronger as a whole unit. The concept of developing a character with skills that help with the quest but also flaws was difficult for these students. They were used to seeing some of their own traits as negative and not focusing on the potential positive nature when working together with others. It was critical that the teacher used his knowledge of students' backgrounds, skills and goals based on their IEPs. For example, he told a student who is somewhat shy and timid that Hagrid saw bravery in him. Another student had difficulty managing his anger, and the teacher reframed it to help him see taking the initiative as leadership that could help everyone succeed. It was important to facilitate the balance between character as a reflection of self-identity and a model that represented possibilities for growth.

The scenario used should allow for easy buy-in by students who may fear unfamiliar situations due to past experiences. In this case, Harry Potter was chosen because all the students had seen at least one of the movies and the class was reading one of the books. This familiarity with characters and the ways of the world saved precious time and increased buy-in by players. Ensuring that negative aspects of fantasy games, like violence and death, are outside the scope of the game was critical. The teacher had to create space for conflict that could be solved without negative words or actions. In this pilot, no character or NPC could die or be mortally injured. The Harry Potter context allowed balance with world-building and familiarity of the students' reality. It provided the attraction of magic without some of the aggressive responses that are acceptable in some traditional fantasy role-playing games. It also meant that the teacher was able to adapt situations and create additional features that maintained the positive environment as the game proceeded. The lessons learned from this pilot can be used to develop and run other similar projects.

ROLLING THE DICE: POTENTIAL USE OF TABLETOP RPGS WITH STUDENTS WITH DISABILITIES

Although this pilot project was limited in several ways, it can provide key ideas for future consideration of tabletop RPGs with students with disabilities. The points briefly discussed below provide ideas and suggestions as well as research and resources that can inform educators as they contemplate using or adapting existing games or creating new versions. Practitioners who have been integrating tabletop RPGs in their classrooms offer valuable insight for those educators interested in trying this for the first time or extending what they may have already considered. Resources below offer a balance of research and reflection on experience.

The pilot provided indication that tabletop RPGs could be used to teach and reinforce academic cognitive and academic goals with students with disabilities. Research supports this, particularly in English Language Arts. The use of narrative structures, such a critical part of tabletop RPGs, is easily aligned with curricular standards. From using a game to help students make meaning and interact with a short story (Cook et al. 2017) or Greek mythology (Zalka 2016), practitioners have described their efforts and provided evidence that RPGs can be effective tools for teaching skills of reading and writing (Darvasi 2018; Doty 2023; Jones et al. 2021; Kaylor 2017; Lazrow 2022k; Prager 2019; Wells 2023). Studies provide ideas that could be adapted and examined for different settings and student populations. Gatsakou and colleagues (2022) propose ways that RPGs could benefit students with dyslexia. Westborg and Bowman (2024) provide a clear outline for the didactic potential of RPGs which can be used as a framework for applications to literacy learning objectives that are on most IEPs.

The use of stories and participatory narratives as tools for immersive and engaged learning in formal education has gained increased popularity and study. Stories and storytelling are effective tools for learning and retention. Storification generally refers to the use of fictional or non-fictional narratives as contexts for learning activities (Aura et al. 2021b). Storification draws from storytelling, gamification and positive psychology to engage students, learn and practice social skills, and increase academic performance (Akkerman et al. 2009). Specific use of Harry Potter to create a familiar story-based environment within classrooms as well as school-wide has shown benefits such as improved interpersonal and social skills and sense of community (Aura et al. 2021a, 2025). This project connected previous studies of storification within gamification.

Closely related to academic curricular content are the skills needed to retain, retrieve and apply that knowledge. The power of tabletop RPGs is also the learning experience itself. The unpredictable way characters and game scenarios unfold assists with application of executive functioning skills. Zagaria and colleagues (2021) define these as a set of cognitive mechanisms, such as planning, attention and self-monitoring, that are used by individuals to select and modify responses to situations. Many students with disabilities lack the skills necessary for successful learning. Goldman (2024) describes the connections between play in *Dungeons & Dragons* and executive functioning skills in life:

> In summary, executive functioning is a collection of mental processes that are fundamental to how we live, work, and interact with the world. These skills are varied and complex, and their effectiveness can significantly impact our daily life. Understanding executive functioning is crucial because it not only helps us recognize our strengths and weaknesses but also offers insight into how we can better manage our cognitive resources.
>
> *(Para. 12)*

Educators will affirm that these skills, so critical to success in learning and life, are often lacking or underdeveloped in students with disabilities. Tabletop RPGs offer a wealth of strategies for using and improving these skills while enjoying the activity. As Nguyen (2021) describes it, gameplay is learning in disguise.

In addition to these academic and curricular benefits, tabletop RPGs help foster affective and social-emotional learning (SEL). Students with disabilities struggle with these, and poor SEL skills may impact successful gameplay. Many students with disabilities have SEL goals on their IEPs. States have adopted SEL standards and educators at all grades are required to integrate these into content lessons (Collaborative for Academic, Social, and Emotional Learning 2020). Stubbs and Sorensen (2025) described the effectiveness of tabletop RPGs as a low-cost, flexible and creative means of developing and reinforcing SEL skills that can supplement any school-wide program. Others provide guidelines for using tabletop RPGs for SEL in classrooms (Lazrow 2022i). Studies addressed the possibilities offered by tabletop RPGs in educational settings to develop these skills in autistic individuals (Atherton et al. 2024; Katō 2019; Nguyen 2021). The term neurodivergent has come to describe a brain that works differently, and includes individuals with ADHD, autism and others. Valorozo-Jones (2021) created *The Neurodivergent Player's Handbook* to assist these players in finding a group in which to play and considering possible adaptations for success. Many others provide additional strategies for supporting neurodivergent players at the table (Dallas 2020; Dice Dragons 2023; Martin and McLaughlin 2024; Lazrow 2022d, 2022e, 2022h).

Related to SEL, students with disabilities often find it difficult to use appropriate communication skills, such as appropriate eye contact, vocal expressions, and gestures. They must process what was said and give a timely and suitable response. Role-playing games allow these students with disabilities to practice these skills in an enjoyable and low-stress space. The use of drama combined with the game play can help (Bowman 2015). The National Council for Curriculum and Assessment in Ireland (n.d.a, n.d.b) created two guides to help primary school teachers teach drama skills to students with mild and severe learning disabilities. Complete with scenarios and lessons, these could be used to prepare students for the demands of tabletop RPGs. For students with disabilities, teaching drama skills and then using them in the structured group setting of tabletop RPGs may help improve communication with peers and adults, leading to greater acceptance.

These are closely related to "soft skills" for workplace success. Recent conversations discuss the need for about like teamwork, collaboration, problem-solving, critical thinking, persistence, interpersonal communication and conflict resolution in employees (Daniau 2016; Hirsch 2017). Studies support the use of games for 21st-century skills (Aura et al. 2023a, 2023b). The Office of Disability Employment Policy (2012), part of the United States Department of Labor, produced a curriculum designed to help youth with disabilities develop and practice soft skills for increased employability, with activities and lessons that mirror tabletop role-playing game actions. Veldthuis et al. (2022) found *Dungeons & Dragons* to be effective as a didactic instrument that aided students in collaboration and creative problem-solving. In this pilot, the teacher found it necessary to help students develop and grapple with soft skills. Tabletop role-playing games require that players take time to plan, consider the perspective of others, sift through information and options, and weigh possible effects. This is done within a social group setting, something with which students with disabilities often struggle. Teachers can use NPCs to simulate realistic conflicts. For example, an arrogant NPC can be a stand-in for a peer and help students learn appropriate peer interaction. Students learn to disagree and come to consensus when faced with conflict. They can see the benefit of prior knowledge and transfer skills from one game session to another to scaffold play. They can reflect on what worked or why something did not go as planned and see that that does not necessarily mean the same action may not work in a future situation (Clarke et al. 2019; Gilsdorf 2018; Wolk 2017).

Research supports the use of tabletop RPGs with individuals with disabilities and mental health struggles. Tlili and colleagues (2022) described the use of this type of game to help students with disabilities learn and practice daily living skills, decision-making and problem-solving. Bystrova and Tokarskaja (2023) discuss the need for consideration of players' disabilities when designing tabletop games. Yuliawati et al. (2024) reviewed studies that demonstrated the benefits of tabletop RPGs as psychological interventions. The therapeutic use of role-playing games is a growing tool for mental health professionals (Arenas et al. 2022; Baker et al. 2022). Therapeutic use of role-playing game has been documented (Connell 2023; Henrich and Worthington 2021; Kilmer et al. 2023). The organization *Games to Grow* provides training to mental health professionals, educators and others on the applied uses of role-playing games (Kilmer et al. 2023) and Connell extends that to provide guidance for the clinician as gamemaster (2023). The "silverware technique" describes the ways gamemasters can maximize the benefits by acting in ways that both support and challenge players (Kilmer et al. 2023). "Offer a fork" means providing players with a clear set of choices. "Spoon feeding" means making a path or option explicit to the players through guided questions or statements. "Twist the knife" refers to prompting player action by using an in-game situation to raise the stakes. This method is similar to the way this teacher candidate managed the game and articulates the importance of teacher or mental health professional to be skilled in facilitation.

Teachers at all grade levels with inclusive classrooms can and should consider trying to implement tabletop RPGs. Studies have explored using tabletop RPGs in STEM areas (Carbajal and Angulo 2019; Chiu and Hsieh 2017; Ehlert 2023). Specific lesson plans that connect to almost every discipline, including art (Lazrow 2022f, 2022g, 2022l, 2022m), are available as first steps. There are ideas to address potential parental concerns and ways teachers can respond (Lazrow 2022b, 2022p). Even educators unfamiliar with using this type of game as a teaching strategy can start with whatever seems the best fit for them. Veterans like Paul Lazrow help interested educators by providing tales of their classroom applications (Lazrow 2022j, 2022n, 2022o). Teacher Sarah Roman describes the reasons she went from using other games to tabletop RPGs and shares her wisdom of experience, even considerations for room logistics (Roman 2018a). These teacher accounts combine with research to demonstrate that games can be integrated to create community and teach any content area. Concrete guidelines and stories of classroom experiences offer points to consider and ways to avoid potential obstacles (Cooper et al. 2024; Lazrow 2022a; Roman 2018c; Youakim 2019). There are guides that walk teachers through the steps and process from the beginning. Videos of actual gameplay with students can serve to show the ways teachers deal with the unexpected (Allan 2024). The website TTRPGkids (Campbell 2024) described steps in shifting from merely generic "educational" to "classroom ready" tabletop RPGs, including a Classroom Ready Toolkit. Any teacher with the willingness to try tabletop RPGs in their classroom can now find both research support and "how to" resources.

Tabletop RPGs have possibilities for academic and social-emotional learning for students with disabilities. Whether traditional *Dungeons & Dragons* play or adapted strategies, characters and scenarios, the potential is great. Resources continue to become available at little or no charge to assist teachers in integrating tabletop games at any grade level, content area or for SEL (Schrier et al. 2024, Trueblood 2022a, 2022b; Zamboni et al. 2024). First-person accounts from experienced educators can assist novice gamemasters in finding success implementing these games into their classroom (Allan 2024; Leach 2021; Martin and McLaughlin 2024; Reznichek 2021; Watson 2018). Wizards of the Coast (n.d.) now has a separate site for *Dungeons & Dragons* education resources and an educator license that makes it easy for teachers to find free materials and ideas for any age group and different formats (after-school club and learning standard-aligned scenarios). There are numerous places for educators to acquire the information, skills and materials needed to integrate tabletop role-playing games into their practice with diverse learners. The particular appeal and learning benefits of using tabletop RPGs to teach students with disabilities are clear (García-Redondo et al. 2019; Sari et al. 2021; Tlili et al. 2022). Educators willing to add "Game Master" to their resume can roll the dice and enter a world of motivation, engagement and learning with their students that is reality, not merely fantasy.

REFERENCES

AbleGamersFoundation. 2022. "Accessible Play Starts Here." Accessed January 3, 2025. https://accessible.games/.

Ahmad, Saghir, Abid Hussain Ch, Ayesha Batool, Khadija Sittar, and Misbah Malik. 2016. "Play and Cognitive Development: Formal Operational Perspective of Piaget's Theory." *Journal of Education and Practice* 7(28): 72–79.

Akkerman, Sonne, Wilfried Admiraal, and Jantina Huizenga. 2009. "Storification in History Education: A Mobile Game in and about Medieval Amsterdam." *Computers & Education* 52(2): 449–459. https://doi.org/10.1016/j.compedu.2008.09.014.

Alexander, Leigh. 2012. "GDC 2012: Sid Meier on How to See Games as Sets of Interesting Decisions." *Game Developer*. Accessed December 30, 2024. https://www.gamedeveloper.com/design/gdc-2012-sid-meier-on-how-to-see-games-as-sets-of-interesting-decisions.

Allan, Bill. 2024. "D&D with High School Students - The Complete Series." *YouTube*, June 10, 2025. https://www.youtube.com/playlist?list=PL-e8SjU6Hfttkld80Wixe4qLrUAM0sjze.

Amauger, Christian. 2023. "The Power of Choice: Player Agency in Tabletop Role-Playing Games. The Tavern (blog), *Medium*. Accessed January 12, 2025. https://medium.com/the-tavern/the-power-of-choice-player-agency-in-tabletop-role-playing-games-446e0be16428.

Anderson, Marc Malmdorf, Julian Kiverstein, Mark Miller, and Andreas Roepstorff. 2023. "Play in Predictive Minds: A Cognitive Theory of Play. *Psychological Review* 130(2): 462–479. https://doi.org/10.1037/rev0000369.

Arenas, Daniel Luccas, Anna Viduani, and Renata Brasil Araujo. 2022. "Therapeutic Use of Role-Playing Game (RPG) in Mental Health: A Scoping Review. *Simulation & Gaming* 53(3): 285–311. https://doi.org/10.1177/10468781211073720.

Atherton, Guy, Rhys Hathaway, Ingela Visuri, and Liam Cross. 2024. "A Critical Hit: Dungeons and Dragons as a Buff for Autistic People." *Autism: The International Journal of Research and Practice* 29(2): 1–13. https://doi.org/10.1177/13623613241275260.

Aura, Isabella, Lobna Hassan, and Juho Hamari. 2021a. "My School Is Hogwarts: Students' Social Behavior in Storified Classes." In *Proceedings of the 5th International GamiFIN Conference 2021*, edited by Mila Bujić, Jonna Koivisto, and Junho Hamari. https://ceur-ws.org/Vol-2883/paper2.pdf.

Aura, Isabella, Lobna Hassan, and Juho Hamari. 2021b. "Teaching Within a Story: Understanding Storification of Pedagogy." *International Journal of Educational Research* 106: Article 101728. https://doi.org/10.1016/j.ijer.2020.101728.

Aura, Isabella, Lobna Hassan, and Juho Hamari. 2025. "*Transforming a School into Hogwarts*: Storification of Classrooms and Students' Social Behaviour." *Educational Review* 77(1): 1–20. https://doi.org/10.1080/00131911.2023.2170332.

Aura, Isabella, Simo Järvelä, Lobna Hassan, and Juho Hamari. 2023a. "Gamified City for 6th Graders: The effect of Gameful Experience on Students' 21st Century Readiness in Finland." In *Proceedings of the 2023 Digital Games and Research Association International Conference*. https://doi.org/10.26503/dl.v2023i1.1903.

Aura, Isabella, Simo Järvelä, Lobna Hassan, and Juho Hamari. 2023b. "Role-Play Experience's Effect on Students' 21st Century Skills Propensity." *The Journal of Educational Research* 116(3): 159–170. https://doi.org/10.1080/00220671.2023.2227596.

Avalanche Software. 2023. *Hogwarts Legacy*. Warner Bros. Games. PC, PlayStation 5, Xbox Series X/S, PlayStation 4, Xbox One, Nintendo Switch.

Baker, Ian S., Ian J. Turner, and Yasuhiro Kotera. 2022. "Role-Play Games (RPGs) for Mental Health (Why Not?): Roll for Initiative. *International Journal of Mental Health and Addiction* 21: 3901–3909. https://doi.org/10.1007/s11469-022-00832-y.

Baranowski, Tom, Richard Buday, Debbe I. Thompson, and Janice Baranowski. 2008. "Playing for Real: Video Games and Stories for Health-Related Behavior Change." *American Journal of Preventive Medicine* 34(1): 74–82. https://doi.org/10.1016/j.amepre.2007.09.027.

Barton, Erin E. 2015. "Teaching Generalized Pretend Play and Related Behaviors to Young Children with Disabilities." *Exceptional Children* 81(4): 489–506. https://doi.org/10.1177/0014402914563694.

Becker, Katrin. 2021. "What's the Difference between Gamification, Serious Games, Educational Games, and Game-Based Learning?" *Academia Letters*, Article 209: 1–4. https://doi.org/10.20935/AL209.

Beidatsch, Cedric, and Susan Broomhall. 2010. "Is This the Past? The Place of Role-Play Exercises in Undergraduate History Teaching." *Journal of University Teaching and Learning Practice* 7(1): 76–96. https://doi.org/10.53761/1.7.1.6.

Bowman, Sarah Lynne. 2010. *The Functions of Role-Playing Games*. McFarland.

Bowman, Sarah Lynne. 2015. "Connecting Role-Playing, Stage Acting, and Improvisation." *Analog Game Studies* 4(3). https://analoggamestudies.org/2015/05/conneccting-role-playing-stage-acting-and-improvisation/.

Brunell-Brutman, David. 2019. *Hogwarts: A Role-Playing Game*. Accessed January 3, 2025. David Brunell-Brutman.com. https://dbb-8.itch.io/hogwarts-rpg.

Bystrova, Tatiana, and Ludmila Tokarskaja. 2023. "Designing Tabletop Games for Individuals with Disabilities through Student Project Activity." In *The World of Games: Technologies for Experimenting, Thinking, Learning*, edited by Daria Bylieva and Alfred Nordmann, 143–159. https://doi.org/10.1007/978-3-031-48016-4_11.

Campbell, Steph. 2024. "Shifting from "Educational" to "Classroom Teady" TTRPGs." *TTRPGkids*. April, 15, 2024. https://www.ttrpgkids.com/2024/04/15/shifting-from-educational-to-classroom-ready-ttrpgs/.

Carbajal, Ricardo Morales, and Carlos Villa Angulo. 2019. "Role Playing Games for Mathematics Education. *Education in the Knowledge Society (EKS)* 20: 1–13. https://doi.org/10.14201/eks2019_20_a7.

Chapman, David F. "Harry Potter - Adventures in the Wizarding World." *Autocratik*. (blog), November 11, 2017. https://www.autocratik.com/2017/11/harry-potter-adventures-in- wizarding.html.

Chiu, Fu-Yuan, and Mei-Ling Hsieh. 2017. "Role-Playing Game-Based Assessment to Fractional Concept in Second Grade Mathematics." *EURASIA Journal of Mathematics Science and Technology Education* 13(4): 1075–1083. https://doi.org/10.12973/eurasia.2017.00659a.

Clarke, Samantha, Sylvester Arnab, Luca Morini, and Heywood, L. 2019. "Dungeons and Dragons as a Tool for Developing Student Self-Reflection Skills." *Games and Learning Alliance 7th International Conference, GALA 2018,* Palermo, Italy, *December 5–7, 2018, Proceedings*, edited by Manuel Gentile, Mario Allegra, and Heinrich Söbke. https://doi.org/10.1007/978-3-030-11548-7_10.

Collaborative for Academic, Social, and Emotional Learning (CASEL). 2020. *CASEL'S SEL Framework: What Are the Core Competence Areas and Where Are They Promoted?* October 1, 2020. https://casel.org/casel-sel-framework-11-2020/.

Connell, Megan A. 2023. *Tabletop Role-Playing Therapy: A Guide for the Clinician Game Master*. Norton Professional Books.

Cook, Mike P., Matthew Gremo, and Ryan Morgan. 2017. "We're Just Playing: The Influence of a Modified Tabletop Role-Playing Game on ELA Students' In-Class Reading". *Simulation & Gaming* 48(2): 199–218. https://doi.org/10.1177/1046878116684570.

Cooper, R. Paul, Mahjabin Chowdhury, Jonan Phillip Donaldson, and Jonathan Mitchell. 2024. "Dungeons & Dragons in the Literature Classroom. *International Journal of Designs for Learning* 15(2): 92–102. https://doi.org/10.14434/ijdl.v15i2.36322.

Cullinan, Maryanne, and Jennifer Genova. 2023. "Gaming the Systems: A Component Analysis Framework for the Classroom Use of RPGs." *International Journal of Role-Playing* 13: 7–17. https://doi.org/10.33063/ijrp.vi13.305.

Dallas, Amy. 2020. "D&D and Neurodiversity: Tips and Tales from the Table." *YouTube Video*, August 25, 2021. https://www.youtube.com/watch?v=xTVQ5Nz85EA.

Daniau, Stephanie. 2016. "The Transformative Potential of Role-Playing Games: From Play Skills to Human Skills." *Simulation & Gaming* 47(4): 423–444. https://doi.org/10.1177/1046878116650765.

Darvasi, Paul. 2018. "Leveraging the Lore of 'Dungeons & Dragons' to Motivate Students to Read and Write." *KQED Mind/Shift*. October 8, 2018. https://www.kqed.org/mindshift/51787/leveraging-the-lore-of-dungeons-and-dragons-to-motivate-students-to-read-and-write.

Davies, Paul, and Kate Lewis. 2023. *Hogwarts Legacy: The Official Game Guide*. Scholastic.

Dewey, John. 1914. *Democracy and Education: An Introduction to the Philosophy of Education*. Macmillan.

Dewey, John. 1934. *Art as Experience*. Capricorn Books.

Dice Dragons. 2023. *How to Play DND as a Neurodivergent Person*. August 28, 2023. https://www.dicedragons.co.uk/blogs/tabletop-tips/how-to-play-dnd-as-a-neurodivergent-person.

DOTS RPG Project. n.d. *Improving Accessibility in Tabletop Roleplaying Games, One Adventure at a Time*! Accessed January 12, 2025. https://www.dotsrpg.org/.

Doty, Gene. 2003. "A Toss of the Dice: Writers, Readers and Role-Playing Games." *Journal of the Fantastic in the Arts* 14(1): 51–67.

Eberhart, Janina, Paes, Tanya M., Michelle R. Ellefson, and Stuart Marcovitch. 2023. "Executive Functions and Play." *Trends in Neuroscience Education* 30: Article 100198. https://doi.org/10.1016/j.tine.2023.100198.

Eberle, Scott G. 2014. "The Elements of Play: Toward a Philosophy and a Definition of Play." *American Journal of Play* 6(2): 214–233.

Ehlert, Julia. 2023. "Dungeons and Dragons - and Chemistry." *Caltech Magazine*. November 3, 2023. https://magazine.caltech.edu/post/dungeons-and-dragons-science-outreach.

Femia, Giuseppe. 2024. "Tabletop Roleplaying Game Studies: An Abundant Site for Disability Media Analysis." *GAME: The Italian Journal of Game Studies* (12). https://www.gamejournal.it/tabletop-roleplaying-game-studies-an-abundant-site-for-disability-media-analysis/

García-Redondo, Patricia, Trinidad Garcia, Débora Areces, José Carlos Núñez, and Celestino Rodríguez. 2019. "Serious Games and Their Effect Improving Attention in Students with Learning Disabilities." *International Journal of Environmental Research and Public Health* 16(14): 1–12. https://doi.org/10.3390/ijerph16142480.

Gatsakou, Christina, Nikolaos Bardis, and Athanasios Drigas. 2022. "The Usage of RPGS as an Interdisciplinary Method of Teaching Dyslexic Students." *Technium Social Sciences Journal* 27: 207–216. https://doi.org/10.47577/tssj.v27i1.5438.

Gilsdorf, Ethan. 2018. "How Playing Dungeons & Dragons Has Helped Me Be More Connected, Creative and Compassionate." *TEDEd* (blog). https://ed.ted.com/blog/2018/09/17/how-playing-dungeons-dragons-has-helped-me-be-more-connected-creative-and-compassionate.

Goldman, Daniel. 2024. "Navigating Life's Quest: Executive Functioning through the Lens of D&D Action Economy." *Geekers Keep* (blog), *Medium*. https://medium.com/geekers-keep/navigating-lifes-quest-executive-functioning-through-the-lens-of-d-d-action-economy-7ddf8cd1219b.

Grafwallner, Peg. (2021). *Not Yet... and That's OK: How Productive Struggle Fosters Student Learning*. Solution Tree.

Grey Ghost Press. n.d. *What's Fudge?* Accessed January 5, 2025. https://fudgerpg.com/about/about-fudge.html.

Haarman, Susan. 2023. "Dungeons & Dragons & Dewey: Toward a Ludic Pedagogy of Democratic Civic Life through the Philosophy of John Dewey and Tabletop Role-Playing Games." PhD diss. Loyola University Chicago. ProQuest (30245953).

Henrich, Sören and Rachel Worthington. 2021. "Let Your Clients Fight Dragons: A Rapid Evidence Assessment Regarding the Therapeutic Utility of 'Dungeons & Dragons'. *Journal of Creativity in Mental Health* 18(3): 1–19. https://doi.org/10.1080/15401383.2021.1987367.

Henry, Elsa S. 2015. "Reimagining Disability in Role-Playing Games." *Analog Game Studies* 2(2). https://analoggamestudies.org/2015/02/reimagining-disability-in-role-playing-games/.

Hirsch, Barton J. 2017. "Wanted: Soft Skills for Today's Jobs." *Phi Delta Kappan* 98(5): 12–17. https://doi.org/10.1177/003172171769035.

Jones, Shelly. 2018. "Blinded by the Roll: The Critical Fail of Disability in D&D. *Analog Game Studies* 5(1). https://analoggamestudies.org/2018/03/blinded-by-the-roll-the-critical-fail-of-disability-in-dd/.

Jones, Karis, Scott Storm, Jennifer Castillo, and Sasha Karbachinskiy. 2021. "Chasing New Worlds: Stories of Roleplaying in Classroom Spaces. *Journal of Language and Literacy Education* 17(1): 1–17. https://openjournals.libs.uga.edu/jolle/issue/view/362.

Kaminske, Althea Need. (2018, August 23). "Learning in Dungeons and Dragons." *Learning Scientists Posts, For Teachers* (blog). *The Learning Scientists*. August 23, 2018. https://www.learningscientists.org/blog/2018/8/23-1.

Kamm, Björn-Ole, and Michael Freudenthal. 2024. "Exploring Access and Accessibility in Analog Role-Playing Games. *Japanese Journal of Analog Role-Playing Game Studies* 5: 1e–9e. https://repository.kulib.kyoto-u.ac.jp/server/api/core/bitstreams/275a0e72-5996-42f1-80fe-442e97cd83bb/content.

Kapur, Manu. 2008. "Productive Failure." *Cognition and Instruction* 26(3): 379–424. https://doi.org/10.1080/07370000802212669.

Kapur, Manu, and Katerine Bielaczyc. 2012. "Designing for Productive Failure." *Journal of the Learning Sciences* 21(1): 45–83. https://doi.org/10.1080/10508406.2011.591717

Katō, Kōhei. 2019. "Employing Tabletop Role-Playing Games (TRPGs) in Social Communication Support Measures for Children and Youth with Autism Spectrum Disorder (ASD) in Japan: A Hands-On Report on the Use of Leisure Activities." *Japanese Journal of Analog Role-Playing Game Studies* 0: 23–28. https://doi.org/10.14989/jarps_0_23.

Kaylor, Stefanie L. B. 2017. "Dungeons and Dragons and Literacy: The Role Tabletop Role-Playing Games Can Play in Developing Teenagers' Literacy Skills and Reading Interests." Master's thesis, University of Northern Iowa. https://scholarworks.uni.edu/grp/215/.

Kilmer, Elizabeth D., Adam D. Davis, Jared N. Kilmer, & Adam R. Johns. 2023. *Therapeutically Applied Role-Playing Games the Game to Grow Method*. Routledge.

Koster, Raph. 2014. *A Theory of Fun for Game Designers* (2nd ed.). O'Reilly Media.

Lacroix, Bobby. n.d. *Wizarding World – The Role-Playing Game*. Accessed January 5, 2025. https://wizworldrpg.com.

Lacroix, Bobby. 2022. "WizWorld RPG." *Facebook*. July 5, 2022. https://www.facebook.com/groups/wizworldrpg/

Lazrow, Paul. 2022a. "And So It Begins: Welcome to Your First Dungeons & Dragons Adventure – Here's All You Need to Know (Plus Free Stuff to Get You Started!)." *The Local*. December 21, 2022. https://nwlocalpaper.com/dungeons-dragons-101-getting-started-on-your-first-adventure.

Lazrow, Paul. 2022b. "D&D and the Satanic Panic — Are My Kids Ok, Really?" *Medium*. May 16, 2022. https://lazrowp.medium.com/d-d-and-the-satanic-panic-are-my-kids-ok-really-ee13038beb50.

Lazrow, Paul. 2022c. "D&D for Kids — How Many Options Are "a Ton of Options"!?!" *Medium*. May 16, 2022. https://lazrowp.medium.com/d-d-for-kids-how-many-options-are-a-ton-of-options-a823057b841b.

Lazrow, Paul. 2022d. "11 Ways to Support Neurodivergent Players at Your D&D Gaming Table." *Medium*. May 20, 2022. https://lazrowp.medium.com/11-ways-to-support-neurodivergent-at-your-d-d-gaming-table-df6640bbd237.

Lazrow, Paul. 2022e. Minds of All Kinds: Supporting Neurodivergent Players in Dungeons & Dragons (and Everywhere). *The Local*. September 26, 2022. https://nwlocalpaper.com/minds-of-all-kinds.

Lazrow, Paul. 2022f. "Teaching with D&D: D&D for Kids — Art Lesson #5." *Medium*. May 9, 2022. https://lazrowp.medium.com/teaching-with-d-d-d-d-for-kids-art-lesson-5-14fd499e7501.

Lazrow, Paul. 2022g. "Teaching with D&D: D&D for Kids — Science Lessons? #4." *Medium*. April 29, 2022. https://lazrowp.medium.com/teaching-with-d-d-d-d-for-kids-science-lessons-4-d8240bc37bd8.

Lazrow, Paul. 2022h. "Teaching with D&D: D&D for Neurodivergent Players?" *Medium*. March 21, 2022. https://lazrowp.medium.com/teaching-with-d-d-d-d-for-neurodivergent-players-719192b9608f.

Lazrow, Paul. 2022i. "Teaching with D&D: D&D Strengthens Kid's Social Emotional Learning (SEL)." *Medium*. April 7, 2022. https://lazrowp.medium.com/teaching-with-d-d-d-d-strengthens-kids-social-emotional-learning-sel-fa9bd07b7e6d.

Lazrow, Paul. 2022j. "Teaching with D&D: Dungeons and Dragons in School?!?" *Medium*. March 21, 2022. https://lazrowp.medium.com/teaching-with-d-d-dungeons-and-dragons-in-school-fef229a37e92.

Lazrow, Paul. 2022k. "Teaching with D&D: Fantastic/al D&D Lesson Plan – 1 Writing." *Medium*. March 23, 2022. https://lazrowp.medium.com/teaching-with-d-d-fantastic-al-d-d-lesson-plan-1-writing-7de5a81a40e2.

Lazrow, Paul. 2022l. "Teaching with D&D: Magical Math D&D Lesson Plan #2." *Medium*. March 25, 2022. https://lazrowp.medium.com/teaching-with-d-d-magical-math-d-d-lesson-plan-2-2bd257eb41fb.

Lazrow, Paul. 2022m. "Teaching with D&D: Stealthy Social Studies Lesson Plan #3." *Medium*. April 11, 2022. https://lazrowp.medium.com/teaching-with-d-d-stealthy-social-studies-lesson-plan-3-120a91f10c23.

Lazrow, Paul. 2022n. "Teaching with D&D: Why You and Your Kids Should Play Dungeons & Dragons." *Medium*. April 30, 2022. https://lazrowp.medium.com/why-you-and-your-kids-should-play-dungeons-dragons-f9dea74e0331.

Lazrow, Paul. 2022o. "The Best Ultimate Guide to Running Dungeons and Dragons Games for Kids." *Medium*. March 28, 2022. https://lazrowp.medium.com/the-best-ultimate-guide-to-running-dungeons-and-dragons-games-for-kids-3eab31458712.

Lazrow, Paul. 2022p. "Uhh Ohhhh……My Kid Is a Murder Hobo!?!" *Medium*. April 4, 2022. https://lazrowp.medium.com/uhh-ohhhh-my-kid-is-a-murder-hobo-f5db0dd48e6c.

Leach, M. (2021). *How Autism Powers My D & D. Polygon*. https://www.polygon.com/22527706/dungeons-dragons-autistic-autism-dungeon-master-essay.

Lillard, Angeline. S. (2015). "The Development of Play." In *Handbook of Child Psychology and Developmental Science: Cognitive Processes*, 7th ed., edited by Richard M. Lerner, Lynn S. Liben, and Ulrich Mueller, 425–468. John Wiley & Sons. https://doi.org/10.1002/9781118963418.childpsy211.

Lillard, Angeline S., Matthew D. Lerner, Emily J. Hopkins, Rebecca A. Dore, Eric D. Smith, Carolyn M. Palmquist. 2013. "The Impact of Pretend Play on Children's Development: A Review of the Evidence." *Psychological Bulletin* 139(1): 1–34. https://doi.org/10.1037/a0029321.

Lillard, Angeline. S., Ashley M. Pinkham, and Eric Smith. 2010. "Pretend Play and Cognitive Development." In *The Wiley-Blackwell Handbook of Childhood Cognitive Development*, 2nd ed., edited by Usha Goswami, 285–311. Blackwell. https://doi.org/10.1002/9781444325485.ch11.

Lockhart, S. 2010. "Play: An Important Tool for Cognitive Development." *Extensions: Curriculum Newsletter from HighScope* 24(7): 1–8. https://www.yumpu.com/en/document/view/10903568/play-an-important-tool-for-cognitive-development-become-a-.

Martin, Monty, & Kelly McLaughlin. 2024. "Game Prep Tips for Neurodivergent Dungeon Masters!" *YouTube*, April 2, 2024. https://www.youtube.com/watch?v=Oyh_ALgjyCo

National Council for Curriculum and Assessment. n.d.a *Primary Drama: Guidelines for Students with Mild General Learning Disabilities*. Government of Ireland. https://ncca.ie/media/3882/p_mild_drama-1.pdf

National Council for Curriculum and Assessment. n.d.b *Primary Drama: Guidelines for Students with Severe and Profound General Learning Disabilities.* Government of Ireland. https://ncca.ie/media/3882/p_mild_drama-1.pdf

Nguyen, Hoa P. 2021. "How to Use Gameplay to Enhance Classroom Learning." *Edutopia.* March 26, 2021. https://www.edutopia.org/article/how-use-gameplay-enhance-classroom-learning/.

Noda, Shota, Kentaro Shirotsuki, and Mutsuhiro Nakao. 2019. "The Effectiveness of Intervention with Board Games: A Systematic Review. *BioPsychoSocial Medicine* 13(22): 1–21. https://doi.org/10.1186/s13030-019-0164-1.

Office of Disability Employment Policy. 2012. *Skills to Pay the Bills: Mastering Soft Skills for Workplace Success.* United States Department of Labor. https://pueblo.gpo.gov/CAARNG/ODEP/PDF/ODEP013.pdf.

Open AI. 2024. *ChatGPT* (Spring 2024 version). https://chat.openai.com.

Plass, Jan L., Bruce D. Homer, and Charles K. Kinzer. 2015. "Foundations of Game-Based Learning." *Educational Psychologist* 50(4): 258–283. https://doi.org/10.1080/00461520.2015.1122533.

Prager, Richard Heinz Patrick. 2019. "Exploring the Use of Role-Playing Games in Education." *The MT Review*, Issue 2. https://mtrj.library.utoronto.ca/index.php/mtrj/article/view/29606/25764.

Reznichek, Zachary Anton. 2021. *The Teacher Gamer Handbook for Dungeons and Dragons.* Wild Mind Training.

Roll 4 Initiative, 2023. "Disability & Accessibility in TTRPGs." *YouTube*, September 19, 2023. https://www.youtube.com/watch?v=3Iff8yTNjPU.

Roman, Sarah. 2018a. "D&D and Education: The Logistics behind the Room and Student Management." *Medium.* February 27, 2018. https://medium.com/@dndlearning/d-d-and-education-the-logistics-behind-the-room-and-student-management-edb4f8b5bd01.

Roman, Sarah. 2018b. "D&D and Education: The Rumblings of Research with Character Creation." *Medium.* February 19, 2018. https://medium.com/@dndlearning/d-d-and-education-the-rumblings-of-research-with-character-creation-487dc6f76ff.

Roman, Sarah. 2018c. "D&D in the Classroom: Making Old Worlds New." *Medium.* February 12, 2018. https://medium.com/@dndlearning/d-d-in-the-classroom-making-old-worlds-new-3a9ee4241d7d

Rowling, J. K. 1998. *Harry Potter and the Sorcerer's Stone.* Scholastic.

Ruiz-Ezquerro, Antonio. 2021. "Rolling Dice and Learning -- Using Role-Playing Games as Pedagogy Tools." *Journal of Campus Activities Practice and Scholarship* 3(2): 50–56. https://doi.org/10.52499/2021022.

Salen Tekinbas, Katie, and Eric Zimmerman. 2003. *Rules of Play: Game Design Fundamentals.* MIT Press.

Sari, Retno Purwani, Iqbal Yusuf Fadillah, Riki Buldan Al Hariri, Muhammad Indra Habibi, and Raiswati Untsa Mega. 2021. "Educational Game Development Based on Role Play Games for Students with Special Needs". *Jurnal Teknologi Informasi dan Pendidikan* 14(2): 178–184. https://doi.org/10.24036/tip.v14i2.

Schrier, Karen, Rachel Kowert, Diana Leonard, and Tarja Porkka-Kontturi, eds. 2024. *Learning, Education, & Games Volume 4: 50 Games to Use for Inclusion, Equity, and Justice*. Carnegie Mellon University: ETC Press.

Sinha, Tanmay, and Manu Kapur. 2021. "When Problem Solving Followed by Instruction Works: Evidence for Productive Failure." *Review of Educational Research* 91(5): 761–798. https://doi.org/10.3102/00346543211019105.

Skilbeck, Adrian. 2017. "Dewey on Seriousness, Playfulness and the Role of the Teacher." *Education Sciences* 7(1): 16. https://doi.org/10.3390/educsci7010016.

Smolucha, Larry, and Francine Smolucha. 2021. "Vygotsky's Theory In-Play: Early Childhood Education." *Early Child Development and Care* 191(7–8): 1041–1055. https://doi.org/10.1080/03004430.2020.1843451.

Sousa, Carla, Sara Rye, Micael Sousa, Pedro Juan Torres, Claudilene Perim, Shivani Atul Mansuklal, and Firdaous Ennami. 2023. "Playing at the School Table: Systematic Literature Review of Board, Tabletop, and Other Analog Game-Based Learning Approaches." *Frontiers in Psychology* 14. https://doi.org/10.3389/fpsyg.2023.1160591.

Stancin, Kristian, and Natasa Hoic-Bozic. 2020. "The Importance of Using Digital Games for Educational Purposes for Students with Intellectual Disabilities." In *SLET 2020: Proceedings of the International Scientific Conference on Innovative Approaches to the Application of Digital Technologies in Education (SLET 2020)*, edited by Jože Rugelj and Maria Lapina, 8–15. https://ceur-ws.org/Vol-2861/invited_paper_1.pdf.

Stancin, Kristian, Natasa Hoic-Bozic, and Sanja Skocic Mihic. 2022. "Key Characteristics of Digital Educational Games for Students with Intellectual Disabilities," *International Journal of Game-Based Learning (IJGBL)* 12(1): 1–15. https://doi.org/10.4018/IJGBL.313637.

Steele, Harlin/Hayley S. 2023. "The Maker Turn in Classroom Games: An Articulation of Gamemaking in Education (GME)." In *Generation Analog 2021: Proceedings of the Tabletop Games and Education Conference,* edited by Evan Torner, Shelley Jones, Edmond Chang, Megan Condis, and Aaron Trammell. Carnegie Mellon University ETC Press, pp. 5–27.

Stokes, Michael. 2017. "Access to the Page: Queer and Disabled Characters in Dungeons & Dragons." *Analog Game Studies,* 4(3). https://analoggamestudies.org/2017/05/access-to-the-page-queer-and-disabled-characters-in-dungeons-dragons/.

Stubbs, Richard, and Nikolas Sorensen. 2025. "Tabletop Role-Playing Games and Social and Emotional Learning in School Settings." *Social and Emotional Learning: Research, Practice, and Policy* 5: 1–10. https://doi.org/10.1016/j.sel.2025.100090.

The Official Fate SRD. n.d. "Fate Accessibility Toolkit." Accessed December 20, 2024. https://fate-srd.com/fate-accessibility-toolkit.

Tlili, Ahmed, Mouna Denden, Anqi Duan, Natalia Padilla-Zea, Ronghuai Huang Tianyue Sun, and Daniel Burgos. 2022. "Game-Based Learning for Learners with Disabilities—What Is Next? A Systematic Literature Review from the Activity Theory Perspective." *Frontiers in Psychology* 12. https://doi.org/10.3389/fpsyg.2021.814691.

Trueblood, Laurie. 2022a. "How Our RPG Characters Drive Our Personal Development." *Adventures to Authenticity*. August 6, 2022. https://www.adventurestoauthenticity.com/blog/how-our-rpg-characters-drive-our-personal-development.

Trueblood, Laurie. 2022b. "The Scientific Benefits of Tabletop Gaming." *Tabletop Games Blog*. April 19, 2022. https://tabletopgamesblog.com/2022/04/19/the-scientific-benefits-of-tabletop-gaming-topic-discussion/.

Valorozo-Jones, Caleb. 2021. "Neurodiversity, Dungeons, and Dragons: A Guide to Transforming and Enriching TTRPGs for Neurodivergent Adults or the Neurodivergent Player's Handbook." Master's thesis. Ontario College of Art and Design University. https://openresearch.ocadu.ca/id/eprint/3498/1/Valorozo-Jones_Caleb_2021_MDES_INCD_MRP.pdf.

Veldthuis, Marcella, Mathijs Koning, and Dave Stikkolorum. 2022." A Quest to Engage Computer Science Students: Using Dungeons & Dragons for Developing Soft Skills" In *CSERC '21: Proceedings of the 10th Computer Science Education Research Conference*, edited by Dave Stikkolorum and Ebrahim Rahimi, 5–13. https://doi.org/10.1145/3507923.3507927.

Watson, Eric. 2018. "Teaching in the Classroom with Dungeons and Dragons." *Pixelkin*. February 28, 2018. https://pixelkin.org/2018/02/28/teaching-the-classroom-with-dungeons-dragons/.

Weisberg, Deena Skolnick. 2015. "Pretend Play." *WIREs Cognitive Science*, 6(3): 249–261. https://doi.org/10.1002/wcs.1341.

Wells, Kade C. 2023. "Supporting Student Development with Role-Playing Games." *Edutopia*. October 12, 2023. https://www.edutopia.org/article/supporting-student-development-role-playing-games/.

Westborg, Josefin. 2023. "The Educational Role-Playing Game Design Matrix: Mapping Design Components onto Types of Education." *International Journal of Role-Playing* 13: 18–30. https://doi.org/10.33063/ijrp.vi13.306.

Westborg, Josefin, and Sarah Lynne Bowman. 2024. "GM Screen: The Didactic Potential of RPGs." In *#EduRPG. Rollenspiel als Methode der Bildung*, edited by Frank R. Roberts and Kathrin Fischer. https://www.diva-portal.org/smash/get/diva2:1814582/FULLTEXT01.pdf

Whitebread, David, Penny Coltman, Helen Jameson, and Rachel Lander. 2009. "Play, Cognition and Self-Regulation: What Exactly Are Children Learning When They Learn Through Play?" *Educational and Child Psychology* 26(2): 40–52. https://doi.org/10.53841/bpsecp.2009.26.2.40.

Willig, James H., Jennifer Croker, Lisa McCormick, Meena Nabavi, Jeremey Walker, Nancy P. Wingo, Cathy C. Roche, Carolyn Jones, Katherine E. Hartmann, and David Redden. 2021. "Gamification and Education: A Pragmatic Approach with Two Examples of Implementation." *Journal of Clinical and Translational Science* 5: e181, 1–7. https://doi.org/10.1017/cts.2021.806.

Wizards of the Coast. n.d. "Educator Resources." Accessed December 12, 2024. https://dnd.wizards.com/resources/educators.

Wolk, Steven. 2017. "Educating Students for an Outdated World." *Phi Delta Kappan* 99(2): 46–52. https://doi.org/10.1177/0031721717734190.

Youakim, Gannon. 2019. "Dungeon Classroom Guide: Using Tabletop Role-Playing Games in the Classroom." Honors Capstone Project. University of Minnesota Morris. 12. https://digitalcommons.morris.umn.edu/honors/12.

Yuliawati, Livia, Putri Ayu Puspieta Wardhani, and Joo Hou Ng. 2024. "A Scoping Review of Tabletop Role-Playing Game (TTRPG) as Psychological Intervention: Potential Benefits and Future Directions." *Psychology Research and Behavior Management* 17: 2885–2903. https://doi.org/10.2147/PRBM.S466664.

Zagaria, Tommasa, Gabriella Antonucci, Serafino Buono, Marilena Recupero, and Pierluigi Zoccolotti. 2021. "Executive Functions and Attention Processes in Adolescents and Young Adults with Intellectual Disability." *Brain Sciences* 11(1): 42. https://doi.org/10.3390/brainsci11010042

Zalka, Csenge Virág. 2016. "Adventures in the Classroom: Creating Traditional Story-Based Role-Playing Games for the High School Curriculum." *Storytelling, Self, Society* 12(2): 173–206. https://dx. doi.org/10.13110/storselfsoci.12.2.0173.

Zamboni, Camilla, Matthew Farber, and William Merchant, eds. 2024. *Roll for Learning: 51 Micro Tabletop Role-Playing Games to Use in the Classroom*. Play Story Press. https://works.hcommons.org/records/crhvk-jwe98.

CHAPTER 5

Cripping Tabletop Role-Playing Games

A Critical Analysis of Disability and Inclusion in Inspirisles *and Beyond*

Hanne Grasmo and Lobna Hassan

INTRODUCTION

If you are a teacher using games to build an inclusive classroom, you will probably get excited by encountering *Inspirisles* (Oxenham, 2021); a tabletop role-playing game (RPG) created together with Deaf[1] youth and aiming to raise deaf awareness. The magic system in the game is dependent on using sign language, the drawings of characters in the rulebook are very diverse when it comes to ethnicity, gender, disabilities and appearance, and the game text well explains deafness/Deaf identity and mentions other disabilities and how to play with them in-game. The game, hence, is not just an entertaining activity in your classroom, but also an educational one. But to what extent would using this game be educational or inclusive?

Tabletop RPGs are used to teach social and emotional skills (Ruff, 2021; Westborg, 2023; Hammer et al., 2024), can reduce bullying in the classroom (Bagès, Hoareau and Guerrien, 2021), and are especially useful when working with neurodivergent students (Grasmo, 2025). Even if tabletop RPG design has a long history of game rules and representations that

DOI: 10.1201/9781003641384-8

essentialize and negatively stereotype minority social groups (Burton, Trammell and Jones, 2024, p. 458), these games have undergone significant transformations in recent years. Many contemporary games, like the new edition of *Dungeon & Dragons*, strive to be more diverse and inclusive, particularly regarding sexuality, gender, and ethnicity, although there remain calls for further improvements.

However, issues of ableism and disablism persist within these games (Jones, 2018). While disablism can be defined by negative practices or assumptions that lead to unequal treatment of people with disabilities (Dolmage, 2017), ableism is the continuous positive valuation of able-bodiedness. The assumptions and norms of the able body permeate our culture in a way that may be seen as compulsory (Kafer, 2003). Ableism takes for granted that everyone is able-bodied and thereby constitutes an approach to the world (albeit a fantastical one) that rewards only those who are able-bodied (Jones, 2018). Previous studies (Henry, 2015, Jones, 2018, see also Hassan, 2024b) have highlighted how disability is often erased or marginalized in tabletop RPGs: through the narrative use of science to "cure" disability, reducing it to mere flaws, or presenting it as a consequence of in-game injury (Henry, 2015). If disabled persons are present in games, they are most likely present as "the other", a weird, strange or even dangerous being. RPGs, both analog and digital, do represent disability, but take part in the flexible normalism when they represent certain people with disability as normal (Ledder, 2018). It is not enough that a game presents disabled characters for it to be inclusive. In fact, the inclusion of disability can work to inadvertently strengthen existing biases, ableism, or internalized ableism even when the game is made by designers and developers with disabilities.

When *Inspirisles* designers and educators (Hatchlings games, 2021) created this tabletop RPG, they had a clear vision to be inclusive of functional diversity (physical disabilities). Teachers should therefore "run to the game" to teach inclusivity. We still think they may want to. *Inspirisles* is both fun and educational. It is inclusive as well, at least at first glance. However, in this chapter, we study the game closer through a "criptical lens." By using crip theory (McRuer, 2006), we reveal discourses of ableism and disablism (Dolmage, 2017) in the game. This is not to deter the reader from using *Inspirisles* in their classroom – we do argue that it is one of the most positive representations of disability – but rather to bring to light how the game – and similar games – could be critically examined and utilized within an educational context. In fact, a previous explorative study shows that experienced role-players are more likely to play a character with weaknesses and less likely to be interested in playing a flawless character (Poeller, Dechant and Mandryk, 2023), so role-playing does not have to be all about "characters' enhanced skills and continuous growth stronger, faster, and 'better'" (Jones, 2018). Meaning that *Inspirisles* should particularly appeal to at least experienced players and also to serve with disability awareness building.

Games can broaden our fantasies about bodies and embodiment, far beyond the binary understanding as either abled or disabled. They can even advocate for understanding the world, and ourselves as "crip" with a positive connotation. The challenge is that if a disability-inclusive game like *Inspirisles* still enforces the abled–disabled binary, it still does not cater for a wider, more inclusive understanding of function variance. If disability is seen as something negative, especially implicitly within inclusive games, games will keep limiting our knowledge about bodies and minds. After all, ableism is everywhere (Dolmage, 2017, p. 40).

We utilize critical discourse analysis (Booth, 2021, chapter 3) in examining *Inspirisles* to unveil the embedded layers of disablism and ableism that can still be there when we design inclusive games. This analysis is helpful for educators and game-makers aiming to design similar games. With a critical disabled framework, we try to crip the understanding of this RPG.

The discussion we are interested in is the understanding of "the crip", when reviewing and preparing games for inclusive education. We refer to these games as "crip-ed" games.

This chapter will introduce crip theory and give examples from *Inspirisles* to discuss; in what ways does the game promote different-abled inclusiveness on the one hand, or on the other hand ableism/disablism through the characters and their magic? The study investigates the digital version of the *Inspirisles* core book (Hatchling games, 2021), which provides game instructions to players and game masters, descriptions of the characters in the diegetic world and the player characters as well as illustrations. We also discuss how game mechanics might evoke ableism or a broad inclusiveness.

CRIP THEORY

An important critical viewpoint of disablism arrived with crip theory (McRuer, 2006), building strongly on queer theory discourse, with methods of deconstructing the disabled–abled binary. Crip theory challenges the dominant social messages that define who and what are normal (Kafer, 2013; McRuer, 2006). Crip is a queer way of looking at individual bodies and the ableist society. Central to crip theory is the idea of compulsory able-bodiedness and able-mindedness. Instead of thinking of people as belonging to either the "abled" or "disabled" group (as in "straight" or "queer"), "the crip" may be every one of us. The title of the book *Crip Theory* is a subversive play on the word "cripple" and invites the readers to "criptical" thinking, moving away from the rhetorical and linguistic framework that casts disability as, at best, impaired function. According to Robert McRuer (2006, see also 2002), queerness and disability can be aligned. Mc Ruer refers to Butler as "queer derives its force precisely through the repeated invocation by which it has become linked to accusation, pathologization, insult" (Butler, 1993), the same can be said about the term "crip" or crippled, even though the implications of those two identities have different cultural and bodily effects and affects.

Crip theory explores the tension between claiming crip as an identity and perpetuating oppressive narratives associated with the categorization of disability. Claiming crip is "a way of acknowledging that we all have bodies and minds with shifting abilities" (Kafer, 2013, p. 13). But claiming crip also feeds into ableist messages that value the categories of disabled and non-disabled. McRuer (2006) asks why we all have to become able-bodied, by tools and assistance, so that our disabilities are as invisible as possible. How can we rather think of the "crip" as desirable? Similarly, Dolmage (2017) states that "seeing disability as fixable is very, very different from seeing disability as desirable" or perhaps even as neutral as discussed. The idea of using "crip" in the same way as "queer" has been advocated by Allison Kafer (2003) reasoning that disability continues to be seen by the larger culture as a medical and/or natural phenomenon rather than a social or political one. Following the scholars of crip theory, we must acknowledge that every one of us is "cripped", at least sometimes in life. A crip-ed game should hence portray disability as fluid and constructed through social expectations and therefore not something for which a label is necessarily appropriate. However, in the immediate future, Kafer explains that able-bodiedness has been cast as separate from politics, as a universal ideal and a normal way of life, in much the same way as heterosexuality had been in the 1970s and early 1980s, coined as "compulsory heterosexuality" (Rich 1986). Crip theory is interested in uncovering "compulsory ableism".

Because disabled people have been oppressed and discriminated against on the basis of their disabilities, many have wanted to appear "normal," "natural," or "healthy" in other aspects of their lives (Kafer, 2003, p. 82). Because of this, we can safely assume that internalized ableism also exists in people with disability (Campbell, 2008) – like internalized homophobia – so even when Deaf teenagers have been part of developing the game we are to analyze, they may have a wish for normalization, and the compulsory ableism affects them as well.

In her later book *Feminist. Queer. Crip.*, Kafer (2013) has visions for alliances between these three identities to build new futures. Where disability politics and theory promote disability rights and normalization of diversity, Kafer rejects the idea of normalization and promotes a crip-political framework for a more just world.

To crip is to expose and reproduce disjunction, to refuse order and embrace messiness, and by this, to illuminate the hypocrisies of the norm. According to McRuer, the point is inflating them into parody. Like queering, cripping names a deconstructive process situated within culture, within everyday life, but at high stakes. Like queering, cripping can be robbed of its subversive power. Abes and Darkwood (2020) explore who is allowed to be disabled and how the student service works for disabled students as well as how disabled students may or may not be their authentic self; "many students engage in passing, maintaining their more comfortable position in the non-disabled/disabled binary" (Abes and Darkow, 2020, p. 223), often a result of ableism.

Inclusive crip-ed games could at best aim to make disability diversify the current cultural knowledge base about differential embodiment (Mitchell and Snyder 2016) and by that even advocate for understanding the world, and ourselves, as crip. On the other hand, a disability-inclusive game like *Inspirisles* may still educate people along the abled–disabled binary and thereby erase and diminish disability, and in this way limit our knowledge about bodies and minds. Our argument, hence, is that games and game studies may be implicitly taking the same ableist stand. Our goal is to unveil the layers of disablism, and ableism embedded in games, even games meant to be inclusive of people with function variations.

We may question the position toward disability when accessing a game, politicizing it instead of individualizing it – it is not about individual (dis/)

abled game-makers or gamers, but a social-cultural system of implicit biases we are all a part of.

METHODS

This work is situated within game studies and is informed by disability studies. We use a framework informed by critical theoretical approaches (Slayter and Johnson, 2023), specifically: crip theory, to do a literary, visual and ludic analysis of the game material, namely the digital core book of the game *Inspirisles* (Hatchling games, 2021). The game can be purchased online, but we have not played the game ourselves but rather analyzed it as is next described. One of the authors has also attended a presentation by the creators of the game at Transformative Play Initiative Seminar (Cullinan and Oxenham, 2022), which has also informed our understanding of the game, but the content of the presentation has not been formally incorporated in the analysis.

We view RPGs as literary-ludic art games (Ensslin, 2018). By that definition, this game is an artistic expression which we analyze both as a cultural narrative, a visual and textual story, and as game mechanics. We also generally examined the accessibility (the playability) of the game according to the needs of different users with visual, auditory, cognitive, motor, and neuropsychiatric disabilities. No formal framework was used in this accessibility analysis, but we outlined the needs for the disability groups through analytical work and a subsequent report by Grasmo and Ling (2023) as part of a postgraduate course on Disability, taught at Tampere University by Lobna Hassan.

Based on this initial analysis, we now chose to further look at the themes relevant for educators, namely representation of functionality (in text, illustrations and game mechanics), inclusion of disabled players, role-play of disabled characters in-game (story and game mechanics), and the language used to describe impairments. In the analysis, we focus on how this game can be understood in the binary abled/disabled discourse versus a "crip" understanding.

As researchers, we believe that we are embodied and situated (Harraway, 1988) when we read and analyze games. Hence, it is important to note that the co-authors have disabilities or identities that may allow them to think of themselves as disabled or cripped. This means that both authors are connected in some ways to the material they analyze, and the target groups of the game. But none of us is part of the Deaf community; hence, we may miss some important points in how this game can work for Deaf students.

Introducing *Inspirisles*: A Fairytale Building Empathy and Awareness

Inspirisles is a tabletop role-playing game (tabletop RPG) for three to five players and one game master, called Grail Guide. The players are humans traveling to the Faerie world to help them heal their kingdom and the World Tree (Figure 5.1). To fulfill their tasks in the game, the role-players need to learn sign language. That's how they can do magical shaping of the world. Each character, called Pendragons by the Fae, has one kind of elemental magic – water, fire, wind, or earth. The better the player can sign, the stronger their magic gets (Figure 5.2). As the rulebook indicates, "While you might only be able to throw a bucketful of water with a weak

FIGURE 5.1 Diverse Pendragons entering the Faerie world of *Inspirisles* role-playing game.

Ill: Lucille Nual. Copyright: Hatchling Games.

FIGURE 5.2 Water magic! The characters in *Inspirisles* make magic by using sign language.

Ill: Lucille Nual. Copyright: Hatchling Games.

shape, at its potent level you could lift the contents of a lake!" (p. 65).[2] The game is family friendly and can even be run by teachers or youth leaders that have never played tabletop RPG before.

Rich Oxenham is the lead designer behind *Inspirisles.* He founded Hatchlings Games as a kickstarter, after running a Dungeon and Dragons role-playing group for teens, while at the same time working at a Deaf charity as a support worker. Oxenham wanted to make an inclusive tabletop RPG especially for deaf awareness, with the aim of teaching sign language. *Inspirisles* had Deaf tutors do consultation on the game material, and the teens from his role-playing group play-tested the game to ensure it was suitable for the intended age group and whether the language learning was achievable (Oxenham, Personal Communication with the author (14.08.2025)).

The game is not targeted especially for the Deaf community, as the designers explain on their website (Hatchling games, 2022); rather, it is a game for the general public. The game singles out three themes that the designers are passionate about promoting: storytelling, empathy (collaboration, work toward a common goal), and deaf awareness (understanding the diversity of Deaf people and learning sign language). A qualitative study of using *Inspirisles* in the classroom (Cullinan and Wood, 2024) showed students learning 50–100 signs by playing the game.

RESULTS

The results are presented from three different analysis angles: the players, the characters, and the game mechanics. The first theme sums up our accessibility analysis. The other two themes are focusing on how the game can be placed along three possible discourses of function variation: compulsory ableism, the abled–disabled binary, and the crip discourse. We will first look at whether the in-game characters are able-bodied, disabled, and crip, and then we analyze the game mechanics and especially discuss the concept of the "super-crip".

Accessibility Analysis

In our accessibility analysis, we found many positive features to foster inclusivity in the game. The diversity of character visuals was striking on impairment, ethnic, and gender representations.

When it comes to audio accessibility, the game is accessible for all who can read or who understand sign language, as the game rules were explained in online videos using sign language. However, while playing the game, non-hearing players will need a Grail guide (an in-game character played by other players) who can sign on their behalf. Deaf players would need an interpreter to part-take with hearing co-players.

Visual accessibility for people with visual impairment was found to be acceptable. The pictures are clear with good contrast and strong colors. The fonts are dyslexic-friendly, and the index table is easy to use. Since the rulebook is digital, visually impaired people can use a screen reader to access it. During gameplay, in-game developments are generally easy to follow through the game's narrative or the conversation of the players.

Motor and mobility accessibility was also found to be acceptable. Tabletop is an excellent form of gaming for people with mobility and motor impairments – especially when the game does not come with small props to place on a game board – since it is mostly about storytelling and imagining what action you can do. As the game is happening around a table, teachers need to plan for accessible locations. Sign language as a game mechanic can be an issue for people with low or no motor hand ability; however, there are suggestions for playing the game online or with dice instead (p. 11). Another suggestion is to pair players up with other players, who can sign for them.

Regarding cognitive accessibility, like any other disability, cognitive disabilities come in many forms and severity levels. Compared to other tabletop RPGs, we find *Inspirisles* to be accessible for people with lighter learning disabilities. The game requires the use of six-sided dice (D6), but without the need for complex calculations or more complex dice variations (e.g., D4, D8, D20 and D100) that other games (e.g., D&D) might require. The system is quite simple also for children and people with cognitive challenges. For instance, each race of Fae has their own Patron (p. 27) which rules one element, and each of the Pendragons (player characters) has one element they can do magic from.

For neurodivergent players, explanations of how to play are clear, for instance, how to differentiate between Narration vs Performance (p. 14). While there are many pages of rules, this is all in all a much simpler tabletop RPG than, for instance, a common Dungeon and Dragons (DnD) tabletop adventure game. There is also an in-game "Sanctuary", a safe space to store magic, which also works as a safe and positive palace that the players themselves imagine before the game starts (p. 59). This can create a way for overwhelmed players to rest in-game, for instance, people on the autism spectrum.

In-Game Characters as Able-Bodied, Disabled, or Crip?

We started by studying how disability in players and characters is portrayed in text and drawings: there are pictures of characters ("pendagrons"), showing characters using wheelchairs, glasses, with skin condition, or with a prosthetic limb, but surprisingly, no one uses hearing aids or has other signs of being Deaf in this game about Deaf awareness. The game is easily accessible to deaf/Deaf people, as long as they can read, since it is text based. It might even be advantageous and cool to be a Deaf player when the magic in the game is actually your own language. The better you are at signing (called "shaping," p. 74), the higher levels of in-game magic (p. 39) you can pursue. Here, we can interpret the Deaf person as a desirable crip, someone we want to be more alike, both in-game and out-of-game (as players). But still, it seems like the "you" in the text address is an able-bodied person, or at least not a Deaf person. For instance, after each game session, the book asks us to reflect on the gameplay by answering the question: "Has your shaping improved?" (p. 72). How is that relevant for people already using sign language, or are they assumed not to be playing the game?

The ableist assumptions about players are also apparent in the description of the "Grail Guide", the facilitator of the game (p. 103), where neither inclusion of disabled players nor a criptical view is mentioned. The book proclaims, "The type of venue isn't important" (p. 12). But if we are all crips, it is. The game takes for granted that accessibility for people with motor functionality variance is not an issue. Ableism is also stated in "Please use as many of the 5 senses as you can (sight, sound, touch, smell, and taste) and describe your Pendragon Sanctuary" (p. 60). The book does not explain or discuss how people with different abilities could play together.

On the other hand, both visually and textually the rulebook is both queer- and crip-inclusive – with more than two genders, non-normative gender expressions, and people of all colors, in addition to a representation of disabilities in character drawings. They have also provided a screen-reader-friendly pdf for better accessibility for the visually impaired and explain how to play the game without the use of sign language (p. 11).

The game is about deaf awareness, and the core player group is most likely hearing students who want to learn sign language (p. 11). The difference between Deaf as an identity and being deaf is explained (in p. 38), and the signing community is in focus (p. 39). Sign language as a game mechanic for all players to use may be a way to crip tabletop role-playing; in fact, the rulebook suggests spreading their methods: "Please feel free to use our sign language for other tabletop RPG games" (p. 39) as well as use "deaf clapping" (p. 77).

In stark contrast to the positive attitude that *Inspirisles* seems to have toward inclusivity, is the representation of function variability in the non-player characters of the game: None of the gods, heroes, fae, or foes characters in the game are described with a disability, apart from a couple of side characters at the end of the manuscript. Why does a game about Deaf Awareness not include positive Deaf role models? A few exceptions are found in a couple of powerful characters with motor impairments; some Wyrms (foes) are without wings (p. 31) and in Merfolk who cannot walk (p. 147). While these visual and narrative representations are there, the disabled identity is neither explained nor are the visual representations sufficient in providing crip role models. Kafer (2003) writes that unless someone identifies herself as disabled or is visually marked as disabled, she is assumed not to be disabled. So, when we read the characters in the game, it is easy to presume that they are hearing, even if the game creators (p. 39) tell us they are all part of the sign community.

There are a couple of drawings of vision impairment (p. 10 and p. 29, an elderly woman). Along with the very old historian Grace (p. 166) who is described as one who cannot travel much anymore, that signals that we may all be cripped if not now, in possible futures (McRuer, 2006). But why not give the historian Grace an explicit impairment of seeing, walking, or hearing? If she could not hear, the player character may have to find other means of communication, and we think that will raise Deaf awareness more.

The clearest in-game possibility for playing a character with motor disability is described in the short chapter "Piskie Inventions" (p. 70). "Some of you may be physically disabled and wish to play a Pendragon to represent your disability. To facilitate this, we have our Piskie inventor Friends," and "This will ensure your full inclusion." The Piskie will provide the characters with magical limbs (Figure 5.3), so they become fully able, not crips anymore. This means being exactly as able in-game as a body-normative able body would be. It also assumes that only players who are physically disabled will desire to play that disability, marking it as fundamentally not desirable. In other words, the game assumes that players without a motor disability don't want to play that in *Inspirisles*.

There is one character mentioned (Giantheld free-climber Darwin) born with one arm. But he has the Piskie prosthetic (p. 166) and is a better climber than anyone else. *Inspirisles* has several examples of *super-crip*, a character that has a disability but ends up being super-able. Another example is the Knockers living in the dark (p. 33, p. 150), in the mines, and who look like moles, but have super-vision. It might have been more inclusive to make them blind, like the animals they are modeled after are. To

FIGURE 5.3 Disabled bodies become super-crip with magic prosthetic from the Piskies.

Ill: Lucille Nual. Copyright: Hatchling Games.

make it possible for characters to play *with* a function variant, and have to struggle or get help, might have cripped the game more, instead of jumping over to the able positions, as it seems *Inspirisles* does.

SUPER-CRIP MAGIC PROMOTES COMPULSORY ABLEISM

We have seen several examples of ableist and disableist discourse in the crip-ed game *Inspirisles*, even if there is room for cripping with the required use of sign language magic. The game is perhaps giving a meta-message of "regardless of how satisfied they may be in their lives, there must be a part of them that longs for a non-disabled body, wishes desperately for a cure, and/or feels woefully incomplete" (Abes and Wallace, 2018). The tabletop RPG presumes compulsory ableism. If a player wants to use their own disabilities as part of a character, the game manuscript asks them to choose a pixie limb, magical sight or pretend hearing ability – in this way, the player becomes an able-bodied "super-crip".

The game appears to want us all to be the same, to be able, to do the same things. The characters use "crip magic," but are not cripped themselves, an especially strong meta-message is that none of the gods (called "Friends", Figure 5.4), heroes, or inhabitants in the magic world are crips themselves.

Kafer (2003) raises the issue of focusing too much on identity, because of the kinds of questions it sparks: Who identifies as disabled? As non-disabled? How and why do they do so? Who do we exclude from such an identification? In the tabletop RPG *Inspirisles*, it seems like a strong identity of Deaf people is taken for granted, and that they are disabled; hence, the authors feel the need to raise awareness. On the other hand, all the characters in the game are supposed to be a part of the Sign Language

FIGURE 5.4 The "Friend" Glow Ruler Water supports Pendragons who have water magic. None of the gods are cripped, not even a hearing disability.

Ill: Lucille Nual. Copyright: Hatchling Games.

community, and disability is seldom mentioned. It is normalized, but more like "none of us are disabled" than looking at the world through a crip lens.

It shows how difficult it is to design for inclusivity, how we are embedded in unconscious bias from the society we live in and how it is hard to step outside what is considered "normal", even with the best intentions. Abled teachers and game designers, even if experienced in working with disabled youths, may unconsciously promote a discourse of non-disabled/ableism, and even compulsory able-bodiedness. *Inspirisles* did have Deaf consultants, but maybe if had been created in cooperation with Deaf youth and used their knowledge and understanding it would be closer to use cripistemology as a framework, meaning knowledge production from a crip perspective. On the other hand, the internal ableism of disabled people might as well create games for escaping disabilities and become super-crips.

If we believe that "to shift views of disability can lessen the burden disabled students face with self-disclosure" (Abes, 2020), it can seem like this game needs more crippin' to allow for that. This is something educators and people who run *Inspirisles*, and other inclusive RPGs, can choose to do.

CONCLUSIONS AND RECOMMENDATIONS

RPGs can create imagined social worlds (Juul, 2008). They can be understood as sociocultural technology for building (queer or crip) *heterotopias* (Grasmo, Sihvonen and Stenros, in press); neither utopia nor dystopia, but just "somewhere else" (Foucault, 1986/1967). Hence, our hope is that crip-ed games create even more inclusive and empowering, or just very different, fantasy worlds. Such a novel experience of disability and function variations may impact not only the role-players playing the game, but our societies and our social politics (Grasmo, Sihvonen and Stenros, in press).

At the same time, it is important to acknowledge that creating empowering gameplay and representative characters is a challenging goal, perhaps one that may never be fully attainable, given the resource limitations of this mortal world (Hassan, Buttler, and Vesa, 2024). It is important to acknowledge the value that games like *Inspirisles* bring to the literal and figurative table. Not only do we have an educational game, but one where we see a remarkable range of diversity represented. While we may have examined the game critically, it is only with the intent to further inclusive game design. We also hope that some of the questions we have raised in our analysis could be used for critical analysis of other games in educational settings, particularly crip-ed games (Figure 5.5).

We imagine players gathered around the game, using some of these questions as openers for reflecting on who, if any, was left behind in this game, encouraging them to widen their awareness of the people around them in society. We imagine the players questioning the abilities given to some characters but not others, discussing if their life experience was fully represented in the game. *Inspirisles* is a conversation opener, one that brings disability, diversity and queerness right to the front, rather than avoiding these taboo topics. We are in need of more such conversation openers. It is our intent, next, to show how further conversation could be opened through intentional game and character design.

FIGURE 5.5 *Inspirisles* is an inspiring attempt to make an inclusive tabletop game for education. To enable this vision of a crip-ed game, the teachers will need to *crip* it even more.

Ill: Lucille Nual. Copyright: Hatchling Games.

Often, games create a figurative magic circle (Stenros, 2012, see also Juul, 2008), an imagined universe within which the game is enacted. Game and play researchers tend to debate this imagined reality and what it feels like to the players and onlookers (Consalvo, 2009). In the context of disability, many tend to imagine this magic circle as an imagined universe within which the players are "free" of their disabilities (see our previous discussion of the pixie prosthetic). In the context of *Inspirisles*, while the players can have many different disabilities, they are freed of their own disability when they play the game. So much so that a character can be read as being an unrealistic super-crip as discussed. We need to exercise caution when reflecting on *Inspirisles* as we are indeed reflecting on a singular game. Yet, this pattern in game design is so common that it is hard to ignore (see Stang et al., 2025, for further examples).

While indeed many players, with and without function variations, may wish to use games as a tool of escapism (Hassan, 2024a), playing a game is, and should be, pleasurable in itself, without focusing on any external goals from playing it (escaping) (Rodriguez, 2006). We argue that escapism does not necessarily need to coincide with the eraser of aspects of identity nor life experience. Creating characters that are simultaneously able and disabled, that have certain powers but lack others, can lead to more complex and especially engaging characters (Hassan, 2024b). Hopefully, these characters are also more realistic, allowing players who perceive themselves as able-bodied and able-minded to understand disabilities from a more cripped position. It may also allow players who do identify as a disabled to expand their identities and see it accepted and a part of a continuum more than a binary. Yet, it is important in this endeavor to keep characters' power in check so as not to end up with super-crips but acknowledge that difficulties both in practical function variations and with discrimination are challenging.

People with disabilities, both as players and characters, come in the same endless variety as any other human, still there is commonalities that can be taught through a crip-ed game: A blind human may have an above-average hearing sensitivity as they may have naturally honed their hearing skills, in the same way that a human with good eyesight would have good driving skills because they have honed their skills. Rarely is the human with good eyesight a super driver and rarely is the blind human an invincible detective because of their heightened hearing.

In that light, it is important to acknowledge that – in a way – superheroes, gods, and some mythical creatures are, by definition, characters with heightened abilities (Figure 5.6). They are rarely human or of this world. That is not true of all mythical creatures and monsters, but it is important to have this awareness when borrowing from heritage and mythology. Characters such as witches, sirens, and lynch have long been examined as problematic representations of especially women (Stang, 2021), and we argue that many other characters are similarly problematic in terms of disability. Especially in crip-ed games whose goal is to be inclusive, this heritage needs to be renewed when borrowed into the world of inclusive games. As noted, in a game

FIGURE 5.6 Traveling the Faerie World on a Kelpie. Mythical creatures with super-powers enhance the pleasure of playing, but educational games can include some function hindering for them too.

Ill: Josh Arklin. Copyright: Hatchling Games.

that promotes inclusivity, when there is no function variance among all the higher-power in-game role models (e.g., gods and faes and heroes) this can be demotivating for players, and show implicit ableism. We hope in the future that the non-player characters can show more realistic role models that can also provide in-game learning on how to be super and deal with in-game challenges of function variation. Our in-game challenge can be, for example, how to communicate with a God that cannot hear, or using the magician's super-powers when they cannot see, move by themselves, or are extremely forgetful. What about a Hero whose help you need, but who gets sudden anxiety attacks that you need to help her with.

We would love to see a game design that ensures both the player characters and the non-player characters like mythical figures, heroes, and gods are relatable rather than a representation of unattainable ideals that leave the player feeling disabled. This is not to say that games can't have super superheroes, they indeed can, and perhaps should, given that many players enjoy these characters and find them liberating, rather we are calling for diversity in all these characters especially in the context of games intended to show diversity.

The most important lesson we learned from the educator's point of view is that it is possible to crip the tabletop RPG games, when it comes to who is allowed to join the game on equal terms (players accessibility), who do we want to role-play as (creating character), and how can we play the game without a binary understanding of abled and disabled (narrative and game mechanics). To look at games through a crip theory framework can help us deconstruct our implicit biases toward disability, and by that allow us to create an even more inclusive and educating game experiences.

NOTES

1 Deaf with capital D is preferred by Deaf people to mark "not hearing" as an identity, while "deaf" can be used to talk about the handicap in general. Both forms are used in this chapter.

2 All page references without any further reference are from the Core rulebook of *Inspirisles*.

REFERENCES

Abes, Elisa and Daniel Darkow (2020) "Using Crip Theory to Create Campus Cultures that Foster Student' Disability Disclosure." *Journal of Postsecondary Education and Disability*, 33(3), 223–231.

Abes, Elisa S. and Michelle M. Wallace (2018) "People See Me, But They Don't See Me": An Intersectional Study of College Students with Physical Disabilities." *Journal of College Student Development*, 59, 545–562.

Bagès, Céline, Natacha Hoareau, and Alain Guerrien (2021) "Play to Reduce Bullying! Role-Playing Games Are a Useful Tool for Therapists and Teachers." *Journal of Research in Childhood Education*, 35(4), 631–641. https://doi.org/10.1080/02568543.2020.1810834

Burton, Adriana, Aaron Trammell, and Katherine Castiello Jones (2024) "Diversity, Equity, and Inclusion in Role-Playing Games." In *The Routledge Handbook of Role-playing Game Studies*, edited by José P. Zagal and Sebastian Deterding. London: Routledge.

Booth, Paul (2021) "What Is Ludic Discourse Analysis of Board Games?" Chapter 3 in *Board Games as Media*. New York: Bloomsbury Academic, ISBN: 9781501357183.

Butler, Judith (1997/1993) "Critically Queer." In *Playing with Fire: Queer Politics, Queer Theories*. Edited by Shane Phelan, New York: Routledge. ISBN: 9780415914178.

Campbell, Fiona Kumari (2008) "Exploring Internalized Ableism using Critical Race Theory." *Disability & Society*, 23(2), 151–162. https://doi.org/10.1080/09687590701841190

Consalvo, Mia (2009) "There Is No Magic Circle." *Games and Culture*, 4(4), 408–417.

Cullinan, Maryanne and Laura Wood (2024) "Getting Inspired: A Qualitative Study on the Use of the *Inspirisles* Role-Playing Game to Teach Middle Schoolers American Sign Language." *Simulation & Gaming*, 55(2), 267–280. https://doi.org/10.1177/10468781241229614

Cullinan, Maryanne and Rich Oxenham (2022) "Getting Inspired: Using the *Inspirisles* RPG to Teach ASL and Cultural Awareness to Middle School Students" Presentation at *Transformative Play Initiative Seminar*, Visby.

Dolmage, Jay T. (2017) *Academic Ableism: Disability and Higher Education*. University of Michigan Press.

Dungeon & Dragons Revised 5th edition (2024). Michigan, USA: Wizards of the Coast. https://www.dndbeyond.com/sources/dnd/dmg-2024

Ensslin, Astrid (2018) *Literary Gaming*. Cambridge, MA: MIT Press.

Foucault, Michel (1986) "Of Other Spaces, Heterotopias." (Based on the lecture from March 1967.) *Diacritics* 16(1), 22–27. https://doi.org/10.2307/464648

Grasmo, Hanne (2025) "Neurospicy Larpers: Role-Play as a Method for Working with Neurodivergent Youth with Challenging Behavior Regarding Sexuality." In *Anatomy of Larp. Thoughts: A Breathing Corpus*. Nadja Lipsyc (ed/coordinator). Knutepunkt Conference Reader, Oslo. https://nordiclarp.org/wiki/Anatomy_of_Larp_Thoughts:_a_breathing_corpus

Grasmo, Hanne, Tanja Sihvonen and Jaakko Stenros (2026), "(Ir)resistible Bodies. Larp as Sociocultural Technology for Building Queer Heterotopias." In *Playing Politics in Digital Spaces Life After Social Media*. Edited By Frank Chouraqui, Alex Gekker, Bram Ieven, Saniye Ince, Frans-Willem Korsten, Sybille Lammes, Sara Polak. Routledge.

Grasmo Hanne and HuiHui Zhang (2023) "*Inspirisles*: A Table Top Role Playing Game. Accessibility Study." In *A Presentation for Tampere University Master Course GS.186* "Disability & Game Studies" autumn 2022.

Hammer, Jessica, Alexandra To, Karen Schrier, Sarah Lynne Bowman, Geoff Kaufman (2024) "Learning and Role-Playing Games." In *The Routledge Handbook of Role-Playing Game Studies*, edited by José P. Zagal and Sebastian Deterding. London: Routledge.

Hatchlinggames.co.uk/signlanguage webpage downloaded 15.11.2022

Hassan, Lobna (2024a). "Gaming (the Pandemic) with Vision Impairment: An Auto-ethnographic Account." In *Gaming and Gamers in Times of Pandemic*, edited by P. Siuda, J. Majewski, and K. Chmielewski. London, UK: Bloomsbury Academic Press.

Hassan, Lobna (2024b). "Accessibility of Games and Game-based Applications: A Systematic Literature Review and Mapping of Future Directions." *New Media & Society*, 26(4), 2336–2384. https://doi.org/10.1177/14614448231204020

Hassan, Lobna, Pekka Buttler, and Mikko Vesa (2024) "Games, Business, and Gamers: How to Facilitate a Game Accessibility Transition across the Gaming Ecosystem?" In *Art and Sustainability Transitions in Business and Society: Theoretical Insights and Engagement*, edited by H. Lehtimäki, S. S. Taylor, and M. G. Lyra, pp. 79–108. Springer International Publishing. https://doi.org/10.1007/978-3-031-44219-3_5

Henry, Elsa S. (2015). "Reimagining Disability in Role-Playing Games." *Analog Game Studies*, II(II) (downloaded Nov 2024).

Inspirisles. Role-Playing with Sign Language (2021) Digital version of the core book. Published by Hatchling Games (downloaded 1.11.2022).

Jones, Shelly (2018) "Blinded by the Roll: The Critical Fail of Disability in D&D." *Analog Game Studies*, 8(9). https://analoggamestudies.org/?s=Blinded+by+the+roll (downloaded 18 Dec 2024)

Juul, Jesper (2008) "The Magic Circle and the Puzzle Piece." *Proceedings of the Philosophy of Computer Games: DIGAREC Series* 1, Postdam.

Kafer, Allison (2003) "Compulsory Bodies: Reflections on Heterosexuality and Able-Bodiedness." *Journal of Women's History*, 15(3), pp. 77–89. Johns Hopkins University Press [Access provided at 25 Oct 2022 11:09 GMT from UIO – Universitetsbiblioteket] https://doi.org/10.1353/jowh.2003.0071

Kafer, Allison (2013) *Feminist, Queer, Crip*. E-book. Indiana University Press. ISBN: 9780253009418.

Ledder, Simon (2018) "On Dis/ability within Game Studies. The Discursive Construction of Ludic Bodies." In *Interdisciplinary Approaches to Disability: Looking towards the Future*, edited by K. Ellis, R. Garland-Thomson, M. Kent, R. Robertson, 1st ed., pp. 30–44. Routledge. https://doi.org/10.4324/9781351053228

McRuer, Robert (2002) "Compulsory Able-Bodiedness and Queer/Disabled Existence." In *Disability Studies: Enabling the Humanities*, edited by Sharon L. Snyder, Brenda Jo Brueggemann, and Rosemarie Garland-Thomson, pp. 88–99. New York: Modern Language Association.

McRuer, Robert (2006) *Crip Theory: Cultural Signs of Queerness and Disability.* New York: New York University Press, 283 pages.

Mitchell, David and Sharon L. Snyder (2016) "The Matter of Disability." *Journal of Bioethical Inquiry*, 13(4), 487–492. https://doi.org/10.1007/s11673-016-9740-2. Epub 2016 Jul 27.

Oxenham, Rich (2021) *Inspirisles - The Downloadable Game.* Hatchling Games, UK. https://hatchlingdm.itch.io/inspirisles

Poeller, Susanne, Martin Dechant, and Regan L. Mandryk (2023) "Playing a Flawless Character? Exploring Differences between Experts and Novices in Tabletop Role-Playing Games and Potential Benefits for Well-Being." In *Proceedings of the 18th International Conference on the Foundations of Digital Games (FDG '23). Association for Computing Machinery*, New York, NY, USA, Article 58, 1–7. https://doi.org/10.1145/3582437.3587180

Rich, Adrienne (1986) "Compulsory Heterosexuality and Lesbian Existence (1980)." In Adrienne Rich: *Blood, Bread, and Poetry: Selected Prose 1979–1985.* New York: W.W. Norton & Company ISBN: 978-0-393-31162-4.

Rodriguez, Hector (2006) "The Playful and the Serious: An approximation to Huizinga's Homo Ludens." *The International Journal of Computer Game Research,* 6(1). ISSN: 1604-7982

Ruff, Tia (2021) *Increasing Social and Emotional Learning Competencies through Use of Tabletop Role-Playing Games.* PhD dissertation, George Fox University. https://digitalcommons.georgefox.edu/edd/155

Slayter, Elspeth and Lisa Johnson (Eds.). (2023) *Social Work Practice and Disability Communities: An Intersectional Anti-Oppressive Approach.* Rotel Pressbooks. E-book ISBN: 978-1-964276-22-9.

Stang, Sarah M. (2021) *Maiden, Mother, and Crone: Abject Female Monstrosity in Roleplaying Games.* PhD dissertation, York University. https://hdl.handle.net/10315/38644

Stang, Sarah, Mikko Meriläinen, Joleen Bloom, and Lobna Hassan (2025). *Monstrosity in Games and Play: A Multidisciplinary Examination of the Monstrous in Contemporary Cultures.* Amsterdam University Press. https://www.aup.nl/en/book/9789048556632/monstrosity-in-games-and-play

Stenros, Jaakko (2012) "In Defence of a Magic Circle: The Social and Mental Boundaries of Play." *Proceedings of DiGRA Nordic 2012 Conference: Local and Global – Games in Culture and Society.* https://doi.org/10.26503/dl.v2012i1.605

Westborg, Josefin (2023) "The Educational Role-Playing Game Design Matrix: Mapping Design Components onto Types of Education." *International Journal of Role-Playing*, 13, 18–30.

FURTHER READINGS

Algayres, Muriel Gaelle (2018) "A Study of Active Learning in Educational Roleplaying Games and Students' Motivation." In *Proceedings from Teaching for Active Learning: TAL2018*, edited by Christopher Kjær, Donna Hurford, and Lotte Dyhrberg O'Neill, 24–29. Denmark: Syddansk University. A Study of Active Learning in Educational Roleplaying Games and Students' Motivation.

Balzer, Muriel (2011). "Immersion as a Prerequisite of the Didactical Potential of Role-Playing." *International Journal of Role-Playing*, 2, 32–43.

Belman, Jonathan and Mary Flanagan (2010) "Designing Games to Foster Empathy." *Cognitive Technology*, 14(2), 5–15.

Chandler, Daniel and Rod Munday (2011) *Queer Theory. A Dictionary of Media and Communication.* Oxford University Press. ISBN: 978-0-19-956875-8.

Cullinan, Maryanne (2024). "Surveying the Perspectives of Middle and High School Educators Who Use Role-Playing Games As Pedagogy." *International Journal of Role-Playing*, 15(June), 127–141. https://doi.org/10.33063/ijrp.vi15.335

Cullinan, Maryanne and Jennifer Genova (2023) "Gaming the Systems: A Component Analysis Framework for the Classroom Use of RPGs." *International Journal of Role-Playing*, 13, 7–17.

Davis, Adam and Adam Johns (2020) "Dungeons, Dragons, and Social Development." In *Integrating Geek Culture into Therapeutic Practice: The Clinician's Guide to Geek Therapy*, edited by Anthony M. Bean, Emory S. Daniel Jr., Sarah A. Hays, 95–107. Fort Worth, TX: Leyline Publishing.

Dipesh, Gopal P., Ula Chetty, Patrick O'Donnell, Camille Gajria, and Jodie Blackadder-Weinstein (2021) "Implicit Bias in Healthcare: Clinical Practice, Research and Decision Making." *Future Health*, 8(1), 40–48. https://doi.org/10.7861/fhj.2020-0233.

Elms, A. C. (1966). "Influence of Fantasy Ability on Attitude Change through Role playing." *Journal of Personality and Social Psychology*, 4(1), 36–43. https://doi.org/10.1037/h0023509

Heyward, Paul (2010) "Emotional Engagement Through Drama: Strategies to Assist Learning through Role-Play." *International Journal of Teaching and Learning in Higher Education*, 22(2), 197–203. https://www.isetl.org/ijtlhe/pdf/IJTLHE751.pdf

Kallam, Michael L. (1984). *The Effects of Simulation Game Play upon Oral Language Development and Internalisation of Locus of Control among Mildly Handicapped Adolescents.* PhD diss, Oklahoma State University. ProQuest Dissertations and Theses Global.

Katherine, Jones (2022). "Celebrate Disability Pride, Uplift Gaming and Disability Communities and Creators with Team Xbox." *Xbox Wire.* https://news.xbox.com/en-us/2022/07/05/team-xbox-celebrates-disability-pride/

Klopfer, Eric, Jason Haas, Scot Osterweil, and Louisa Rosenheck (2018) *Resonant Games: Design Principles for Learning Games that Connect Hearts, Minds, and the Everyday.* Cambridge, MA: MIT Press.

Leonard, Diana J. (2021) "Playing for Pain: Benefits, Pitfalls, & Strategies for RPing Marginalized Characters - Diana Leonard." *Transformative Play Initiative. YouTube*, September 24.

Long, TiMar (2016) "Character Creation Diversity in Gaming Art." *International Journal of Role-Playing*, 7, 23–29.
MacLean, Graham (2016) "One Way to Create Educational Games." *International Journal of Role-Playing*, 6, 51–54.
Meinen, Lisanne (2023) "Share the Experience, Don't Take It: Toward Attunement with Neurodiversity in Videogames." *Games and Culture*, 18(7), 919–939. https://doi.org/10.1177/15554120221149538
Preuß, Anna K. (2021) "The Learning Process in Live-Action Simulation Games: The Impact of Personality, Motivation, Immersion, and Flow on Learning Outcome in a Simulation Game." *Simulation & Gaming*, 52(6) (November 17), 775–795.
Turi, Bálint Márk and Mátyás Hartyándi (2023) "Playing With The Fictitious 'I': Early Forms of Educational Role-Playing in Hungary, 1938–1978." *International Journal of Role-Playing*, 14, 47–60. https://doi.org/10.33063/ijrp.vi14.355
Wernbacher, Thomas, Michael Wagner, Doris C. Rusch, and Joerg Hofsstaetter (2011) "Learning by Playing." In *Proceedings of European Conference on Games Based Learning*, 775–777.
Wendel, Viktor, Stefan Krepp, Michael Oliver Gutjahr, Stefan Göbel, Ralf Steinmetz (2015) "Game Mastering in Collaborative Serious Games." *International Journal of Game-Based Learning*, 5(4), 27–49. https://doi.org/10.4018/ijgbl.2015100103
Westborg, Josefin (2024) *Placing Edu-larp on the Map of Educational Learning Theories: A Critical Discourse Analysis of Ideas about Learning in the Edu-larp Community*. Master's thesis, Gothenburg University.
Westborg, Josefin and Sarah Lynne Bowman (2024) "GM Screen: The Didactic Potential of RPGs." In *#eduRPG. Rollenspiel als Methode der Bildung*, edited by Frank J. Robertz and Kathrin Fischer. Gelsenkirchen: SystemMatters Publ. Available at Academia.edu in English: https://www.academia.edu/109659917/GM_Screen_The_Didactic_Potential_of_RPGs
Zheng, Lucy R., Catherine M. Oberle, W. A. Hawkes-Robinson, and Stéphane Daniau (2021) "Serious Games as a Complementary Tool for Social Skill Development in Young People: A Systematic Review of the Literature." *Simulation & Gaming*, 52(6), 686–714.

VIDEO-SOURCES

McCabe, Jessica Lauren. 2010. "Tips to Make Your Tabletop RPG Game More ADHD Friendly! (Ft - Elizabeth Kilmer)." How to ADHD. *YouTube*, February 14.
Nerback, Lars. 2013. "Three Ways to Make Games More Inclusive - Lars Nerback." Nordic Larp Talks. *YouTube*, April 18.
Kim, Yeonsoo Julian, Shayna Cook, and Lee Foxworthy. 2018. "Walking the Talk: Working Disability into Gaming." Roundtable at Living Games Conference 2018. *YouTube*, August 16. https://www.youtube.com/watch?v=JLEV3UzTYas

PART III

Class Features

Discipline-Specific Practices

CHAPTER 6

At the Crossroads of Creative Writing, Technical Writing, and Composition

A Proposal for Teaching Tabletop RPG Design in Higher Education

Keely Mohon-Doyle

INTRODUCTION

The act of writing is at the heart of all role-playing games, particularly tabletop role-playing games (tabletop RPGs). The authors of these games build entire worlds, establishing the theme and tone, describing the landscape and characters. They also outline the rules within which players must work to interact with the game world and progress across the map. However, this skill is only tangentially acknowledged in much of the scholarship concerning pedagogical applications of these games. When writing is discussed, it is often in the context of how existing games can be played in the classroom and used as a springboard to inspire other forms of writing that are semi-divorced from or simply set in the world

DOI: 10.1201/9781003641384-10

of play (Boss 2019; Schultz Colby and Colby 2008). In other cases, tabletop RPGs are used to teach basic literacy skills and support language acquisition (Cook et al. 2017; Kaylor 2017). Often, tabletop RPG writing is done by the instructors, rather than students, in an attempt to gamify a topic and enhance student motivation (Anto 2021; Etheridge et al. 2022; Stroessner et al. 2009; Zalka 2016). Broadening the scope to include all tabletop games, Steele (2023) points to a rise in Gamemaking in Education (GME), an approach derived from project-based and experiential learning; however, even as students are tasked with designing and writing games, the learning outcomes emphasize mastery of the content knowledge. Creating the game, then, becomes about getting students to analyze and reflect on the topic being studied. What appears to be missing from the literature is a discussion of how to teach students specific writing skills by collaboratively designing their own tabletop RPGs.

While acknowledging the challenges of using tabletop RPGs for any pedagogical purpose (Shoenberger 2024), this chapter will argue that tabletop RPGs' positioning at the crossroads of creative writing, technical writing, and composition—major fields within English and humanities departments in higher education—provides students with the unique opportunity to develop key skills associated with each. Creative writing scholars view tabletop RPGs as an excellent starting point for learning world-building and character development (Hergenrader 2014a); technical writing scholars have explored how rulebooks serve as examples of "cool and useful" document design (Christensen 2022); and composition scholars have stressed the concepts of process (Murray 1972), collaborative writing (Restaino 2014), and multimodality (Bourelle et al. 2019).

In addition to outlining the writing skills that students can learn through the process of tabletop RPG design, this chapter will detail strategies and assignments that can be adapted to fit instructors' specific pedagogical contexts. How can you introduce your students to the rhetorical conventions of a tabletop RPG? What kind of tabletop RPG will they create? Will they create a new world or a transmediated paratext, a game that builds on an existing one in popular fiction (e.g. a game based on *Star Trek* or *Lord of the Rings*) (Booth 2015)? Will they have the option to choose between the different dice-rolling systems? Will they create a player's guide or a one-shot? It will also provide suggested scaffolding to help walk students through the process from planning to playtesting.

WHAT STUDENTS CAN LEARN FROM WRITING TABLETOP RPGS

Tabletop role-playing games offer a unique opportunity for students to acquire important transferable skills across multiple writing areas, including creative writing, technical writing, and composition. While I will discuss them individually below, it is important to remember that these are not, in practice, separate. The success of a tabletop RPG relies on the author of the text acquiring and utilizing skills from all areas.

Creative Writing

Students in creative writing can use tabletop RPGs to build their craft. In an attempt to reconcile the argument between ludology and narratology, mechanics and story, Jenkins (2002) reminds the reader that games are not narratives in the traditional sense. Instead, they are spatial, and, thus, work in different ways: "spatial stories can evoke pre-existing narrative associations; they can provide a staging ground where narrative events are enacted; they may embed narrative information within their mise-en-scène; or they provide resources for emergent narratives" (123). This idea is echoed in Ekman and Taylor's (2009) discussion of the approach to critical world-building in fantasy and science fiction that they call "World-Architecture," in which the author "transforms space into place" by building up its form, function, and meaning through embedded histories and objects, setting the stage for storytelling (13).

What this means is that narrative in tabletop RPGs is a collaborative endeavor between author and players. While players ultimately determine what specific stories are told and how they progress, tabletop RPGs rely on the elements of narrative created by the author to construct the world with(in) which play occurs. The author establishes the genre, setting, and tone through descriptions in the rulebook. In the case of one-shots, the author creates the underlying plot through which players weave and the major non-player characters that are encountered. It is possible that players may choose to countermand these narrative elements, but it is a choice in response to what the author has set forth and maintains the collaborative nature of the game. Tabletop RPGs in which an author has concretized the narrative and disallowed significant collaboration are considered "on rails" and tend to be viewed negatively by players.

The act of writing a tabletop RPG, then, can serve as a form of constrained writing, broadly defined here as a technique that provides the writer with a specific set of limitations and affordances. This technique is often associated with poetic forms—haiku, villanelle, sonnet, etc.—however, the concept of constraints has been applied to creative multimedia, including comics, graphic novels, and screen production (Baetens 2003; Taylor 2019). Not only does this technique "cultivate skills that would otherwise go undeveloped," but it also "break[s] down complex topics of craft and technique" (Vigna 2021, 86–87).

Hergenrader's (2014b) cataloging assignment offers an example of how writing tabletop RPGs, as an exercise of constrained writing, could help improve students' fiction. In this assignment, students work collaboratively to build a game world guided by questions provided by the instructors, beginning with its social, economic, and political underpinnings. From there, they use a template that dictates content and formatting requirements to create wiki entries of people, places, and objects that populate the world. Students then engage in creative play within the world they have created, using the shared catalog to develop story ideas. Hergenrader (2014a) explains that his "incremental storytelling is a move from the macro element of story to the microelements of craft," preparing students to create more complex narratives than they otherwise would have been able to (169).

Technical Writing

Asking students to write (for) a tabletop RPG can also enhance their skills as technical writers. Even in the example offered by Hergenrader (2014b), there is an implicit acknowledgment of the technical aspects required to effectively communicate the game world. In his assignment, templates provide consistency for players; maps offer a visual demonstration of how cataloged elements relate to each other in space. Narrative writing on its own is not enough to support a playable tabletop RPG. Christensen (2022) identifies three metrics for judging the technical effectiveness of a tabletop RPG rulebook: "cool (appealing, attractive), useful (actually playable), and accessible (usable by a wide spectrum of users)" (151). Translated into aesthetics, usability, and accessibility, these metrics sit at the heart of technical communication, and students could be asked to consider how they appear in the various elements they create for their own games.

Writing a rulebook requires writing rules, and Jara (2013) points out that "rules affect player (as well as game master) expectations for the game, thus influencing their input in the narrative" just as much as the setting does (42). The author of a tabletop RPG must ensure that these rules are clearly explained and organized, so players can understand them and reference them quickly should the need arise. Games that do not achieve this tend to have much smaller player-bases no matter how interesting the world may be. In addition to learning how to write coherent rules that correspond to the game world, students learn to visually organize this information into chunks, figures, and flowcharts that provide accessible scaffolding (Yucel 2014).

As equal partners in the gaming ecology, players and their agency cannot be ignored in the creation of the documents that frame their play (Eyman 2008). As with any manual, technical writers must consider how their audience will engage with these documents, anticipating questions, challenges, and creative usage. Game designer Jason Morningstar (2014) provides an example of how the skill of user testing, in this case playtesting, can be learned through tabletop RPG design. For his tabletop RPG *Night Witches*, a game in which players take on the role of female aviators in World War II, Morningstar sought to create a character sheet that would be easy to navigate and aesthetically pleasing. After several playtests, he realized some of his favorite elements from the original design inhibited play, and he made revisions based on player feedback. The final document separated information into three sections depending on how much the information would change throughout a game: static, stable, and volatile. Visual elements that would help with immersion in the narrative world, such as medals, character pictures, and airplane diagrams, were added. The latter was included because players were already adding these images to the sheets themselves. The character sheet was printed as a single page instead of a booklet to aid navigation; character stories were removed due to lack of use; and a list explaining player moves was reduced to avoid confusion and clutter. Playtesting, while sometimes frustrating for the author, ensures that the completed document meets the technical writing requirements of a well-written tabletop RPG: cool, useful, and accessible.

Composition

Writing (for) tabletop RPGs can introduce students to or reinforce basic composition concepts and theories. The planning, design, and playtesting of a game mirror the writing process—from prewriting to revising—initially advocated for by Murray in 1972 and still used in first-year college writing courses to this day; however, game design also lends itself to a post-process approach that views the writing act as public ("a product of our communicative interaction with others"), interpretive (semantically unstable), and situated (determined by specific contexts) (Katsman Breuch 2002, 133). Process serves as the training wheels that teach students how to break larger projects into smaller steps that they can revisit and revise. Post-process asks students to consider the rhetorical nature of their writing through an iterative process that takes the audience and the context into account. In the case of writing (for) tabletop RPGs, particularly rulebooks that must lay out the rules and world of the game while also anticipating how those are taken up by players, both approaches are needed.

Students writing (for) tabletop RPGs will also learn how to analyze and incorporate multimodal elements into their writing. Research into and projects incorporating multimodal composition have risen with the increasing ubiquity of computers and the internet as a source of information and entertainment, and the expanded definition of composition from simple text on a page to fully multimodal productions has been embraced by composition and rhetoric scholars teaching in higher education (Palmeri 2012; Selber 2004; Shipka 2011; Takayoshi and Selfe 2007). One of the more common methods to ease students into this way of writing is the use of a re-mediation project where students transform a traditional essay written earlier in the semester into a multimodal project, such as a podcast, video, or comic. Along this line, Schultz Colby (2017), in her study on how writing instructors use games in their classrooms, describes how some respondents ask students to create persuasive games either in place of or as a re-mediation of a traditional argument paper to reach a wider audience. While tabletop RPGs may begin as simple text on a page, the visual elements—illustrations, maps, fonts, colors, arrangement of elements—help bring it to life for the players.

Commercially available tabletop RPGs are often the products of multiple authors, editors, and artists. Creating such large multimodal projects opens a space for students to practice collaborative writing. Voss (2018) discusses how assigning a collaborative digital project encouraged her students to develop metacognition surrounding cultural capital associated with their knowledge of the medium, using that knowledge to assign responsibilities within the group. In the case of tabletop RPGs, students with more experience as players could assume leadership roles and aid other students in their understanding of the genre. Additionally, collaborative projects provide students with the "diverse vantage points of their peers," which may lead to conflict, but also requires them to learn how to understand and negotiate new ideas (Restaino 2014). Collaboration in composition, particularly multimodal composition, prepares students for future success as members of interactive communities.

PROPOSAL FOR TEACHING WRITING THROUGH TABLETOP RPG DESIGN

While many instructors who incorporate games into their writing classrooms tend to limit instruction to their specific area of writing expertise, doing so reinforces academic silos that do not exist outside of the university. Writing (for) a tabletop RPG requires that the arbitrary walls between creative writing, technical writing, and composition become bridges. In this section, I will offer a planning heuristic and propose strategies and assignments that introduce students to the interdisciplinary act of writing (for) tabletop RPGs and that instructors can adapt to fit their specific pedagogical contexts. Note that this heuristic and course curriculum were developed following several moderately successful attempts to teach games as a unit in an Advanced Composition course. While it is possible to teach parts of this curriculum within a constrained unit, a dedicated tabletop RPG writing course provides the instructor with the opportunity to address some of the challenges mentioned in the following section and allows students time to develop their gaming knowledge base.

Challenges and a Heuristic

Teaching using games can be challenging, but the allure of trying something new can cause some instructors to ignore these challenges to their students' detriment. Knowledge and experience are significant hurdles that must be overcome when teaching with games. If the instructor is not knowledgeable about the basic mechanics of the game, they will be unable to effectively explain how to create them. If students lack experience, they can be taught; however, lack of experience or preconceived ideas about gaming may inhibit students' motivation in the course. They may not see games as serious assignments and produce work that reflects this stance (Andrievskikh 2024). Hergenrader (2014b) and Reed (2015) also point out that the amount of time required to induct students into gaming knowledge economies and to build complex gaming systems can be prohibitive.

As the instructor begins planning their class, they should consider the aforementioned challenges and use the following heuristic to address them:

- **What is the instructor's experience and knowledge of tabletop RPGs and games in general?** If the instructor is a casual gamer who has dabbled in boardgames or videogames, they will need to induct themselves into the world of tabletop RPGs. Review player handbooks from different systems and watch livestreams of gaming sessions. Talk to gaming friends or visit a local game store (LGS) to find a gaming group and play a one-shot or campaign. If the instructor is well acquainted with tabletop RPGs, now is the time to try serving as a game master. It is also strongly encouraged that the instructor attempt to write their own rulebook or one-shot, so they are aware of the time and knowledge required to do so effectively and can set realistic deadlines and expectations. While it is possible to learn alongside the students, it is wiser to wait until the instructor is comfortable with tabletop RPGs before incorporating them into a writing course.
- **What is the instructor's academic specialty, and how can they become familiar with the other specialties involved?** The instructor does not have to be an expert in all areas to run this course successfully, but they do need to be willing to grow their knowledge base. While the most obvious way to do this is through research and consultations with fellow instructors who are experts, another option is to share the burden. Seek partners within the department who would be willing to guest lecture or even co-teach the course. If the university supports learning communities, consider proposing two courses that teach different areas of writing but work toward the same final project.
- **What is the anticipated gaming experience of the instructor's students?** Unless the instructor has reason to believe differently, it is best to assume that students have little experience with gaming beyond casual party games. During the first class, conduct a survey of students' experience and adjust the assignment details and rubrics accordingly. If students have different levels of experience, design assignments that offer them options they can choose from based on their comfort level.

- **Will this be a new course, or will the instructor adapt the assignments of a pre-existing course?** It may be more difficult to get a new course based solely on games approved by the curriculum committee, requiring significant planning, presentation of the existing literature, clear alignment with department goals, and assurances that you are not stepping on anyone's toes. At the university level, the instructor may have to defend the course by demonstrating how the learning outcomes translate to real-world skills valued by potential employers. Working games into pre-existing courses, however, can be a little easier. If a technical writing course already includes a unit on writing manuals, the instructor could make the manual a rulebook. If they teach a nebulously defined Advanced Composition course, they can use "writing for and about games" as a theme.

- **At what academic level will the course be taught? Who will be eligible to enroll?** Deciding whether this is a 1,000-level course, 4,000-level course, or somewhere in between will help the instructor determine which of the assignments to emphasize, how to design grading rubrics, and what type of instruction will be required in each of the three areas: creative writing, technical writing, and composition. Students new to thc university will require stronger grounding in the basics and may need stricter guidelines for how to approach their games. Upperclassmen majoring in the department have likely already taken courses in one or more of the three areas and can be introduced to more complex gaming mechanics and systems.

- **What learning outcomes would the instructor like students to achieve?** Based on their area, department, and university goals, the instructor will need to determine which learning outcomes to prioritize and adapt the assignments to meet them. When evaluating the final product, they will need to remember to focus on these outcomes. It is not fair to students to emphasize writing clear and concise rules all semester in feedback and lectures and then penalize them because their game based on *Euphoria* or some other popular media was not original enough.

- **How much time can the instructor dedicate to designing the tabletop RPG in the course?** The amount of time students have to work on the project will help the instructor determine what scaffolding assignments they will be able to incorporate and how polished the final project will be. If the instructor can only dedicate a unit to the project, they may not require students to create a final rulebook. Instead, students could submit a detailed proposal for their game.

- **How can the instructor ensure that collaborative elements are truly collaborative?** Contracts that establish the rules of collaboration and regular instructor check-ins that hold students accountable can be effective methods for ensuring equal participation. While some students may feel comfortable informing the instructor of issues with their groupmates, the responsibility for creating clear reporting pathways lies with the instructor.
- **How can the instructor emphasize the important transferable skills students are learning?** Students (and parents and administrators) want to know how the skills they are learning will help them upon graduation, specifically in regard to employment. They may believe that gaming is something done for fun; it is not a serious area of study. As students progress through the different assignments, explain the utility of each skill and provide students with concrete examples of those skills being implemented in other contexts.

Once all of these questions have been addressed, the instructor can begin designing their curriculum.

Assignments

Assignments in the course should provide students with adequate scaffolding to introduce them to the genre of tabletop RPGs and provide them with support as they work through worldbuilding, document design, and eventual playtesting of their games. The following is a suggested sequence of assignments that could be taught over the course of a 15-week semester dedicated to writing (for) tabletop RPGs. While options will be discussed in many of the assignment descriptions, instructors are highly encouraged to alter, skip, or even add assignments to better fit their context and pedagogical goals.

Reflection Journal

Students should maintain a weekly reflection journal. Ideally, this journal will be a low-stakes writing assignment that serves as a metacognitive exercise and record of the students' progress throughout the semester. Students can use it to document their contributions to the collaborative project, discuss the writing skills they have practiced and the lessons they have learned, and pose questions regarding the challenges they are facing in their game design. This type of assignment allows the instructor to ensure that all students are on target and to intervene early if there are any academic or interpersonal issues. They can also provide a useful resource for students' future gaming projects, as they preserve orphaned ideas.

Genre Analysis

A genre analysis of the specific characteristics that define a tabletop RPG will allow students to familiarize themselves with the type of project they will be asked to create. Written texts, such as rulebooks and one-shots, can be analyzed to determine the type of information included, how this information is organized, how narrative and instruction interact and the ratio between the two, and what visual elements are included and for what purpose. In addition to assigning rulebooks and/or one-shot scenarios for this assignment, it is important that students be required to engage in or observe actual gameplay, as tabletop RPGs are not complete texts without the input of the players. Even if students have extensive experience as players or game masters (GMs), they likely were not thinking about their gameplay analytically, considering the affordances and limitations that the rules and world impose or how they chose to either adhere to or ignore them. If it is possible, the instructor could run a brief one-shot during one of the first weeks of class. If not, assigning an episode of a livestream, such as *Critical Role* or *Dimension 20*, could give students an idea of how the written text translates to actual play.

Proposal

Once students have become more familiar with what a tabletop RPG is, they can begin to think about the type of game they would like to work on throughout the semester. Students could be given the option between writing a full-blown rulebook or a one-shot within an existing game world, using the mechanics established therein. If they create their own tabletop RPG, the completion of something similar to Hergenrader's (2014b) world-building survey could be a required section, as it walks students through fleshing out the details of the world and its social, economic, and political structures. Alternatively, they could choose to transmediate an existing text into a tabletop RPG rulebook. For example, games like *Call of Cthulhu*, *Harlem Unbound*, and *Delta Green* are transmediations of H.P. Lovecraft's eldritch horror stories. Students could create a tabletop RPG for *Adventure Time* or *The Office*, or whatever is popular right now, and they could explain the narrative elements, such as characters, locations, and objects, that would be pulled over and the mechanics that would dictate interactions. If students choose to create a one-shot, they should explain why they chose the specific rulebook and how they plan to add to it narratively and mechanically. Stress to students that they are not yoked to every detail of the proposal; as they develop their games, they should feel comfortable revising their ideas and testing other approaches.

Students will also have to decide what rules system to use. The instructor should consider the students' experience and the amount of time they have to complete their project before introducing options. The Gumshoe system, with its straightforward 1d6 skill checks and emphasis on storytelling over dice rolls, or a simple dice pool system, where players roll a number of the same type of die based on their skills or attributes, may be ideal for students or classes that do not have much experience with tabletop RPGs. These systems take very little time to explain and can easily be adapted to most genres, including science fiction (e.g. *Ashen Stars*), cyberpunk (e.g. *Shadowrun*), fantasy (e.g. *Swords of the Serpentine* and *The Burning Wheel*), vampires (e.g. *Night's Black Agents* and *Vampire: The Masquerade*), horror (e.g. *Fear Itself*), and mystery (e.g. *Bubblegumshoe*). The d20-based system's skill modifiers and use of different dice for actions like damage rolls may be too complex for students to master in one semester. Games in this system tend to work well for dungeon crawlers, where combat is a significant element (e.g. *Dungeons & Dragons* and *Pathfinder*). Students could also be introduced to several systems and allowed to choose or adapt them to fit the game they are designing. The instructor should not let the choice of rules system become an impediment to the main goal of writing.

In addition to beginning the brainstorming process for their project, the proposal is also a good location for students to negotiate the rules of collaboration. Who will be responsible for what elements? When will students meet throughout the semester to work on things together? When should items be submitted for consideration by the group? How will they notify the instructor if someone is not doing their work? Determining these rules early on can help students feel more confident about the collaborative process and provide them with a document they can point to if things fall behind.

Narrative Drafts

The narrative elements that set the tone and build the world of play may be completed as a single draft or in a series of smaller drafts throughout the semester. Students should consider how the narrative will be shared with players and how much description is needed to set the stage for the type of play they hope will be enacted. In a rulebook, narrative drafts may include extensive catalogs of people, places, and objects that can be used to populate the play space. It can also include an introduction to the rulebook or to the individual sections within the text that sets the tone and evokes the world. For example, the character creation section of the tabletop RPG *Ashen Stars* clearly establishes a space western feel where the player characters serve as mercenaries or unofficial lawmen:

> They call you Lasers. Or scrubbers, regulators, or, out in the Scylla Outzone, shinestars. To the lawless denizens of the Bleed, whether they be pirates, gangsters, or tyrants, you're known in less flattering terms. According to official Combine terminology, the members of your hard-bitten starship crew are known as Licensed Autonomous Effectuators. You're the seasoned freelancers local leaders call, when a situation proves too tough, too baffling, or simply too weird to handle on their own. In the abandoned fringe of inhabited planets known as the Bleed, you're as close to a federal authority as they come.
>
> (*Laws 2011, 3*)

If students are planning a one-shot within an existing world, the amount of cataloging required is significantly diminished and replaced by the need to plot out a full interactive narrative. One-shots tend to have a more traditional beginning, middle, and end. How players get through these plot points is still largely up to them. While he is specifically speaking about videogame RPGs, Jenkins (2002) offers some examples of how students can think of narrative within a one-shot. Evocative spaces are transmediated spaces that trigger knowledge of existing worlds. For example, an author may describe a table in the woods set for tea that players would associate with *Alice in Wonderland* and that would cause them to anticipate some form of chaos. Enacted stories are localized incidents that encourage exploration and drive a plot; these stories offer the players choices and allow them to interact with the game world. Embedded narratives are stories within the main narrative that offer additional information about the world, so players may run into characters or become embroiled in events that provide them with details that could help them as they progress. Emergent narratives are unstructured stories that develop through play. While the author does not have much control over these player-driven narratives, they can attempt to anticipate them and/or allow space for them to occur.

Rulebook/One-Shot Prototype

Once the narrative elements and rules have been written, they need to be presented in a way that is both aesthetically pleasing and easy for players to follow. While it does not have to be perfect, the rulebook/one-shot prototype should be the closest students can get to a completed, polished document in the time they are given. It should reflect effective technical writing, including clear organization of information on and across pages and visual elements that add to the narrative or help explicate the rules. Additionally, it can include paratexts associated with play, such as location maps and character sheets.

Students should be introduced to document design tools that will aid them as they seek to create a cool, useful, and accessible text. While Adobe InDesign is an extremely versatile tool, it may not be accessible to students due to cost or the steep learning curve associated with it. Currently, the tools available to most students are Word, Google Docs, and Canva, a website that offers free templates and editing tools. While Word and Google Docs may seem ubiquitous, it is important to understand that students may not know all of their features, so some instruction may be necessary. For the creation of maps, students could hand-draw them or use a program like Inkarnate, which offers a free version.

Playtest and Revision Plan

Playtesting, ensuring that players not only understand the world and rules but that they interact with it in ways that the author expects, is an important part of the tabletop RPG design process. Playtesting could take several forms: students could test each other's games in a type of peer review; they could ask their friends and family to serve as testers; or the instructor could put out a call to the student body or on-campus gaming group. Play testers should be provided with any materials they will need in advance, so they have the opportunity to adapt to the game world, create their character (unless pre-generated characters will be assigned), and review the rules.

During playtesting, one of the group-members could serve as the GM, while the other member(s) takes notes about how the players interact with the game world and the rulebook, questions and comments that arise during play, and the overall satisfaction of players during and at the end of the session. Follow-up feedback should be solicited from players through surveys and/or interviews. The group member serving as the GM should also provide notes on the experience of running the table. Once feedback has been reviewed and analyzed, students should write up a formal plan outlining successes and areas for revision.

CONCLUSION

Tabletop RPGs offer writing instructors across the areas of creative writing, technical writing, and composition the opportunity to break out of their silos and offer students assignments that highlight the interdisciplinary nature of writing beyond academia. While instructors must acknowledge and address potential challenges to incorporating games into the curriculum, it is possible to create academically rigorous assignments that introduce and reinforce important writing skills that students will need as they progress through college and into their communities and careers.

While I have focused on writing in this chapter, here at the end, I would like to offer a peek at how we can continue to break down the walls between disciplines using tabletop RPGs. As multimodal texts, tabletop RPGs offer the opportunity to partner with departments of art and music through the creation of client-based projects, where writing students share their games and receive complementary creative compositions in exchange. Students in history departments could be consulted to develop rich settings and characters based on real events. In a time when the Humanities are undervalued, it is important for us to look for ways to support each other.

REFERENCES

Andrievskikh, Natalia. 2024. "Student-Created Tabletop Foresight Games as Advocacy." *prompt* 8 (1): 28–37. https://doi.org/10.31719/pjaw.v8i1.169.

Anto, Christina. 2021. "Remediating the Tempest as a Playable TTRPG Module." Master's thesis, Ryerson University. https://doi.org/10.32920/16906654.v1.

Baetens, Jan. 2003. "Comic Strips and Constrained Writing." *Image and Narrative* 7. https://www.imageandnarrative.be/inarchive/graphicnovel/janbaetens_constrained.htm.

Booth, Paul. 2015. *Game Play: Paratextuality in Contemporary Board Games.* Bloomsbury Academic.

Boss, Suzie. 2019. "Gaming as a Tool for Narrative Writing." *Edutopia*, May 6. https://www.edutopia.org/article/gaming-tool-narrative-writing.

Bourelle, Tiffany, Angela Clark-Oates, Andrew Bourelle, Matthew Irwin, and Breannae Potter. 2019. "Thinking beyond Multimodal Projects: Incorporating Multimodal Literacy into Composing and Reflection Processes." In *Bridging the Multimodal Gap: From Theory to Practice*, edited by Santosh Khadka and J. C. Lee. Utah State University Press.

Christensen, Kasen. 2022. "Cool and Useful: Tabletop Roleplaying Games as Aesthetic Technical Communication." *SIGDOC* 149–151. https://doi.org/10.1145/3513130.3558994.

Cook, Mike P., Matthew Gremo, and Ryan Morgan. 2017. "We're Just Playing: The Influence of a Modified Tabletop Roleplaying Game on ELA Students' In-Class Reading." *Simulation & Gaming* 48 (2): 199–218. https://doi.org/10.1177/1046878116684570.

Ekman, Stefan, and Audrey Isabel Taylor. 2009. "Notes toward a Critical Approach to Worlds and World-Building." *Fafnir: Nordic Journal of Science Fiction and Fantasy Research* 3 (3): 7–18. https://journal.finfar.org/articles/notes-toward-a-critical-approach-to-worlds-and-world-building/.

Etheridge, Brian C., Christian Duncan, Jeremy J, Mhire, Jean Gourd, John Worsencraft, and Heath Tims. 2022. "Serious Analog Game Development across Disciplines." *Analog Game Studies* 4 (2). https://analoggamestudies.org/2022/05/thinking-without-borders-serious-analog-game-development-and-trans-disciplinary-education/.

Eyman, Douglas. 2008. "Computer Gaming and Technical Communication: An Ecological Framework." *Technical Communication* 55 (3): 242–250. http://www.jstor.org/stable/43095345.

Hergenrader, Trent. 2014a. "The Narrative Potential of Tabletop Roleplaying Games." In *Proceedings of the Games+Learning+Society*, edited by Amanda Oschner, ETC Press.

Hergenrader, Trent. 2014b. "Dense Worlds, Deep Characters: Role-Playing Games, World Building, and Creative Writing." In *Proceedings of the Games+Learning+Society*, edited by Amanda Oschner, ETC Press.

Jara, David. 2013. "A Closer Look at the (Rule-)Books: Framings and Paratexts in Tabletop Role-Playing Games." *International Journal of Role-Playing* 4: 39–54. https://doi.org/10.33063/ijrp.vi4.228.

Jenkins, Henry. 2002. "Game Design as Narrative Architecture." *Computer* 44: 118–130.

Kastman Breuch, Lee-Ann. 2002. "Post-Process 'Pedagogy': A Philosophical Exercise." *JAC* 22 (1): 119–150.

Kaylor, Stephanie L. B. 2017. "Dungeons and Dragons and Literacy: The Role Tabletop Role-Playing Games Can Play in Developing Teenagers' Literacy Skills and Reading Interests." *Graduate Research Papers*. 215. https://scholarworks.uni.edu/grp/215.

Laws, Robin D. 2011. *Ashen Stars*. Pelgrane Press.

Morningstar, Jason. 2014. "Visual Design as a Metaphor: The Evolution of a Character Sheet." *Analog Game Studies* 1 (5). https://analoggamestudies.org/2014/12/visual-design-as-metaphor-the-evolution-of-a-character-sheet/.

Murray, Donald M. 1972. "Teach Writing as a Process Not a Product." *The Leaflet*, 11–14.

Palmeri, Jason. 2012. *Remixing Composition: A History of Multimodal Writing Pedagogy*. Southern Illinois University Press.

Reed, A. A. 2015. "Telling Stories with Maps and Rules: Using the Interactive Fictional Language 'Inform7' in a Creative Writing Workshop." In *Creative Writing in the Digital Age: Theory, Practice and Pedagogy*, edited by Michael D. Clark, Trent Hergenrader, and Joseph Rein. Bloomsbury Publishing.

Restaino, Jessica. 2014. "Writing Together: An Arendtian Framework for Collaboration." *Composition Forum* 30. https://compositionforum.com/issue/30/writing-together.php.

Schultz Colby, Rebekah. 2017. "Game-Based Pedagogy in the Writing Classroom." *Computers and Composition* 43: 55–72. https://doi.org/10.1016/j.compcom.2016.11.002.

Schultz Colby, Rebekah, and Richard Colby. 2008. "A Pedagogy of Play: Integrating Computer Games into the Writing Classroom." *Computers & Composition* 25: 300–312. https://doi.org/10.1016/j.compcom.2008.04.005.

Selber, Stuart A. 2004. *Multiliteracies for a Digital Age*. Southern Illinois University Press.

Shipka, Jody. 2011. *Towards a Composition Made Whole*. University of Pittsburgh Press.

Shoenberger, Michael. 2024. "Tertiary Learning Usage of Tabletop Roleplaying Games: Affordances and Challenges." In *Revitalising Higher Education: Insights from Te Puna Aurei LearnFest 2022*, edited by Tracy Bowell, Nicole Pepperell, Anthony Richardson, and Maria-Teresa Corino. Cardiff University Press.

Steele, Samar H. 2023. "The Maker Turn in Classroom Games: An Articulation of Gamemaking in Education (GME)." In *GENeration Analog 2021 Proceedings*, edited by Evan Torner, Shelly Jones, Edmond Chang, Megan Condis, and Aaron Trammell. ETC Press.

Stroessner, Steven J., Laurie S. Beckerman, and Alexis Whittaker. 2009. "All the World's a Stage? Consequences of a Role-Playing Pedagogy on Psychological Factors and Writing and Rhetorical Skill in College Undergraduates." *Journal of Educational Psychology* 101 (3): 605–620. https://doi.org/10.1037/a0015055.

Takayoshi, Pamela, Cynthia L. Selfe. 2007. "Thinking about Multimodality." In *Multimodal Composition: Resources for Teachers*, edited by Cynthia L. Selfe. Hampton Press.

Taylor, Andrew. 2019. "There Is No 'E' in 'Constraints': Teaching Creativity in Higher Education Screen Production." In *The Palgrave Handbook of Screen Production*, edited by Craig Batty, Marsha Berry, Kath Dooley, Bettina Frankham, and Susan Kerrigan. Palgrave Macmillan.

Vigna, John. 2021. "The Value of Constraints in the Generative Workshop." *Writing in Education* 83: 86–88.

Voss, Julia. 2018. "Who Learns from Collaborative Digital Projects? Cultivating Critical Consciousness and Metacognition to Democratize Digital Literacy Learning." *Composition Studies* 46 (1): 57–80.

Yucel, Ibrahim. 2014. "Rules for Writing Rules: How Instructional Design Impacts Good Game Design." *Analog Game Studies* 1 (3). https://analoggamestudies.org/2014/10/the-rules-for-writing-rules-how-instructional-design-impacts-good-game-design/.

Zalka, Csenge V. 2016. "Adventures in the Classroom: Creating Traditional Story-Based Role-Playing Games in High School Curriculum." *Storytelling, Self, Society* 12 (2): 173–206. https://doi.org/10.13110/storselfsoci.12.2.0173.

CHAPTER 7

Role-Playing Games and Narrative Identity as Pedagogical Tools in Teaching Fiction

A Reflection from Inside the Classroom

William Stratton

INTRODUCTION

On the first day of classes a few years ago, one student made their way through the lingering chatter of the crowd as it filtered slowly out into the hall. It was my first time teaching a class I had designed to, according to the learning outcomes set forth by the department: "explore complex ideas through reading and writing" and "apply multiple analytical frameworks" to those ideas and to further examine our roles both in the ideas and their frameworks, as well as the assumptions that are inherent in them. That can be an intimidating ask for students who have only been out of high school for a few months and are entering a college classroom for the first time, so I when I was approached by a tentative-looking student after class,

DOI: 10.1201/9781003641384-11

I was eager to hear what they had to say about what we'd talked about that day--mostly introductions and explanations, but also the syllabus and overview.

"I see why you chose RPGs to use for this class," they said.

"You do?" We had touched briefly on how we would be approaching the subject matter and curriculum, but I was curious to see how this student would engage and apply their own experience to the ideas.

"Yeah--I can't think of anything else that gives you so much to do and so many ways to do it--so much to think about and so many options. All that, and they're fun."

We went on talking for a few minutes, asking questions and expressing excitement for the semester, but it was that first moment that really hit me, for two reasons. First, I realized that tabletop role-playing games (RPGs) had become so big, so pervasive, that many of my students had built their own library of experience and relationship with the systems and games—and that was a key to bridging the gap between what can sometimes be perceived by students to be abstract academia and the relatability of their own lives. Indeed, most of those who did not have previous experience playing tabletop RPGs had enough cultural understanding to recognize what they were, how they operated, and broadly speaking that they wield some not-inconsiderable influence in the world at large. Secondly, they recognized with only the bare minimum of pre-emptive scaffolding, some things these systems might have to offer—not only for our shared academic experience, but also for their lives beyond school.

Realizing the reach of tabletop RPGs, their impact on contemporary culture and society, their swelling economic fingerprints, and how many students have participated in the movement of tabletop RPGs from the proverbial basement to earning hundreds of millions of players—and a proportionate amount of dollars—was not only incredibly useful for my class work, but also a relatable and entertaining ride for my students.

I'd spent almost my entire life playing tabletop RPGs of one form or another. The summer after I turned 10, I wandered into a bookstore in Lake Placid, NY, and found a copy of Advanced Dungeons and Dragons 2nd Edition Player's Handbook. The art on the cover, the small bits of text I sampled as I skimmed it, and the idea that it was some sort of game I could play all combined and completely infatuated my sense of adventure. From that day on, I was a convert to the world of tabletop

RPGs, and as my educational experience and contextual understanding of teaching in the world of higher education increased, I itched to put my decades of experience and passion for the games to use in my educational world/life. For many years, I shied away from trying to use it in classrooms, fearing the stigma from academia that I'd already encountered when I taught science fiction and fantasy classes, or used video games to reach the students. It was only when I began to realize the extent that tabletop RPGs had become mainstream culture and outsized in their influence that I was able to find the synthesis between the systems and my curriculum, allowing my pedagogy to grow and reflect my knowledge base.

For all the ways in which we as educators approach the use of tabletop RPGs in our curriculum and pedagogy, perhaps none of them are so uniquely tied to the system, history, lore and everyday use of those tabletop RPGs than is fiction, especially speculative and, under that umbrella, fantasy fiction. If we consider for instance the case of Dungeons and Dragons, whose creator Gary Gygax cited the Conan books as a major source of inspiration (and, though he famously snubs Tolkien, the influence does appear to be obvious and inescapable). It seems to follow, then, that we ought to be able to find a myriad of uses for tabletop RPGs when teaching students about writing creatively within or without the previously mentioned genres. While I do think RPGs have some interesting things to teach young writers about setting, plot, and theme, this chapter will focus more specifically on character and ways in which I have previously found success using these games to help developing writers in that regard.

To begin with, the recognition of systemic ties to character in RPG is a valuable one for the students and should be a relatively simple gap to bridge. One of the most popular aspects of any contemporary RPG is character creation. Nowhere is this more apparent than the hundreds of hours of video with millions of views on YouTube for Baldur's Gate 3 character designer (modded or vanilla, take your pick). The content creator Fextralife, for example, has 884,000 views on a video that only covers race choice, which is only one of the six steps included in character creation (Fextralife, 2023). While perhaps not as observably popular, many Dungeons and Dragons players will tell you that their own character creation process is one of their favorite parts and typically consumes a good deal of time and energy.

SYSTEMS AND CHARACTER

Some part of why this process gains so much attention and is so attractive lies in the emotional exploration of a systemic approach to creation. Our tabletop RPGs offer us "stats" by which to measure the respective strengths and weaknesses, abilities and tendencies, capabilities and potential pitfalls of the characters we are soon to inhabit for potentially long periods of time. Those measurements adhere to and are central to the functioning of the system as it exists, but it also offers the players a window into the possibilities of the characters themselves. Somewhere inherent in the idea of tabletop RPG is the undertaking of the heroic, semi-heroic, or in some other way, potentially high-stakes plot. In turn, that implies potential circumstances in which the relative humanity of these characters, through the stats previously mentioned here, has a chance to become realized within the context of the game. This humanization nearly encompasses all the things we look for in good character work and embodies some of the more recognizable and important ones (Vermeule, 2011). When your clumsy character drops the magic artifact and nearly destroys the world with an accident, it is not only wildly entertaining, but also a moment in which the character moves in some small way from being numbers on paper to being a real person. The system allows and encourages players to explore these possibilities even in the first steps of realizing a character in the creation process.

Another piece of this puzzle lies in the relative level of detail in the design process. Character creation processes which are too simple can lose the attention of players before the game even starts. Conversely, there seems to be a much higher tolerance for the optional deep dive into the relative minutia of creation in character and their backstory. This is reflective, I think, of good fiction writing habits as well. A character who is big and strong is fine and well, but knowing what kind of hat they wear or that they have a scar on the webbing between thumb and forefinger affords the player an opportunity to explore important questions about that character, such as: why? In turn, that exploration has the potential to lead to a better understanding of what makes that character a person, instead of a trope.

NARRATIVE IDENTITY THEORY

In a similar way, we might inquire as to what makes a person who they are. While not conclusive or comprehensive, the theory behind narrative identity is a solid approach point for the examination of character both in tabletop RPG and fiction. In brief, the idea that the self (or whatever we consider to be the self in terms of a working thesis for identity) is formed by stories the brain tells itself about itself through the integration of experience and its transformation into narrative (Mehl-Madrona and Mainguy, 2022). The games here allow access to both the process of making those experiences into values used by a system to forward narrative but also encourage the telling of stories beyond the bounds of its own narrative in the strictest sense (Lacy, 2006). In the same way that an author might write backstory for their characters before the construction of a novel, so too do most tabletop RPGs incorporate an inherent sense that the story does not materialize out of nothing when the game begins but rather picks up where the interesting bits are most relevant. For a character obviously had a life before the game started, and the player must fill in those blanks as best dictated by the system of the game itself, and most often, well beyond that as the contextual clues indicate. So too do characters exist before the book is written—babies make poor protagonists—and it behooves an author to consider well how the intersection of those ideas/experiences came to a confluence and created the person they are writing. It is not too great a stretch, following these ideas, to understand that the remembrance or reconstruction of a character's past, the character's perception of present experience and sensory intake, and the projected future of this character is not greatly or functionally dissimilar from our own remembrance, perception, and imaginings.

To follow through a bit further on this idea, certainly we can assume that physical characteristics crucially inform what a person does, how they act and interact with the world, what they might think or feel, and how others view them. So does experience and the stories that person tells themselves about themselves, and about the world (Armstrong, 2020). Both internally and externally, that process becomes informative at the same time and in the same space in which it is creative. Learning and practicing that process through RPGs is a potential asset and tool to add to the box for any creative writer. Because of its relatively easy access, its systemic approach to quantifiable character composition, and the ability to create via this system as many different characters as the player (author) would like, RPGs are a resource that has great potential to help explore, refine, and understand what makes characters compelling and real.

Also worth exploring is the idea of how a communally constructed narrative relying heavily on character creates and experiences itself simultaneously, and how what might appear to be stories constructed by one person are more likely a gathering of communal experiences to guide a creation process. Whatever we say we might use as the base of our character creation process, inevitably we draw from our own experience, even if that experience is second or third hand and/or contextual. Tabletop RPGs, as a system in which we create a cooperative narrative (Cole, 2017), allow us to experience not only our own ideas about character (and self) and how they fit into the larger composition of narrative, but also how that works for others. Another player's character evolution informs not only our own, but also our ideas about what characters are, and how they act, interact, and change as life happens to them. Even if the only other players are, as they might be in a video game, the developers and writers who made the rest of the world the player interacts with, those are still potentially new and essentially informative ideas and experiences about and involved with the character, each of which has the potential to influence and integrate into the player and author's ideas.

CLASSROOM PRACTICES

One of the exercises I find useful in this regard is to have the students access DnD Beyond and create an account. It's free, and relatively unobtrusive. Should you choose, however, you can find free character creators online as well. From there, the students can access the character creation process simultaneously as a class, and we can walk through the system together. While many of my students are already familiar with at least the basic ideas, some are not, and the early exploration of the system is often an eye-opening experience for them. Regardless, during the creation process, the goal here is to get them to think about and discuss what the system says about what makes a person who they are.

During this first phase, I try to let the discussion develop naturally, asking questions when needed about what makes certain characteristics and scores relevant, what they reflect in the real world, how they might be indicative of other character trends or ideas relevant to the construction of narrative. The process can be a long one, as I've found students are often interested in exchanging ideas about what scores reflect in terms of behavior or abilities/actions in life. Does wisdom influence your shopping skills? Would being a sorcerer enhance or hinder your math skills? Etc. Once they've completed the character, I give them the opportunity (through an assignment, usually) to explore who this character is based on what they've made of them through the system. In this way, they can place their new character in any setting and write the story of how they came to be the way and things that they are. Why are they so charismatic, but so foolish? What happened in their life to make them go down the path of becoming a secluded woodland druid? The inquiry is central to the process, asking the important questions and pursuing them is a way for students to understand not only the character, the ideas that formed it, and the ways in which they conceive of them as a person, but also of their own various roles in that creation (Harrell and Harrell, 2012).

Students often find the process itself contains high value to their thinking and writing. The process of running the normal system backward (first rolling scores, then explaining why) is another way to explore what makes characters compelling, alive, and emotionally worth investing in. All characters have some abilities, but following through on why, how, in what ways, and the further construction of meaning is the piece of the puzzle most often missing from young writers' skill sets. A written character becomes more than unidimensional through the same process—the realization of experience and the narratives that form whatever self they have or are. An author, especially one at the beginning of their writing journey (relatively speaking), will likely benefit from the practice and exploration this process offers. If the students are presented the opportunity to explore what makes people interesting, what things they might be able to quantify in terms of their experiences and individual narratives, it's not a far stretch to see how this might help them understand not only what forms compelling characters, but how those things can be framed, further explored, and understood.

To preface this, I ask the students the week before to write a short backstory for a character, a page or so will do. I don't ask them to consider yet what makes a character compelling or feel real, but rather what kind of a person they have created, and what kind of a story has led them to be that person.

Another way of approaching something similar is to have what I call a self-character-creation day. I start by having the students assign themselves ability scores and skills within the system used (any system should work, so long as it has scores that represent character traits and abilities). To begin with, they're completely in the camp of the system as it exists, but as we move along, I start to pull them into our world. What skills do they have that might measure on a character sheet?

As an example, a student who spends every winter weekend on the slopes and has been doing so since they were 10, might give themselves a +3 skiing skill. Meanwhile, another student who frequently plays first-person shooter games might assign themselves a +2 shooting skill. Yet another, who goes to the local pool twice a week, gives themselves a +4 swimming. Some students will see the fun/appeal in giving themselves negatives here, which works just as well for the purposes of the exploration. I've seen things like: −2 emotional regulation, −3 mood, or things like +4 clumsiness. This is also key to the creation process, as expressing flaws and exploring internal conflict is a vital component to compelling character (Corbett, 2019). The possibilities here are really open ended, and the students usually have a good time exploring the potential. More importantly, they're also framing how experience informs who we are on certain levels, and as a result, how characters are or can be.

Next, I ask them to assign themselves classes and levels—similar to the previous portion, they're now considering what things they've grown to be accomplished at. Most will quickly label themselves as a mid-level student, for example, and many will build on early jobs they've had. I have had many fifth-level babysitters, food service experts, and grocery store employees, for example. There's obvious fun and investment for the students here, and the conversations that spring up around this part are often centered around what level denotes what measure of skill, or how much time would be required to be considered beginning, proficient, or expert level at a thing. In addition, the students will frequently examine how they can measure these outcomes, or how they reflect in their regular lives.

This is crucial to the construction of character, as part of the process is anticipating how, for example, a protagonist who has worked in food service might respond to a certain situation versus one that works on a dairy farm—or whatever the circumstances may be. Characters, in the context of this conversation, gradually shift from vehicles for plot movement to three-dimensional beings which are worthy of examination, thought, personality, and emotional involvement (Pelican, 2020). The recognition that their own lives are influenced on a regular basis in some part because of the experiences they've accumulated, and that the same must therefore be true of any significant character they might spend the time writing, has the potential to be profound in terms of their respective writing process.

This integration of various real-life disciplines, experiences, habits and skills can lead to some exciting realizations about what makes a character interesting, as well as what powers their own life. In my experience, the longer the students spend with this in both conversation and in practice, the more they will develop insight into their own characters, and themselves as human beings. I try to use myself as an example, suggesting that I might be a level 10 teacher given the decades of experience I have, but only a level 1 fast food maker, in reference to the summer I spent working at Burger King. I usually find that I have to end this exercise artificially, because the students will not easily tire of the comparison, examination, and continued expansion of the application of systemic value to real-life skill sets as they apply to their own lives.

Ultimately with this exercise, one of the core principles is the exploration of what makes a person a person, and in turn, how we can make characters feel more lifelike, more activated, more inhabited by real experience. There are many different approaches to writing compelling characters, but most will benefit from this exploration. Finding flaws, as expressed earlier, is one key component to turning an otherwise flat series of tropes into something that might resemble a compelling book character (Corbett, 2019). Many tabletop RPG systems have flaws built in, or at least have the option to use them. Even if the system does not, prodding the students to find those flaws, understand, and explore them, is a great way for them to work the system and the character creation process. The above is one way we can use a well-tested and widely known system to propel ourselves past the surface-level stereotypes that young writers often fall into when they begin to explore character, especially in fiction and doubly so for genre fiction.

RPGs have their own tropes to struggle with, but by and large, they fall into similar categories as fictional tropes. The tortured genius, the hero with a dark past, the chosen one, etc. all offer young players (and writers), among other things, access to their ideas about what might be. Giving them a way to explore and honor this while challenging some of the assumptions that old tropes make is a useful tool that makes for both a fun class and a useful approach.

Another approach I like to take is to consider what makes a character in a tabletop RPG appealing as a player and consumer of the narrative. In most RPGs, the narrative is co-created, even so, the players themselves are the base consumer, and while they have influence over and might decide key details of the story as it progresses, the level of investment they have in it often comes down to their attachment to or feelings toward the character they play (Bopp et al., 2019; Mallon, 2014). Because I teach in a school that has a lot of video game enthusiasts, one of the things I like to do is ask them who their favorite game protagonists are. While there is a wide variety in the responses given, and the list is likely to continue to evolve as time goes on, I've found that some characters have staying power. For example, even six years on from the game's release, Arthur Morgan (of Red Dead Redemption II) remains a popular choice. From there, it's fairly easy for me to access a more detailed exploration of why those characters made such an impression.

Once I have the list of characters (assuming I'm familiar with at least one or two of them), we can start with how the character interacts with the system it inhabits, as well as the world it lives in. Arthur, for example, has a certain set of skills that help define who he is, where he came from, and where he might go from here. HIs deadeye skill is the one that really sets him apart from the NPCs (non-player characters), and though it might be considered a mechanic, we can infer that the gunslinger he has become has some relation to that ability—the students might discuss whether it was his experiences that led to this skill, or that his skill led to the experiences he had—but both are great ways to explore the character's development. The world he lives in is harsh and violent, and it's clear his mentors/parental figures are, at first appearance at least, amoral people. So, while riding around the fictional old west world and committing crimes, the players who are controlling the character are discovering the world through Arthur's filters, and having more experiences that seem to fit the theme of Arthur's life in general. This bit of RPG fiction is understood and valued almost singularly because of the character through which the player gets to experience it. It's not hard for them to see the connection to their own writings, here. This example also serves to blur the lines between tabletop RPG and fiction, the students will often ask whether RDR2 is more of a narrative work or an RPG. For that matter, they may start to question where the lines between tabletop RPGs and narrative are, or if they exist at all. I always encourage these discussions as a sort of cultural discourse and often prod them on mythos, community, and identity (Cragoe, 2016). The distinction isn't terribly important to resolve, so long as they are demonstrating an understanding of how character is formed, explored, and operates for the larger system and story.

Likewise, through the filter of RPGs in general, the players can experience what makes a character compelling even as they decide which actions (to a greater or lesser degree) the characters themselves make or take. Though there is a large divergence in practice, system, and ideas between video game RPGs and tabletop RPGs, both operate heavily within the realm of character-forward art and narrative, and both can afford students the opportunity to explore how, why, and in what ways that matters.

CONTINUATION AND DEVELOPMENT

When the students have become more comfortable, as the semester has evolved its way into a space of community, I can introduce more complex exercises and expectations for my RPG-playing writers. I sometimes have the luxury of teaching the entire semester's worth of tabletop RPG-related material, and as such, these further explorations are helpful. One in particular that I have found to get good response rates and feedback from students is the one-room adventure. This requires a bit of setup on my part, the designing of a brief, open-ended scenario with a single goal and simple parameters. For example, breaking a friend out of a jail cell, or finding the crate on the deck of a guarded ship. The single room is more of a guideline and reminder to myself to keep things simple and easy, rather than a rule. Once I have the NPCs in place and the scenario as well explained as possible, I split the class into groups of 4–5, let them use the characters they made earlier in the semester, and ask them to solve the problem, in character.

This is an exercise about dialogue, development, and understanding how characters interact with the world. I remind the students to speak to each other in character as much as possible. I don't require (or even recommend) voice acting here, just that they consider what their characters know, how they think, how they feel, and how that influences their dialogue and thought processes. I don't police the exercise tightly, but I do sometimes have to remind them to think about how they are approaching it. After a few minutes, I throw in a new wrinkle or dynamic. A guard, for example, has entered the area, or perhaps they hear screaming somewhere. They are role-playing in this exercise, but they're also investing time and energy into considering how their characters think, feel, act and react. I do my best to answer questions and guide them along the way (writers, I've found, have a knack for pushing the boundaries, which is great here), but ultimately the exercise is asking them to form an emotional and mental bond with this character, and explore how it affects thought, feelings, dialogue, and problem solving.

The success of this particular activity is not only its analytical frameworks and approaches, but also the sheer joy of it for the students. There's almost always laughter involved as the various unpredictable real-time solutions come forth, and while they're not all realistic or, strictly speaking, practicable within the system as I've set it up, in some ways, that has very little to no impact on the exercise itself. The students have the opportunity to learn just as much about their specific characters, and in turn how character functions within a story, but also about themselves and the ways in which they not only approach problem solving but also (if I've done my job correctly and followed through after) how they think about character.

In the before-and-after comparison that accompanies the gradual understanding of effectiveness in my pedagogy and approach, I have observed that these exercises have altered student approach to reading and analyzing characters in the texts we engage. There is a palpable change in empathetic understanding as expressed in classroom discussion following the self-character class, as well as a desire to push the exploration and inquiry to previously unexplored avenues of thought. I believe these two things to be especially valuable for young writers to engage with as they move forward with their creative process. While I have no quantitative data of value (only volunteer informal student polls), the fairly obvious change in engagement, and in turn production and quality of character exploration and development is easily observed in not only the classroom interactions of students, but ultimately their thought processes, and in turn their writing.

I most often use *Dungeons & Dragons* as my example system not necessarily because I consider it to be in some way superior to other systems, but because it is the most commonly recognized and played, and often grants easy access (at least as an idea or cultural phenomenon) to students who might otherwise feel ostracized or overwhelmed when it comes to interacting with RPGs. That said, I have used, with similar (and sometimes greater) success, a number of other TTRPG systems for a wide variety of course utility, particularly for compare and contrast analyses, research materials, or just as venues to further explore the genre in terms of both systems and how they apply to our learning objectives and assignments. It is not the particular system that necessarily matters (though I do think the particulars of the system matter, such as narrative emphasis vs "crunch" or simulation), but rather that it is a system at all, and that it involves playing a character within a set of rules and a world to describe them.

FURTHER CONSIDERATIONS AND REFLECTIONS

The previously outlined student activities are day-to-day operations; they are commonplace and easy to make connections with. While many students have expressed feeling as though their studies are an abstraction, or in some way distant from those thing they are interested or invested in on regular basis, these systems, games, and exercises are ways in which we as educators have an opportunity to bring complex curricular demands, in-depth analytical thought processes, and iterative potential practices to our pedagogy and classroom approaches, and further have a chance to bridge whatever real or imagined gaps exist between academia and the day-to-day lives of our students, and ourselves.

Tabletop RPGs are systems our students are often already familiar with, or at least familiar with the idea of. They engage concepts and ideas that have infiltrated pop culture and reflect some non-insignificant percentage of our media consumption. They allow us access to practices and problems which might, if utilized constructively, afford students new ways to hone their respective crafts, interact with and understand one another and the world at large, and give a relatively safe space from which to risk making mistakes in those realms.

I remember a presentation at one of the Association of Writers & Writing Programs conferences I attended about techniques some successful writers have used in order to explore how characters grow, become three dimensional, and navigate problems. They included things like putting the character into conflict situations and asking them how they'd navigate them or imagining them encountering ordinary surprises and stresses and observing their reactions. RPGs give students and writers a chance to practice exactly these things and give us a structure by which we can navigate them efficiently and uniformly, which is useful for teaching in a group setting. The classroom offers an exceptional environment for tabletop RPG as a tool for essentially unlimited exploration of character, utilizing a system which grants access not only to the creation process, but also growth, arc, depth, and the development of characters that feel, think, and act as real people might, all in service to a larger narrative.

REFERENCES

Armstrong, Paul B. 2020. *Stories and the Brain: The Neuroscience of Narrative*. Baltimore, MD: Johns Hopkins University Press.

Bopp, Julia Ayumi, Livia J. Müller, Lena F. Aeschbach, Klaus Opwis, and Elisa D. Mekler. 2019. "Exploring Emotional Attachment to Game Characters." In *Proceedings of the Annual Symposium on Computer-Human Interaction in Play (CHI PLAY '19)*, 313–324. New York: Association for Computing Machinery. https://doi.org/10.1145/3311350.3347169.

Cole, Alayna M., Dakoda J. Barker, and Jessica Zammit. 2017. "Impossible Identities: The Limitations of Character Creation Systems." Extended abstract, Authors & Digital Games Research Association (DiGRA). UniSC Research Bank, University of the Sunshine Coast.

Corbett, David. 2019. *The Compass of Character: Creating Complex Motivation for Compelling Characters in Fiction, Film, and TV*. Cincinnati, OH: Writer's Digest Books (Penguin Random House).

Cragoe, Nicholas G. 2016. "RPG Mythos: Narrative Gaming as Modern Mythmaking." *Games and Culture* 11 (6): 583–607. https://doi.org/10.1177/1555412015574195.

Fextralife. 2023. "Baldur's Gate 3 Best Race: Which Race Is Best for Your Class?" *YouTube video*, 16:21, August 4, 2023. https://www.youtube.com/watch?v=BCj2s0hcTXs.

Harrell, D. Fox, and Sneha Veeragoudar Harrell. 2012. "Imagination, Computation, and Self-Expression: Situated Character and Avatar Mediated Identity." *Leonardo Electronic Almanac* 17 (2): 74–91. (DAC09: After Media: Embodiment and Context)

Lacy, Ken Nozaki. 2006. *Narrative and Identity in Fantasy Role-Playing Games*. PhD diss., New York University. ProQuest.

Mallon, Bride, and Ronan Lynch. 2014. "Stimulating Psychological Attachments in Narrative Games: Engaging Players with Game Characters." *Simulation & Gaming* 45 (4–5): 508–527. https://doi.org/10.1177/1046878114553572.

Mehl-Madrona, Lewis, and Barbara Mainguy. 2022. "Neuroscience and Narrative." *Anthropology of Consciousness* 33 (1): 79–95. https://doi.org/10.1111/anoc.12144.

Pelican, Kira-Anne. 2020. *The Science of Writing Characters: Using Psychology to Create Compelling Fictional Characters*. New York: Bloomsbury Academic.

Vermeule, Blakey. 2011. *Why Do We Care About Literary Characters?* Baltimore, MD: Johns Hopkins University Press.

PART IV

Critical Encounters

Games That Challenge and Change

CHAPTER 8

Distributed Role-Play

A Proposed Game Mechanic for Exploring Difficult Social Concepts

Caleb Probst

INTRODUCTION

The pedagogic reasons for using role-play in a classroom are as diverse as the teachers who do it. A growing body of research suggests that games and play can be effective tools for understanding concepts, developing personal identity, fostering collaboration, and building healthy and just communities (e.g., Abdul Jabbar & Felicia, 2015; Bers, 2001; Gee, 2004; Gilliam et al., 2018; Squire, 2021). By facilitating the exploration of other people's perspectives, traditional role-play activities can create powerful learning opportunities in these areas. However, their use in teaching challenging topics dealing with oppression or violence is controversial. While writing this chapter, I did a web search for news stories about teachers using role-play to explore difficult histories. In short order, I found examples of teachers from four different US states—Indiana, Georgia, New York, and Wisconsin—who faced severe backlash to their instructional decisions (Chapman & Brown, 2018; Herron, 2019; Martin, 2017; Rahman, 2021). It is harder to find examples of these activities going well, but they certainly exist (e.g., Schweber, 2003). The pursuit of authentic experiential learning is a tantalizing endeavor, but it can lead some teachers to overlook

DOI: 10.1201/9781003641384-13

the potential for role-playing to cause unnecessary discomfort or harm to students. In this chapter, I introduce distributed role-play as an alternative pedagogic strategy to traditional role-play. I then use findings from a case study of students playing a game about sexual consent to suggest that distributed role-play can be a helpful play mechanic in designing games that safely facilitate critical exploration of difficult social concepts.

BACKGROUND: PROMISES AND PROBLEMS WITH ROLE-PLAYING SEXUAL CONSENT

The literature around what adolescents and emerging adults think about sexual consent, though sparse, shows two things. First, young people can often correctly articulate what school policies say about how intimate and sexual relationships should look (e.g., Lofgreen et al., 2017; Williamson et al., 2023). The phrase "a sober *yes*" comes to mind for many of them. Second, undergraduate students tend to believe that their schools' consent policies do not present a realistic guide for how to conduct oneself while hooking up with another person (e.g., Curtis & Burnett, 2017). Therefore, while students may possess declarative knowledge of consent (i.e., they know what it is), they seem to lack procedural knowledge (i.e., they do not know how to do it). Thus, there is a need for teaching young people some know-how when it comes to engaging in consensual sexual activity.

It is likely obvious to readers that adults providing practical instruction to young people on how to have sex presents an array of concerns. I am not advocating for educators to violate their personal or professional ethics. In fact, I am suggesting quite the opposite. The vast majority of parents, regardless of their political ideology, want their children to receive comprehensive sex education, and they want it to include practical information about healthy relationships and sexual consent (Kantor & Levitz, 2017). Students want to learn this information as well (Astle et al., 2021). Parents and caretakers, however, often struggle to effectively communicate these topics with their children (Flores & Barroso, 2017). Teachers, therefore, have an opportunity to take up this mantle in a thoughtful and professional way.

Simulation and role-play are tools that educators who teach social-emotional learning can use to help students develop the skills needed to establish healthy relationships (e.g., Cassie, 2022; Schrier, 2022). The topics of such interventions often include how to set personal boundaries and resolve conflict with other people. They do not, however, tend to involve acting out the negotiations of an imagined sexual encounter. Young people can certainly apply these interpersonal communication skills to their navigations of sexual intimacy; learning scientists would call this *transfer*. However, researchers have observed that transferring knowledge to a novel situation can sometimes be difficult for students, especially when the superficial features do not resemble what they saw in class (Bassok & Holyoak, 1989). Thus, it seems dubious to assume that what students learn about boundary setting from role-playing non-sexual scenarios will consistently transfer to sexual ones.

Whether it is part of a tabletop game or a live-action role-play (larp), traditional role-playing generally involves individual players choosing to embody individual characters; the player-to-character ratio is one-to-one. This can provide a wealth of learning opportunities for people because they adopt the perspective of their characters and experience—to varying degrees—the social, emotional, and psychological consequences of their choices (Hromek & Roffey, 2009). Participating in such explorations within the confines of a fictional game world yields a learning environment that is often safer than the everyday world. Everyone stays alive during a medical role-play, for example, even if players fail to enact proper treatment.

While game worlds may be safer, that does not mean they are always entirely safe. Well-designed and facilitated role-plays have the power to be transformational (Bowman & Hugaas, 2019), but that same power can make them abusive if they are run poorly (Wright-Maley, 2014). As such, scholars and activists do not agree whether games and simulations are appropriate for teaching difficult issues involving the violation of human rights. The Anti-Defamation League, for instance, strongly discourages simulating events relating to the Holocaust, suggesting they over-simplify the atrocities and reinforce stereotypes (Anti-Defamation League, 2016). Schweber (2003) is also generally skeptical that Holocaust simulation is an effective pedagogic strategy, but she writes about one remarkable classroom-based role-play that prevents her from shutting the door on the idea completely.

In their criticism of role-playing through difficult issues, scholars like Schweber raise several important questions. Why role-play? What is learned by exploring violence in a game? Who benefits and who is harmed? Developing students' empathy for people who have experienced violence is often regarded as an important learning outcome of role-play activities. However, empathy alone may not bring about the positive social changes for which so many educators hope (Boler, 1997). As such, teachers who invite students to explore a topic like the history of American slavery through role-play should think deeply about how students, particularly students of color, will experience the game. They should critically consider whether the learning outcomes for some students are worth the potential harm to others. Games compress damaging impacts (Schrier, 2015). Using role-play to compress historic abuses of human rights can traumatize the participants or minimize the gravity of the event. Neither of these outcomes is acceptable. However, mediating something as unbearable as slavery or sexual violence through a game can make it just tolerable enough to meaningfully explore and then critically discuss (Mortensen & Jørgensen, 2020).

In creating a role-play game to meaningfully teach a concept like sexual consent, designers must contend with several challenges. First, exploring sexual consent will almost certainly involve exploring aspects of sexual violence. It therefore becomes necessary to consider the impact of *bleed* on players. This phenomenon occurs "when feelings, thoughts, emotions, physical states, cognitive constructs, aspects of personality, and similar 'bleed over' from player to character or vice versa" (Hugaas, 2024, p. 13). This could result in players discovering something about conducting healthy sexual relationships that they will use in their lives after the game. However, it could also activate past trauma. The former would be a positive outcome of role-playing, whereas the latter would not.

Taking care to avoid traumatizing players is an ethical concern for designers, but that does not mean they must avoid negative or uncomfortable experiences altogether. Experiencing the consequences of inappropriate choices is part of the social/emotional learning process. By designing for—and later facilitating with—*play-external seriousness* (Jørgensen, 2014), those who create educational role-play games about difficult or controversial topics can provide participants with the opportunity to engage reflectively with the content. This can result in what Montola (2010) describes as a *positive negative experience*, where a superficially unpleasant event leads to a deeply meaningful outcome. The participants in Montola's study were "gamers...convinced of the value of non-fun games," who role-played extreme sexual violence. There are differences in design considerations, however, when a role-play is intended for leisure versus when it is meant for education (see Westborg, 2023). If a role-play game is to be used for educational purposes, it needs to be able to safely facilitate positive negative experiences for all kinds of players—even those resistant to role-play and non-fun games.

DEFINING DISTRIBUTED ROLE-PLAY

To balance the transformational learning opportunities of role-play games with their potential to cause harm to players, I propose a design mechanic I am calling *distributed role-play*. Distributing role-play in games intended to teach learners about difficult issues can serve to mitigate some of the harms associated with game-world experiences and their potential to bleed into players' ordinary lives. This is distinct from a "distributed role" described elsewhere in literature on educational role-play, where a player takes on a role that is very different from their own lived experience (Kot, 2012). For example, a legal intern role-playing as a named partner in a law firm during a workplace training would be taking on a distributed role. By contrast, the role-play itself can be distributed when, like cognition (Hutchins, 1993) and instruction (Halverson et al., 2015), the act is stretched across "people, tools, and task" (Hutchins, 1993, p. 37). The result is a role-play situation in which there is not a one-to-one relationship between players and characters, because multiple players are acting as a single character. Distributed role-play games spread the task of character decision-making, as well as the effects of ensuing consequences, across multiple players.

A CASE STUDY OF *THE HOOK UP GAME*

Distributed role-play is the primary game mechanic in *The Hook Up Game* (Probst, 2023). I designed this game with a collaborator based on a decade of experience as a sexual consent educator. As part of our process, we consulted with sexual assault prevention experts, and we incorporated feedback from adolescent play-testers. My colleague and I grounded our decisions in the learning theories of constructionism (Papert, 1980) and transformational play (Barab et al., 2010).

Game Design

The Hook Up Game is a cooperative social game; players succeed or fail together. The goal is to work as a group to construct a story of a hook-up that is safe and pleasurable for the characters. This resembles what Grasmo and Stenros (2022) call a "story-telling erotic roleplay," in which players *agree* on the diegetic actions from outside the narrative itself. Groups of four to eight players create the story of a sexual encounter through their distributed role-play of two characters' intimate interactions. At the start of the game, players choose two characters, a setting (e.g., library, car, party, and dorm room), and a backstory describing the moments before the story (e.g., studying together, on a date, and watching a movie). The characters have their own personal desires and boundaries, and they must communicate these to each other to ensure their interactions are consensual.

The characters communicate with each other through actions and dialogue chosen by the players. Each player holds five action cards (e.g., "Caresses partner's face" and "Kisses partner") and five dialogue cards (e.g., "I'm super into you," "I'm not into this," and "Is this cool?") in their hand at all times. They also have an option to create their own actions or dialogue for a character by writing on blank cards. Players take turns placing cards describing their characters' actions and dialogue on the table (see Figure 8.1), reading them in-character as they do so. This serves to *adjust* the sexual intensity of the role-play (Grasmo & Stenros, 2022) to a level appropriate to educational settings (i.e., no physical contact between players), while maintaining a realistic story. The use of cards also provides a way to scaffold the role-play during the game; players can individually choose the degree to which they want to embody the characters.

This kind of role-play brings players, their content knowledge of sexual consent, and the context in which they apply it into a dynamic relationship. Players become invested in the characters because they have agency over the direction of the story, which can be transformational (Barab et al., 2010). As the story evolves, what *yes* looks like may shift and become more contextual. This creates the possibility of a character violating the other character's boundaries, perhaps unintentionally. For example, it would not be consensual for a character to take off their own shirt after the other character has said, "I want to keep our clothes on." Each player has a Whoa There! card to use if something like this happens. If someone holds up a Whoa There! card, the game pauses, and players discuss the situation. As a group, players must agree on how to revise the story (e.g., replacing the offending card with another) to make it consensual.

The game ends after 20 minutes or when the story is complete, whichever comes first. Limiting the time is a trauma-informed design feature that allows players to know exactly how long the game will take (McInerney & McKlindon, 2014). By the end of the game, players have

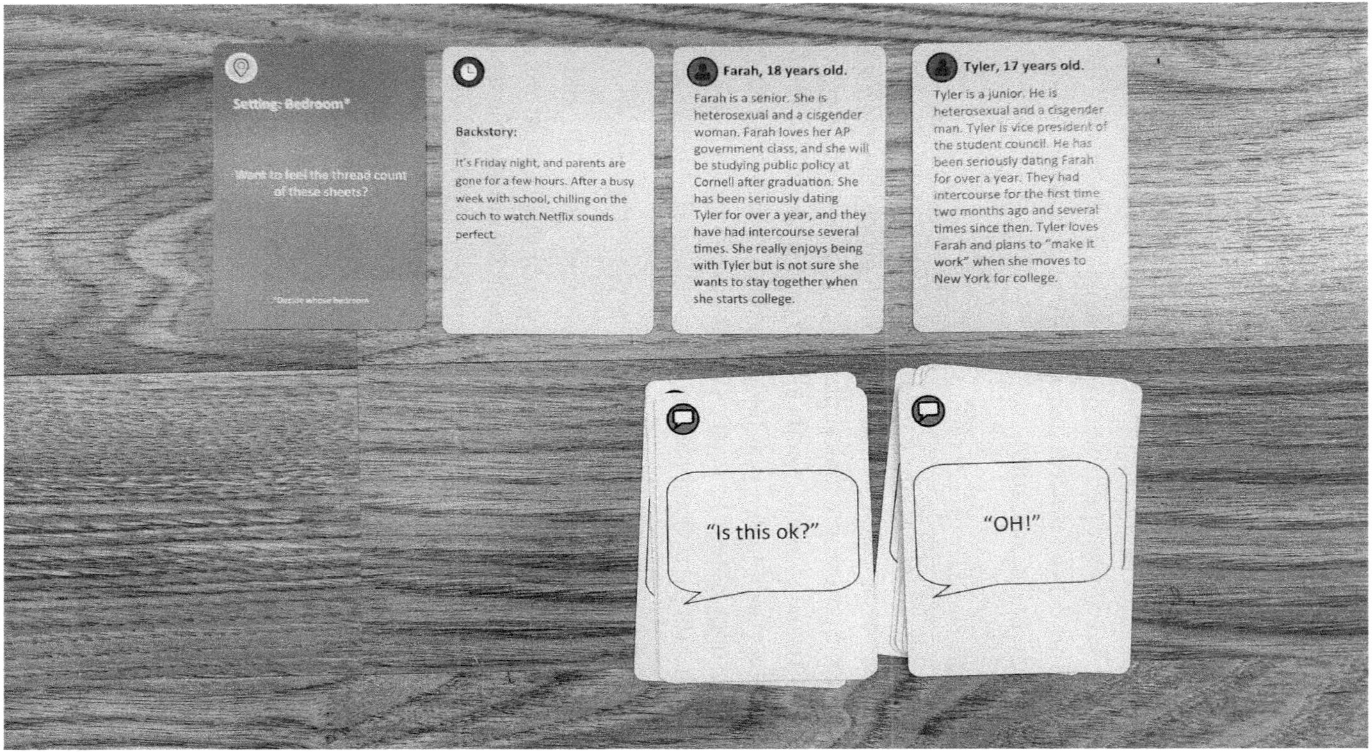

FIGURE 8.1 *The Hook Up Game* in progress. Photograph by the author.

created numerous interactions between characters, thus constructing a nuanced story they can use to think about sexual consent. The action and dialogue cards enable players to role-play intimate interactions between characters, creating sexual encounters that are authentic and specific. The game therefore provides space to explore the difficult social concept of sexual consent in context, rather than in abstraction. During the post-game discussion, facilitated by a consent educator, players talk about their story, what parts were consensual, and how they felt during the game. This debrief process helps solidify the transformational learning (Bowman & Hugaas, 2019).

METHODS

To examine the potential affordances of distributed role-play, I conducted an instrumental case study (Stake, 2000) with people playing *The Hook Up Game*. The purpose was to look at players' interactions while exploring the concept of sexual consent, specifically, to gain insights into the possibilities of exploring difficult social topics through distributed role-play generally. In groups of four to seven, 40 participants played the game seven times, with each participant playing once.

Participants

Most participants were undergraduate students (n = 34), and a few of the participants were graduate students (n = 6). All of them were at least 18 years old and affiliated with a large university in the United States. To recruit participants, I made short presentations about the study to four different university classes, and I asked for volunteers to write their email addresses on a signup sheet. The participants in each group knew each other from the class they had together, and some also appeared to be friends outside of school. I knew some of the participants from passing them on campus, but I was neither a colleague nor a course instructor for any of them at the time of the study.

Study Site

The participants played *The Hook Up Game* and discussed their experiences in a private study lounge in a building on campus. The room's privacy protected the players from the gaze of others who were not part of the game. I arranged the chairs and couches around a large coffee table and provided snacks. I did this to create the comfortable atmosphere of a game night, hopefully mitigating some of the unseen influences of being in a university space.

Data Collection

Before beginning gameplay, I verbally explained the study to everyone. I told them I was interested in observing them play *The Hook Up Game* and hearing them talk about it afterwards. The university Institutional Review Board (IRB) exempted this study, so it was not necessary for participants to provide written consent. However, in explaining the study, I made clear that participation was voluntary. Because of the sensitive nature of the game's content, I also provided information for university resources related to mental health and sexual assault. Finally, I explained that the gameplay would last 20 minutes, and that I would then facilitate a 40-minute post-game discussion.

During gameplay, I remained largely silent. If participants asked questions about the game, I would answer them. I did not, however, serve as a facilitator or gamemaster. In the post-game discussion, I conducted a semi-structured group interview. I began by asking the participants to summarize the characters' actions. I then asked them to describe which ones they thought were consensual and which ones were not. I ended by asking them to talk about how the story they had constructed related to broader aspects of society and culture.

I made video recordings of each gameplay session and post-game discussion using a single camera in the corner of the room. This captured what participants said, their vocal intonations, and gestures. From these recordings, I made two transcripts. The first described what the participants said and did, and the second described what was on each card they played during the game.

Data Analysis

I analyzed these data utilizing principles of video analysis (Derry et al., 2010) and interaction analysis (Jordan & Henderson, 1995). I watched the videos multiple times, pausing them to take notes on how participants engaged with the game, its content, and one another. These observations were brief (i.e., less than one minute) and closely tied to the observable video content. I then generated analytic memos from these observations. Finally, I inductively coded the transcripts and memos, looking for common themes between the ways participants interacted across the different groups.

FINDINGS

The findings show that players nearly always discussed the characters' actions using third-person language. To begin the post-game discussion, I would ask, "Can someone summarize what happened in the story you just made?" A player from one group said, "*They* seemed to be off all night" when describing the interactions between the two characters he role-played with the group. Someone from another group said, "*She* might have felt pressured," rather than something like "*I* felt pressured."

When I asked participants to describe character interactions as consensual or not, they rarely referenced an individual player's contribution. For example, one player said, "*We* seemed to struggle," referring to the whole group having a hard time explicitly communicating boundaries and desires for their characters. Similarly, when players wanted to discuss an action from the game that was not consensual, they generally assigned responsibility for it to the character and not the player.

An Example of Distributed Impact

While it is possible that creating distance between players and characters and removing a sense of personal accountability for specific choices could inhibit individual player's personal learning, Alex[1] provides an example to the contrary. Alex was part of a group role-playing the characters *Erin* and *Matty*. The character card stated that *Erin* did not want to get fully naked during the encounter, and the players worked together to explicitly communicate this boundary. One player used a dialogue card that said, "I want to keep our underwear on" and another used a card that said, "Just hands, ok?" Later in the game, Alex played an action card for *Matty* to "forcefully remove" *Erin's* underwear, a clear violation of the previously established boundary.

Three players quickly held up their Whoa There! cards, and Alex's shoulders immediately slouched. As the group engaged in a spirited discussion about whether the card should remain in play, Alex laid his cards on the table and stared at the floor. He said very little to explain or defend his choice, instead choosing to remain quiet with his eyes cast down for 45 seconds—a substantial portion of a game lasting only 20 minutes. Alex seemed to continue processing the consequences of his action card long after the rest of the group decided to continue the game. He avoided eye contact with the other players for nearly two minutes. Eddie eventually cracked a joke that made everyone laugh, at which point Alex began interacting with other players again.

While discussing the game afterwards, the group talked about this moment extensively. Carla initiated the conversation by saying the "removes underwear part was pretty rough." Alex chuckled sheepishly and nodded. He then listened quietly while the other players shared their thoughts about that part of their game. As they did so, each talked about the characters *Matty* and *Erin*, not the player Alex. They discussed when, if, and how boundaries can be renegotiated during a sexual encounter, as well as ways to consensually navigate "rough" sex. Throughout these conversations, nobody seemed to make Alex feel directly attacked. When Alex decided to explain his choice, he said, "I saw it as passionate, but yes… it [was] against consent." Carla responded, "It would have been better if it said *passionately*." Alex responded, "True. True." He later said that playing the game had shown him some of the social complexities inherent to sexual encounters that he had not previously considered. Perhaps to show that she held no hard feelings, Carla told Alex: "That's what this is all about, right?"

Not Consensual, but "Pretty Accurate"

Another group also constructed a story of sexual assault during their playthrough. Seven undergraduate women created a hook-up between a fraternity member named *Trevor* and a first-year student named *Mariana*. It was not consensual. *Mariana* did not want to have intercourse but was open to oral sex. The participants found ways for her to explicitly express this boundary several times. They used dialogue cards like "What if I just go down on you?" and "I don't want to go all the way." At the same time, however, they played cards that created manipulative responses from *Trevor*. He seemed intent on extracting a "yes" from *Mariana*. This closely follows the typical sexual script of a man persuading a woman to agree to sex after she has refused (Hust et al., 2017). *Trevor* then got *Mariana* drunk, and she vomited. When *Trevor* asked explicitly for sex at this point, *Mariana* said "yes" and put a condom on *Trevor*. The two characters then had sex in the bathroom of fraternity house during a party.

The group role-playing *Trevor* and *Mariana* was distinct from the others who played the game; all the members were cisgender women. This was the only group without gender diversity. Each of the players took turns creating *Trevor's* violating behaviors, as well as the range of *Mariana's* responses. They gasped and giggled as their story unfolded, seeming to be both shocked and titillated by what they were doing. No one played a Whoa There! card, and unlike Alex, no one seemed to feel personally responsible for the violence unfolding in their story. When the game ended, the women reflected on what had transpired.

While discussing this story filled with sexual violation, the group agreed it was not consensual. However, Cynthia said "most girls in her situation wouldn't say, 'I was raped last night.' They would just say, 'well we were both drunk' and try to forget about it." Several members said they should have used their Whoa There! cards more often, but Elizabeth lamented "we just treat this like it's normal." Allison agreed, adding that their story of a college hook-up was "pretty accurate, unfortunately." As they reflected on the game, they seemed to have personal distance from the characters, but they were not disconnected from the story. The women talked about the fraternity party as if they had all been there with the characters. They were disgusted with *Trevor.* "He has a girlfriend!" "He just cheated on her with a girl who was trying to wait for marriage!" They felt bad for *Mariana*. "She said 'no,' but then she said 'yes,' but she was so drunk… This is something that can be very, very confusing." The players also said *Mariana's* friends let her down. "They thought she was fine," but "they weren't on top of it."

This group's debrief was qualitatively different from the others. Whereas Alex's group, for example, used their time to discuss a moment of harm that happened in the game, the women in this group used the game to think about their own experiences at college parties. They completed each other's sentences and knowingly nodded whenever someone made a connection between the game and campus life. Allison said, "this happens to a lot of people," and Danielle added, "it's more common than you think." The room became somber. Given how commonplace the women believed this story to be, I asked about their university's sexual consent education. Danielle said, "This [situation] is too nuanced… This isn't something that's talked about [during the consent workshops]."

DISCUSSION

Talking about sexual consent in a meaningful way can be difficult. Research suggests that most young people do not believe the formal education they receive on the subject is very helpful, and the participants in this study confirmed this. One reason for this, as Danielle explained, is that conversations about consent need to be nuanced if they are to be useful. Traditional role-play offers young people opportunities for this. However, the intensity created by individually embodying characters involved in such an intimate—and possibly violent—situation makes this a risky proposition.

In developing *The Hook Up Game*, my co-designer and I sought to create a game mechanic that could mitigate some of the harms associated with bleed, while maintaining some of the other affordances of traditional role-play. Based on an analysis of player interactions during and after the game, it appears that distributing role-play activity across the group helped to create distance between players and characters. They referred to the characters in third person—rather than first person. They also took collective responsibility for the narrative actions (e.g., "We seemed to struggle…"), or they held the characters—not individual players—responsible. It seems individual players had an *alibi* "that deflect[ed] negative inference[s] from displayed behavior to [their] identity" (Deterding, 2017, p. 268) while maintaining the *play-external seriousness*. Players like Alex, Carla, and the seven undergraduate women appeared to have meaningful and possibly transformational experiences, without needing to leave the game.

Alex offers a nearly ideal example of what we had hoped distributed role-play could provide to game-based pedagogies for teaching difficult social concepts. Had he enacted his in-game choice with an actual romantic partner, he would have violated her explicitly communicated boundary. Had he made his in-game choice during a traditional role-play, where individual players embody individual characters, the impact of his action on the other player would have been intense and could have been traumatizing. The distance between player and character appears to have mitigated this potential for harm, without diluting the experience too much. By playing the game, Alex had a powerful learning opportunity that he may not have otherwise had. Based on my time working in sexual assault prevention, people who have experienced sexual violation do not often want to explain it to their former partners.

Indeed, social justice activists have long held it should not be the responsibility of those who experience systemic harm to teach people in power about oppression. The young woman assaulted at a college party should not be expected to explain the complexities of gender-based violence to the members of a campus fraternity. The Black teen surveilled and harassed by a police officer while walking to school should not have to explain the history of American racism to his fellow students. Traditional role-play games designed to grapple with difficult issues can sometimes fall into the trap of positioning learners from minoritized backgrounds as critical educators. However, interacting with people from marginalized groups and learning from their experiences have been shown to change attitudes, resulting in public policy reforms. Rapid increase in support for gay rights and same-sex marriage provides one recent example of this (Lee & Mutz, 2019).

Distributed role-play provides designers and educators with a tool to balance the competing perspectives on creating role-plays that deal with difficult social concepts. *The Hook Up Game* gave Alex space to learn from his mistake by showing him the effects of his decision from multiple perspectives. However, by distributing the impact of his choice across the entire group, no individual player had to fully embody the harm of an imagined sexual violation. Further, Alex learned something about sexual violation without someone who had experienced it having to explain it to him.

Distributed role-play offered a different opportunity to the seven women who role-played *Trevor's* assault of *Mariana*: the permission to be subversive. Distributing *Trevor's* choices across the entire group appears to have relieved each of them of personal responsibility for his actions. This allowed them to construct a fictional hook-up that clearly violated their university consent education. The result, however, was a story that each of them recognized as "pretty accurate, unfortunately." What they specifically learned about consent is difficult to see, because they already understood they were playing out a story of manipulation and violence. It is beyond the scope of this study to debate whether this constitutes learning, but the sober tone of their debrief suggests that it was meaningful.

LIMITATIONS AND FUTURE RESEARCH

To the best of my knowledge, scholars have not widely investigated distributed role-play as a design mechanic. The above case study offers a glimpse into its potential for facilitating experiential learning of difficult issues in a safe way. Most participants did not discuss personal experiences with sexual violation, and no one disclosed whether prior traumas had been reactivated while playing. Thus, I do not intend to make definitive claims about the protective nature of this game mechanic.

Furthermore, this was a qualitative case study; I did not conduct a controlled experiment. As such, I am not implying a causal relationship between distributed role-play and participant experiences. I am an individual researcher who brought his individual experiences to the analysis. It is possible that another researcher would have highlighted other things and made other conclusions. However, my life experience includes ten years of facilitating sexual consent education workshops and conversations with more than 10,000 high school and college students. I have seen what it looks like for students to struggle to recognize the perspectives of someone who has experienced sexual violation; I have seen what happens when an activity activates prior trauma. So, while I do not want to suggest that distributed role-play is the definitive solution to these problems, the findings from this study indicate that further research into distributed role-play and learning difficult social concepts could be fruitful.

CONCLUSION

Exploring challenging subject matter like sexual violation or systemic oppression through role-play can be controversial. The positive negative experience can lead to deep learning and transformational outcomes, but it comes with a risk that in-game harms will bleed out into players' lives. This can happen for people on either side of the diegetic violence. As such, educators should critically consider the benefits and costs of incorporating role-play into their pedagogy around such topics.

This study of players' experiences with distributed role-play in *The Hook Up Game* offers a new possibility for real-world violence to be safely examined through games. During this study, 13 people across two groups role-played stories of sexual violation. Afterward, they discussed the perspectives of the characters involved in a deep and nuanced manner. The students reflected on their experiences in the game and connected them to their lives outside. Alex, Carla, and the seven undergraduate women show us the opportunities that exist for distributed role-play in games about difficult social topics to have a meaningful impact. Perhaps, designers and educators can use this mechanic to help students develop the knowledge they will need to construct a more just and equitable world.

NOTE

1 All participants are identified by pseudonyms.

REFERENCES

Abdul Jabbar, A. I., & Felicia, P. (2015). Gameplay Engagement and Learning in Game-Based Learning: A Systematic Review. *Review of Educational Research, 85*(4), 740–779. https://doi.org/10.3102/0034654315577210

Anti-Defamation League. (2016). *Holocaust Education: Why Simulation Activities Should Not Be Used* (p. 2). Anti-Defamation League. https://echoesandreflections.org/wp-content/uploads/2018/07/WhySimulationActivitiesShouldNotBeUsed-1.pdf

Astle, S., McAllister, P., Emanuels, S., Rogers, J., Toews, M., & Yazedjian, A. (2021). College Students' Suggestions for Improving Sex Education in Schools beyond 'blah blah blah Condoms and STDs.' *Sex Education, 21*(1), 91–105. https://doi.org/10.1080/14681811.2020.1749044

Barab, S. A., Gresalfi, M., & Ingram-Goble, A. (2010). Transformational Play: Using Games to Position Person, Content, and Context. *Educational Researcher, 39*(7), 525–536.

Bassok, M., & Holyoak, K. J. (1989). Interdomain Transfer between Isomorphic Topics in Algebra and Physics. *Journal of Experimental Psychology: Learning, Memory, and Cognition, 15*(1), 153–166. https://doi.org/10.1037/0278-7393.15.1.153

Bers, M. U. (2001). Identity Construction Environments: Developing Personal and Moral Values through the Design of a Virtual City. *Journal of the Learning Sciences, 10*(4), 365–415.

Boler, M. (1997). The Risks of Empathy: Interrogating Multiculturalism's Gaze. *Cultural Studies, 11*(2), 253–273. https://doi.org/10.1080/09502389700490141

Bowman, S. L., & Hugaas, K. H. (2019, December 10). Transformative Role-Play: Design, Implementation, and Integration. *Nordic Larp*. https://nordiclarp.org/2019/12/10/transformative-role-play-design-implementation-and-integration/

Cassie, J. (2022). Don't Split the Party: Using Games to Enhance Social-Emotional Learning Strategies. In D. Seelow (Ed.), *Teaching in the Game-Based Classroom* (pp. 114–120). Routledge.

Chapman, B., & Brown, S. R. (2018, December 12). EXCLUSIVE: City Fires Bronx 'Slave' Teacher – New York Daily News. *Daily News*. https://www.nydailynews.com/2018/10/19/exclusive-city-fires-bronx-slave-teacher/

Curtis, J. N., & Burnett, S. (2017). Affirmative Consent: What Do College Student Leaders Think About "Yes Means Yes" as the Standard for Sexual Behavior? *American Journal of Sexuality Education, 12*(3), 201–214. https://doi.org/10.1080/15546128.2017.1328322

Derry, S. J., Pea, R. D., Barron, B., Engle, R. A., Erickson, F., Goldman, R., Hall, R., Koschmann, T., Lemke, J. L., Sherin, M. G., & Sherin, B. L. (2010). Conducting Video Research in the Learning Sciences: Guidance on Selection, Analysis, Technology, and Ethics. *Journal of the Learning Sciences*, *19*(1), 3 53. https://doi.org/10.1080/10508400903452884

Deterding, S. (2017). Alibis for Adult Play: A Goffmanian Account of Escaping Embarrassment in Adult Play. *Games and Culture*, *13*(3), 260–279. https://doi.org/10.1177/1555412017721086

Flores, D., & Barroso, J. (2017). 21st Century Parent–Child Sex Communication in the United States: A Process Review. *Journal of Sex Research*, *54*, 532–548. https://doi.org/10.1080/00224499.2016.1267693

Gee, J. P. (2004). Learning by Design: Games as Learning Machines. *Interactive Educational Multimedia*, *8*, 15–23.

Gilliam, M., Jagoda, P., Jones, I. B., Rowley, J., & Hill, B. (2018). Embedded Game Design as a Method for Addressing Social Determinants of Health. *American Journal of Sexuality Education*, *13*(3), 378–398. https://doi.org/10.1080/15546128.2018.1445572

Grasmo, H., & Stenros, J. (2022). Nordic Erotic Larp: Designing for Sexual Playfulness. *International Journal of Role-Playing*, *12*, Article 12. https://doi.org/10.33063/ijrp.vi12.292

Halverson, E., Lowenhaupt, R., & Kalaitzidis, T. (2015). Towards a Theory of Distributed Instruction in Creative Arts Education. *Journal of Technology and Teacher Education*, *23*(3), 357–385.

Herron, A. (2019). Indiana Middle School Cancels "Slave Ship" Role-Play Less after Parents Raise Concerns. *IndyStar*. https://www.indystar.com/story/news/education/2019/09/09/indiana-westen-middle-school-howard-county-cancels-slave-ship-role-play-lesson/2234566001/

Hromek, R., & Roffey, S. (2009). Promoting Social and Emotional Learning with Games. *Simulation & Gaming*, *40*(5), 626–644. https://doi.org/10.1177/1046878109333793

Hugaas, K. H. (2024). Bleed and Identity: A Conceptual Model of Bleed and How Bleed-Out from Role-Playing Games Can Affect a Player's Sense of Self. *International Journal of Role-Playing*, *15*, Article 15. https://doi.org/10.33063/ijrp.vi15.323

Hust, S. J. T., Rodgers, K. B., & Bayly, B. (2017). Scripting Sexual Consent: Internalized Traditional Sexual Scripts and Sexual Consent Expectancies among College Students. *Family Relations: Interdisciplinary Journal of Applied Family Studies*, *66*, 197–210. https://doi.org/10.1111/fare.12230

Hutchins, E. (1993). Learning to navigate. In S. Chaiklin & J. Lave (Eds.), *Understanding Practice: Perspectives on Activity and Context* (pp. 35–63). Cambridge University Press.

Jordan, B., & Henderson, A. (1995). Interaction Analysis: Foundations and Practice. *Journal of the Learning Sciences*, *4*(1), 39–103.

Jørgensen, K. (2014). Devil's Plaything: On the boundary between playful and serious. *Proceedings of Nordic DiGRA 2014 Conference* (May 29–30, Visby, Gotland, Sweden). Digital Games Research Association.

Kantor, L., & Levitz, N. (2017). Parents' Views on Sex Education in Schools: How Much Do Democrats and Republicans Agree? *PLoS ONE*, *12*(7). https://doi.org/10.1371/journal.pone.0180250

Kot, Y. I. (2012). Educational Larp: Topics for Consideration. In S. L. Bowman & A. Vanek (Eds.), *Wyrd Con Companion* (pp. 118–127). Creative Commons.

Lee, H.-Y., & Mutz, D. C. (2019). Changing Attitudes toward Same-Sex Marriage: A Three-Wave Panel Study. *Political Behavior*, *41*, 701–722.

Lofgreen, A. M., Mattson, R. E., Wagner, S. A., Ortiz, E. G., & Johnson, M. D. (2017). Situational and Dispositional Determinants of College Men's Perception of Women's Sexual Desire and Consent to Sex: A Factorial Vignette Analysis. *Journal of Interpersonal Violence*, 1–34. https://doi.org/10.1177/0886260517738777

Martin, J. (2017, October 13). "You Are My Slave:" School's Civil War Day sparks mom's ire | AP News. *Associated Press*. https://apnews.com/article/f39d2500af6a44e48eab4c3297f999ca

McInerney, M., & McKlindon, A. (2014). *Unlocking the Door to Learning: Trauma-Informed Classrooms and Transformational Schools* (p. 24). Education Law Center.

Montola, M. (2010, January 1). The Positive Negative Experience in Extreme Role-Playing. *Proceedings of Nordic DiGRA 2010 Conference: Experiencing Games: Games, Play, and Players*. https://doi.org/10.26503/dl.v2010i1.500

Mortensen, T. E., & Jørgensen, K. (2020). *The Paradox of Transgression in Games*. Routledge.

Papert, S. (1980). *Mindstorms: Children, Computers, and Powerful Ideas*. Basic Books, Inc.

Probst, C. (2023). Narrative Construction Game as Consent Knowledge Assessment. In P. Blikstein, J. Van Aalst, R. Kizito, & K. Brennan (Eds.), *Proceedings of the 17th International Conference of the Learning Sciences-ICLS 2023* (pp. 1230–1233). https://doi.org/10.22318/icls2023.156665

Rahman, K. (2021, April 14). "How Will You Punish This Slave" Assignment Prompts Teachers' Resignation—Newsweek. *Newsweek*. https://www.newsweek.com/how-will-you-punish-this-slave-assignment-prompts-teachers-resignation-1583459

Schrier, K. (2015). Ethical Thinking and Sustainability in Role-Play Participants: A Preliminary Study. *Simulation & Gaming*, *46*(6), 673–696. https://doi.org/10.1177/1046878114556145

Schrier, K. (2022). Using Games for Empathy, Compassion, and Care. In D. Seelow (Eds.), *Teaching in the Game-Based Classroom* (pp. 136–150). Routledge.

Schweber, S. (2003). Simulating Survival. *Curriculum Inquiry*, *33*(2), 139–188.

Squire, K. (2021). *Making Games for Impact*. https://doi.org/10.7551/mitpress/12883.001.0001

Stake, R. E. (2000). Case Studies. In N. K. Denzin & Y. S. Lincoln (Eds.), *Handbook of Qualitative Research* (Second Edition, pp. 435–454). Sage Publications.

Westborg, J. (2023). The Educational Role-Playing Game Design Matrix: Mapping Design Components onto Types of Education. *International Journal of Role-Playing, 13*, Article 13. https://doi.org/10.33063/ijrp.vi13.306

Williamson, L., Bayly, M., Poncelet, E., & Lawson, K. (2023). A Qualitative Exploration of Undergraduate Student Perspectives of Sexual Consent within a Sexual Script Framework. *Canadian Journal of Human Sexuality, 32*(1), 39–50. https://doi.org/10.3138/cjhs.2021-0069

Wright-Maley, C. (2014). In Defense of Simulating Complex and Tragic Historical Episodes: A Measured Response to the Outcry Over a New England Slavery Simulation. *Canadian Social Studies, 47*(1), 18–25.

CHAPTER 9

Teaching Masculinities

The Transformative Potential of Blood Feud

Kristian A. Bjørkelo

INTRODUCTION

In a series of four managed play sessions of the GM-less role-playing game *Blood Feud* (Malmberg and Persson 2021), I observed how the mechanics of toxic masculinity are negotiated and experienced within "the magic circle" (Consalvo 2009; Stenros 2012). As a game scholar, situated in a feminist discourse and a dedicated university educator, I was drawn to *Blood Feud* for its transgressive potential (Mortensen and Jørgensen 2020). Reading the rules and playing the game I found that it had a remarkable focus on masculinity, which motivated reflective conversations for the players, and I decided to keep notes from play sessions. As a game, *Blood Feud* uses resource mechanics to motivate antagonistic and harmful behaviors among the player characters. This was to emulate the toxicity associated with aggressive and honor-based masculinity. It does not provide as much insight into Viking society and history as an understanding of the social rules and mechanics that govern masculinity and masculine behavior toward women, other men, society, and themselves. Throughout the game, the rules put the players in situations where their honor is constantly at stake. This leads to a fear of losing face in front of women and

DOI: 10.1201/9781003641384-14

other men in the many social conflicts that arise, and this fear motivates actions and reactions that can be characterized as toxic (Kupers 2005; Elliott 2018; Waling 2019; Harrington 2021).

Toxic masculinity as a term originates in feminist discourse as a way of suggesting male flaws, often without a clear definition (Harrington 2021). It could be understood as "the constellation of socially regressive male traits that serve to foster domination, the devaluation of women, homophobia, and wanton violence" (Kupers 2005, p. 714), and more simply, the socialized behavior of men that keep them pinned in a system that harm women, children, and the men themselves. Toxic masculinity is often seen as an important factor of, or reason for, violent extremism (Pearson 2019). Andrea Waling (2019) sees the use of toxic masculinity as a way "individualizing toxic/healthy binary that serves to reproduce gender hierarchies" (Harrington 2021, p. 347). In fact, there is reason to argue against the efficacy of using the term in academic concepts and research interviews as it does more to alienate the subjects and subject matter than to elucidate (Harrington 2021; Waling 2019). In this chapter, toxic masculinity is understood in the way portrayed by the game, as a way of performing masculinity that is about honor, power, and (violent) strength and dominance, which is harmful to both men and women, and includes misogyny and homophobia.

The underlying motivation of *Blood Feud* is to present the players with problematic aspects of masculinity, and it is after all tagged as a game about toxic masculinity. My first experiences playing the game at gaming conventions in 2021 and 2022 showed *Blood Feud*'s strength in teaching them what is meant by toxic masculinity and how this harms men as much as anyone else. Through fun and, at times, outrageously transgressive play, the players gained insights into the social contract that drove their fathers and male contemporaries, as the majority of the participants in these two games were teenage girls. *Blood Feud* also provided a source of laughter and spoofing of male stereotypes, a natural release of tension from what would otherwise be a serious subject. Seeing how well the game did this, was both a surprising and thought-provoking experience for myself and the other players, and my notes from these playthroughs motivated me to bring the game into an educational setting, and had me asking the question if *I could teach toxic masculinity through play*, and if *Blood Feud* was a game that could potentially *counteract harmful masculine behavior* through play?

Following up on the initial observations of play, I included the game as part of a six-hour seminar with graduate students taking a course in gender and technology that took place in the fall of both 2023 and 2024. After a class on toxic masculinity, they were given the rules to learn, and were then given an oral introduction to the game and its mechanics by me and my teaching assistants. The first class was divided into half a dozen groups of four players, who proceeded to play the game, creating their own unique scenarios and conflicts, diverging in tone and explicitness. The second class had ten groups of four players each.

Play sessions of *Blood Feud* are structured to be ended with a debrief session, where players discuss how the session was experienced, and how their notions of masculinity were part of it. This allowed for insights into how the different groups of players had approached and understood the subject matter, and provided ample opportunities for me to take notes both during the convention games and in the classroom. These debrief conversations, along with my notes from playing and observing the discussions after play, serve as the empirical foundation of this chapter.

TOXIC VIKING MASCULINITY

The tabletop role-playing game *Blood Feud* is partially inspired by the master thesis *The Making of a Man: The Hegemonic Masculinity of the Viking Age* (Sandquist 2012) by Siri Sandquist, who also served as a playtester for the game, providing a blurb for the back of the book. Her master thesis is a thorough review of academic literature on masculinity in the Viking age, based on archeology and sagas, she concludes that Viking masculinity was

> [...] shaped by complex codes of manly and unmanly behavior deriving from a need of separating oneself from children and women, and placing oneself in opposition to these categories.
>
> *(Sandquist 2012, p. 40)*

Masculinity is reliant on skills as a warrior (Raffield 2019) and the accumulation of wealth, as well as being hospitable and giving gifts. Furthermore, a proper man

> [...] could not show weakness or cry and you could not show fear. To die of old age or sickness was viewed as weak and homosexuality

> was demeaning since it meant that one was more of a woman than a man.
>
> *(Sandquist 2012, p. 40)*

Of course, a man would not practice magic or be involved in other "womanly" activities. These are familiar notions in modern conceptualizations of masculinity as well as Vikings, and these are traits that are often included in the understanding of toxic masculinity. Contemporary enactment of masculinity can seek legitimization in notions of past masculinities and ideas of the Viking and medieval era (Mayer 2019), perhaps most evident in personas like the American far-right political influencer Bronze Age Pervert (Prewitt 2021; Vandiver 2021) and the Swedish bodybuilding Neonazi YouTuber the Golden One.

However, it is important to keep in mind that the actual masculinities of the Viking age were both complex and nuanced, much like contemporary masculinities, and a product of social, cultural, economical, and technological contexts that changed over time (Skogstrand 2016), and

> [...] the significance of warrior ideals and notions of the unmanly in the construction of masculinity depended on the accessibility of the warrior role to most men and the actual freedom of choice and availability of other opportunities.
>
> *(Skogstrand 2016, p. 131)*

Meaning that Viking and Bronze Age masculinity were not just one thing, but myriad, and dependent on specific situations. However, contemporary imaginaries and medievalism have coded this masculinity as a particular kind of violent and tough masculinity that fits our imaginary of Viking warriors, which can be understood as toxic, as is the case with the masculinity presented in *Blood Feud*.

MEN DOING MEN IN THE "VIKING AGE"

Vikings are not a new topic in gaming (Lasausse 2024), and the Viking imaginary plays an important role in video games such as *Skyrim* (Bethesda Game Studios 2011), *Assassin's Creed: Valhalla* (Ubisoft Montreal 2020), *God of War: Ragnarök* (Santa Monica Studio 2022) and *Hellblade: Senua's Sacrifice* (Ninja Theory 2017) to mention just a few high-budget successes.

The list of video games that take inspiration from this particular period of northern European history is long, and the academic papers on them are equally so. The theme holds a certain appeal due to its raw, emotional, and violent aesthetics that somehow present a pure and sometimes "masculine" experience. Fewer, however, are instances of tabletop role-playing games featuring Viking histories and cultures. It is often relegated to supplement established systems and worlds. Some Viking-themed games, however, do stand out, such as *Sagas of the Icelanders* (Dalstål et al. 2013) and the Norwegian language game *Kvad* (Kristoffersen 2023) where the players will enact great ideas they sum up with a Norse poem (kvad) at the end. *Blood Feud* stands out among these with its very strong focus on a singular theme, and the mechanics to support this:

> [...] modern media depictions of Vikings are rife with bloodshed, power struggles, and wanton mayhem caused largely by toxic masculine attitudes. Because of this, the Viking world is a perfect microcosm for looking at and learning about toxic masculinity. It is simultaneously far enough in the past that no one alive has experienced it, yet familiar enough that we all have a clear image of it.
>
> *(Malmberg and Persson 2021, p. 4)*

Blood Feud is played as a freeform tabletop role-playing game that strongly emphasizes improvisation and social drama over combat and physical challenges. It shares DNA with both Nordic larp (Stenros 2014; Stenros and Montola 2010) in that it relies heavily on improvisational work and indie role-playing games originating from the Forge community (Bjørkelo Forthcoming; White 2020a) with its player-facing approach. Meaning that the mechanics are narrative tools provided for the players make use of in creating the game narrative. Where tabletop role-playing games traditionally involve a group of players performing the role of their individual player characters (PCs) in a world defined and narrated by a gamemaster who among other things narrate events, play the non-player characters (NPCs), and arbitrate rules with the help of dice or other mechanics, *Blood Feud* defies all these conventions in favor of improvisation and communal world building. Being GM-less means that the players all share responsibility for narrating the world, arbitrating rules and embodying NPCs.

The players begin the game by defining their characters and establishing the relationships between them, situating them in the localized context of the village. The PCs are all male, but they will also design female NPCs that have different familial relationships with the characters – they are not just passive witnesses to the action, but through being played by players whose characters are not involved gain some agency.

Throughout the game, the players take turns in "setting the scene" as in improv work. Each scene involves at least two male characters and one woman. The player setting the scene chooses one or more male characters to take part in the scene. The remaining players take control of any NPCs in the scene, including *at least* one woman character. Together they then play out the scene, which through the incentives provided by the character traits (such as what they want from other characters) and the honor pool tend toward tense social conflict. If at any point the woman leaves the scene, it ends, no matter how unsatisfying. The scene needs the woman as a witness and motivation for the men's behavior.

Through the myriad stories told through *Blood Feud*, it is possible to see how the mechanics tend toward showing how toxic masculinity harms other men, women, and the community. In addition, it is also possible to see that through this harmful behavior, they also hurt themselves.

TRAITS AND HONOR

The PCs have four or five positive and/or negative traits that define their masculinity. Whether they are married, have strong sons, beautiful daughters, own land, or battle scars, and so on, are considered positive traits and grant honor. Negative traits include having no sexual interest in women (possibly being gay), having a weak (feeble) child, fearing death, performing magic (a woman's task), or being in debt, and so on. The latter does not grant honor.

More honor is garnered when players decide who their characters look up to; or down on and what they want. Honor is represented by tokens or beads, and the game revolves around managing this resource, and the rules refer to it as the "honor economy" (Malmberg and Persson 2021, p. 32). Through this process they create their imaginary "Viking" world, no instructions are given to make this world authentic or according to history books, as the "Viking" context is only there to inspire a certain kind of storytelling and feel that resonates with the player's imagination of Viking masculinity. Players in *Blood Feud* are encouraged to dominate others' PCs and to "acquire" the most desirable women through trade or aggression creating a harmful circle.

PLAYER MOVES AND MECHANICS OF TOXICITY

The player character's actions are governed by a set of possible "moves," all of which affect the honor economy. The moves cover a wide range of social interaction, affect the different characters in the game differently, and are governed by the honor economy. Meaning that a move usually involves paying honor, metaphorically putting your honor at the stake, or, alternatively, a move involves *taking* honor from other PCs. These effects are also modified by who witnesses the moves. Moves include insulting or praising a man or woman in front of them or behind their back. Another move is having sex with a woman or man, and in the latter case, a man loses honor for being the "passive" partner (bottom), or gains honor for being the "active" partner (top). This illustrates the very toxic or problematic relationship masculinity has with homosexuality and affection between men – it becomes a power play, and a way of dominating the other.

The drama intensifies when someone chooses to escalate a social situation, by insulting another man, and who then reciprocates. This becomes a bidding war, where a pool of honor is built up until the point that one of the players runs out of honor or yields (either by choice or by not being creative enough to escalate the conflict further). It is at this point that the game becomes truly dangerous, as an honorless man has nothing to lose and may opt to kill his opponent. No dice rolls necessary, the statement of the intention to murder is all that is needed for this move, the only counter move being striking a simultaneous and equally fatal blow. The death of a player character often serves as the end of a hort game, or, in a longer game, it is the start of a generational blood feud, where the two families will start fighting each other over the pool of honor.

The core theme of *Blood Feud* is thus the competitive nature of honorbound masculinity, which makes it harmful or toxic. The mechanics incentivize dominating other PCs, and every social interaction becomes a power struggle with the women being witnesses, the prize, or even the instigators of the struggle if they so wish. They may also be the victims.

Through very simple mechanics, *Blood Feud* facilitates the socialized behavior we often consider toxic. That is, they "serve to foster domination, the devaluation of women, homophobia, and wanton violence" (Kupers 2005, p. 714), and are harmful to everyone in the community. Including the men themselves who in *Blood Feud* find themselves in a zero-sum bidding war over honor that more often than not leads to death. I refer to these social game mechanics as the mechanics of toxicity – the need to own women (literally) and other men (symbolically), to never lose face, and to dominate. The competitive nature of these mechanics is reflected in the masculinity suggested by toxic meritocracy (Paul 2018), where a competitive edge and one-upmanship are lauded as masculine and positive traits.

The game closes with a debrief session in which players' experiences with the game are explored collectively through conversations. The players are instructed by the rulebook, and often, someone taking on the role of a facilitator, to discuss their experiences. The players are asked questions about what happened, the level of discomfort they experienced, and if they can see any real-world parallels. This conversation invites the players to reflect on the mechanics of the game and on masculinity in and outside the game, as they have experienced and performed acts of imagined masculinity that they would not otherwise be privy to, or be able to reflect on through the frame of playing a role-playing game.

Blood Feud, thus, in the words of Stéphane Daniau, is a tabletop role-playing game that helps "participants realize that they can co-create a fictional world and adapt to it, and then to invite them to explore the meaning of their playful experience through their own personal journey" (Daniau 2016, p. 424). This reflection is of a transformative nature, allowing players to change their outlook, and even behaviors, based on game experiences and debrief. *Blood Feud* should therefore be considered a transformative role-playing game (Daniau 2016) that invites players to change and reorient themselves based on play experiences (Bowman and Hugaas 2021).

THE GAME SESSIONS

This chapter is based on notes and observations from four different occasions of playing *Blood Feud* outside of my own familiar gaming groups. They were not set up as formal research situations, but provided observational data through participating in play and the debriefs. In lieu of formal research interviews, I have my notes from observations and the debrief sessions from all four occasions. Two of these occasions were in an academic context, as it was played in a class on gender and technology. These included a large number of participants, wielding varied observations. The observations made in these sessions proved valuable and interesting, as I was allowed to see how the players reflected on their game experiences. As this was primarily designed as entertaining and educational projects, and not formal studies, I have not collected consent forms from participants, though they were all informed that this was part of my research. For these reasons, I refrain from directly quoting any participants, students or otherwise, and rely solely on my personal observations and notes to protect their anonymity. I am encouraged by this to perform more formal studies of *Blood Feud* and other games in educational settings.

The first occasion was a game at Regncon, a local gaming convention that has been organized since the early 1990s, and which focuses on tabletop games of all kinds. I have been a participant at this "con" since 1994 facilitating different role-playing games and chamber larps, and have also served as one of the organizers of the convention for several years. I took the opportunity to facilitate *Blood Feud* at Regncon soon after the game was published in 2021, and in this first game I participated alongside three teenagers. The second occasion was the same con in 2022, with a more mixed group, recruited by the teenagers from the year before who had recommended the game to others. At this occasion, I took a more backseat role and facilitated the game with as little intervention by myself as possible.

On both these occasions, the players were familiar with role-playing games, and some had special interest in smaller scale "chamber larps" (Bowman and Westborg 2024; Mochocka et al. 2018) which *Blood Feud* resembles. However, they did not have a strong sense of the cultural background of the themes at play in this game.

In 2023, the third occasion was the more formal one, as the culmination of class I had given on toxic masculinity. The students were given the rules to read through and reflect on beforehand. We set aside a six-hour day for the seminar, and I recruited two teaching assistants for the occasion. They, a boy and a girl, were both role-players but neither had experience with *Blood Feud*. The class was divided into six groups of four each.

The fourth occasion, in 2024, was another seminar. I had not been able to teach the students beforehand, but they had followed the class, as it was taught by someone else. This class consisted of 40 students, who were divided into ten groups of four. I recruited teaching assistants from the previous year to help me out, as well as third newcomers who were not familiar with the game, and the current teacher of the class who had no experience with role-playing games.

None of the students in the 2023 group reported any lengthy experience with tabletop role-playing games, but some had knowledge based on popular mediatized actual plays (Chalk 2023; Švelch 2022; Torner 2021). However, some of the students in the 2024 groups were familiar with tabletop role-playing games and even reported that the seminar was a motivating factor for signing up for the class. They were familiar with me from Regncon and previous courses I had taught at the university.

The teaching assistants and I explained the rules and mechanics of the game to the best of our abilities, creating a set of characters between ourselves and playing out different moves as a demonstration. In this, we attempted to show both the humorous situations that could arise and the seriousness of it, and how it relates to what we know about Viking society and masculinity, as well as contemporary expressions of masculinity.

The majority of the students were motivated and eager, and engaged with the game to the best of their ability, despite only a handful of them having role-playing experience from beforehand. Owing to the size of the class, the 2024 group took the longest time to get into the mechanics and started playing. When the students were divided into groups, they proceeded to play the game. Generating diverse stories, with different avenues of drama, shows the different ways in which the mechanics of toxicity influence characters' lives and communities. The assistants and I would wander from group to group to provide aid where the game had stalled and motivate the players who felt they were falling behind. Additionally, we would observe the play that took place.

OBSERVATIONS

While my main focus for the 2021 and 2022 con games was on whether or not the players were enjoying the game, I spent more time observing whether the lessons were understood through play. The different groups varied in their levels of outrageousness and transgressivity (Pötzsch 2019). For some, the games and mechanics lend themselves to a safe space, or "magic circle" (Consalvo 2009; Stenros 2012), where they were allowed to perform playful and aesthetic acts of transgression (Mortensen and Jørgensen 2020) within the framework of "play."

The two con games were dominated by fun and outrageousness in particular. The players in these games engaged with the game in a voluntary playful manner, as they were there to have fun by acting out. For some, it became a way of testing the boundaries of gender identity and sexuality, while others leaned heavily into emotional and relational drama. The groups that played at the con were more familiar with the concept of role-playing games than the student groups described in the section below, and less time needed to prepare them. Even preliminary discussions were had about masculinity, and this discussion brought up several elements that also appeared during play, and the debrief that followed the game sessions. As these were groups of primarily teenage girls, their responses to how masculinity worked mechanically resulted in both snickering and guffaws at the foolishness of it all, as well as recognition as they related it to experiences with particularly men of older generations. Some aspects of the mechanics such as the notion of being dominant or submissive in sexual relationships between men required more explanation – careful and thoughtful explanation – and served as an eye-opener for the competitiveness of masculinity (Paul 2018) and how this is expressed in a harmful manner. For some players it also highlighted the nonsensical way that homophobia would manifest. Similarly, the competitiveness in trying to impress the women character present in every scene, shone light on the how competitive masculinity was harmful to everyone in the community aspect, and in the second of the group ended with the women of the community turning the table on the men and having them all killed.

The student groups were influenced by the classroom context and would in general take a longer time to catch on to what was probably an unusual classroom assignment. This showed itself in how willing they were to indulge in role-*playing* and how they would to a varying degree explore and transgress boundaries. One of the groups was *very* sexually explicit, exploring sexual violence and domination to its very limits, while the other groups focused more on ownership or relationships with women in their imagined village. In general, the student groups warmed up the assignment, and I could see how the mechanics of *Blood Feud* incentivized social role-playing. This lends strength to the argument that games provide, if not a "magic circle," some kind of frame for performing acts and identities that elsewhere would not be allowed. This frame can be understood in a Goffmanian sense, meaning that it is the structure we use to make sense of social situations and interactions (Goffman 1974). Games and play are examples of such a structure or frame that not only allows, but also requires us to act in a certain way that to uphold the citation.

The frame provides what Sebastian Deterding refers to as an alibi for play (Deterding 2018). This frame or magic circle is porous (Bjørkelo 2022; Stenros 2012), allowing for an exchange between intraludic and extraludic values, knowledge, and experiences. Without this frame, the players would not feel safe to perform outrageous and fun acts, or to explore the drama in the free manner that they did. I observed that the students, in spite of being novices in improv and role-playing, almost without fail engaged enthusiastically in the plot-building and role-playing. Given that the majority of the students were unfamiliar with role-playing games, I believe it is safe to assume that both playing as a class assignment provided a framework for free play and engagement with the subject matter.

The playful frame being porous enough to allow for the exchange between the intraludic (inside of play) and extraludic (out of play) is what allows the play experiences to be useful as a tool for teaching and to be considered transformative (Daniau 2016). Bleed[1] is the term used for how play and players are influenced by their life outside of play, and vice versa; the life outside is influenced by play experiences (Bowman 2015; Hopeametsä 2008; Waern 2011; Montola 2010). That latter part of bleed is particularly interesting for teaching purposes, as play experiences become teachable moments and experiences. In particular, so-called positive—negative experiences are understood as particularly useful to induce bleed (Montola 2010). These are experiences that can be characterized as negative, transgressive, or even traumatic experiences in play that are experienced as positive or transformative outside of play. Markus Montola argues that players experience a double consciousness as "players both acknowledge and deny the nature of play" (Montola 2010, p. 2). This might rely on what Kristine Jørgensen has called out-of-play seriousness (Jørgensen 2014), where the playfulness of play is partnered with the seriousness in out-of-play reality and reflection. This is also reflected in the concept of transgressive realism, where negative experiences in play are considered more realistic because the feelings of discomfort are real (Bjørkelo 2019; Bjørkelo and Jørgensen 2018). Due to these effects, the players are able to recognize their real-life knowledge and experience within the play setting, and they are able to recognize their experiences from playing outside the game. Following this, games that are difficult or transgressive may be more conducive to educational situations, as bleed will be more common.

On all four occasions, the players would bring up how they recognized the mechanics of toxicity had been at play in their lives, as well as how the intraludic experiences changed their opinions and understanding of extraludic events. Indicating not only that their real-life experiences influenced their play, but also that their play experiences helped put real-life experiences into a perspective of harmful masculinity. In other words, that real life bled into their play, and their play experiences have value out of the play context.

The outrageous behavior, tinged by sexual violence and other transgressive acts that were observed in the game, is also important in this regard. They can be understood as "fun" and aesthetic transgressions (Mortensen and Jørgensen 2020), the play setting giving them a free pass to behave in ways that would otherwise not be allowed. The majority of players engaging in this kind of play were girls, and one had to ask why they played in this particular manner. Their gleeful embracing of the freedom to be "toxic" males, turning the common situation upside down and allowing *them* to be sexual predators and brutes, would otherwise be avoided. For once, perhaps, being allowed to mess around playfully without consequence in a way that has been argued is the freedom and privilege of predominantly white males (Trammell 2023).

This is the freedom of *role*-playing, but the nature of their engagement also speaks to their internalized understanding of the violent and brutish sexuality of toxic masculinity and the male seeking to dominate all others. I understand this as an expression of *their* experience or understanding of toxic masculinity bleeding into the game, allowing for a cathartic reenactment of it. This was an eye-opening experience, and it was regretfully not possible to follow up through interviews.

The rules of *Blood Feud* instruct the players to create and shape their own vision of "Viking" society and the males inhabiting it, while the mechanics incentivize them to act out in harmful and "toxic" manners. This behavior is still grounded in the world they have created together, and that is informed by their understanding of "Vikings" and masculinity. Their transgressive and outrageous play acting is an expression of their experiences and understanding of this "Viking" masculinity. It would appear that for some of them, the more violent and brutish, the more explicitly and transgressively sexual, and the more engaging and *realistic* the experience feels. Realism after all is a feeling of something being true, authentic, or real in accordance with one's own preconceived notions (Bjørkelo 2019; Pötzsch 2017). And this suggests that transgressive play acting, which usually induces discomfort and censure, becomes a form of transgressive realism – a realism carried by very real feelings of discomfort and transgression (Bjørkelo 2019; Bjørkelo and Jørgensen 2018).

TEACHING VALUES

Blood Feud is a game that incentivizes freeform improvisation and playfulness, encouraging a "fun" engagement with a world of their own creation. At the same time, the underlying themes are serious, and mechanics strongly enforce and strengthen these themes. Here, the educational and transformative potential of the *Blood Feud* rests. Plass, Homer, and Kinzer (2015) argued that while engagement with material and educational games and play is important, *playfulness* is a much greater factor in the learning process:

> Often the argument is made that the motivation provided by games is their most important feature with regard to their potential for learning, but we believe that it is at least as important that games are able to facilitate the kind of learning engagement—on a cognitive, affective, and sociocultural level—that promotes learning in ways other media cannot. In fact, it can be argued that much of the reasoning of using games for learning can be reduced to the playfulness of the learning process that games afford.
>
> *(Plass, Homer, and Kinzer 2015, p. 277)*

Through its freeform and creative nature, removing the authorial voice of the GM and history lessons, *Blood Feud* creates a playful experience that centers the players and their agency in the play experience.

The educational value of role-playing games has long been noted. Already in 1981, Gary Alan Fine wrote in one of the first academic works dealing with tabletop role-playing games that "while they are not for a didactic purpose, it is easy to see how they might be used in school systems to teach folklore and mythology, or cultural differences" (Fine 1981, p. 275). Based on my observations, I propose that *Blood Feud* is a game that *does*, or at least *can*, teach the mythology of masculinity and socialized gender roles through its mechanics.

Blood Feud is, however, not in itself a didactic or "educational game" or simulation, and along the lines of eduLarps and eduRPGs (Bowman and Westborg 2024; Bowman 2014), it sets the stage and has the necessary affordances to be a transformative role-playing game (Daniau 2016).

The key difference is that the main focus and motivator for the game is not *education* but transformative learning experiences, underpinned by bleed, negative—positive experiences, and out-of-play seriousness. The distinction is perhaps a weak one, allowing for considerable overlap. And the transformative aspect, in my experience, does not exclude educational outcomes if prepared in the right context.

It is possible to see how *Blood Feud*, under other circumstances, could also be played subversively, and undermine the themes and messages of the game. It does allow for a game to be *just* about strategic resource management, ignoring the themes of masculinity altogether. Creating the proper pedagogical backdrop and preparing the game in a classroom context were important. One thing is spending the time to explore the rules before play, taking into consideration that the majority of students had no previous experience with tabletop role-playing games, but for a game to have the necessary transformative or educational impact it is important to "prime" them for the situation (Bjørkelo 2017; Bjørkelo and Jørgensen 2018). In the case of the two classes taking part in the game, they did so as part of a course on gender and technology, and previous classes had discussed masculinity and problematized the notion of toxicity beforehand. The first of these groups of students had a class on toxicity by myself, and I had the opportunity to tailor the teaching to the game we were going to play in the following week. In order for a game to work as an educational tool, this kind of preparation and introduction to the concept in play seems necessary for its full effect. It also has the added effect of "priming" the students to think and react in a certain way based on the classroom work (Bjørkelo and Jørgensen 2018).

Just as important as preparation, though, is the debrief that the rulebook calls for explicitly. This allows the players to put the play experiences into their real-world, and theoretical in the case of the educational situation, context. It also allows to unpack any difficult experiences and emotions that may have turned up in the game, perhaps related to personal experiences with aggressive masculinity, although this should also be addressed before play, as well as through the safety tools made available to the players. Playing any game is not necessarily safe and comfortable, and transformative games even less so, and educators should take the necessary precautions with this in mind. Following current trends in tabletop role-playing games, *Blood Feud* includes tools to ensure the players' safety by excluding topics and allowing for opting out of certain narrative paths (Zabala, Zvelebilova, and To 2024; White 2020b). In order for *Blood Feud* and similar role-playing games to work in educational contexts, such precautions are necessary to ensure students' safety and ability to play freely.

Blood Feud intends to reproduce a feminist ideology and discourse that hopefully strengthens anti-toxic values. In my observations, the players became more aware of the harmful aspects ingrained in toxic masculinity and how it harms communities. This awareness is the first step in identifying and changing them. Therefore, *Blood Feud* can be a teaching tool for communicating positive values. In addition, toxicity and harm can be identified as a product of game mechanics, rather than the individual itself, in the same way that these same aspects of masculinity are products of culture and socialization and are not inherent to men or masculinity. The same identification of the mechanics of toxicity also allows for combating or negotiating toxicity in a positive and constructive manner. As one male player objected to the premise, one could just choose *not* to fall for the incentives of the honor economy and behave constructively. *Blood Feud* is therefore a transformative role-playing game that has great potential for teaching and re-learning masculinity, which deserves further study.

CONCLUSION

The mechanics of toxicity at play in *Blood Feud* are clever in their simplicity, incentivizing the PCs to act out in a harmful, gendered manner, causing damage to themselves, their fellow PCs, women, and the community. As it boils down to an honor economy, it suggests that toxic masculinity is about interchange of power and honor between men, within a social structure that incentivizes domination of others above all else – even personal growth or comfort.

Preliminary observations of three different occasions of play with several groups of players show that these themes of toxic masculinity emerge naturally in play using these systems. Allowing the players to act out outrageous, stereotypical, and almost farcical imaginations of masculinity in the Viking age simultaneously elucidates contemporary issues with how masculinity is socialized. This elucidation leads to awareness, the ability to see the root causes in culture, and the ability to afford avenues of change. To counteract the harmful aspects of how contemporary masculinity – or toxic masculinity – is socialized.

As such, *Blood Feud* is also considered a transformative role-playing game, as it does not necessarily teach or educate but encourages transformation through reflection and awareness. This opens up for further study and more structured observations and interviews of the players to be conducted in the future, which will provide a strong framework for further intentional transformative use of *Blood Feud* in educational settings. The game's strength as an educational element lies in its focus on theme, and how the mechanics support this theme without shying away from making an entertaining and engaging experience. Similarly designed games can be used to explore different themes and topics both in- and out-of-classroom settings to provide transformative and educational experiences.

NOTE

1 Originally coined by Emily Care Boss at Ropecon 2007.

REFERENCES

Bethesda Game Studios. 2011. 'The Elder Scrolls V: Skyrim'. PC Windows, Xbox 360, Xbox One, Xbox Series X/S, PS3, PS4, PS5, Nintendo Switch. The Elder Scrolls. Bethesda Softworks.

Bjørkelo, Kristian A. 2017. 'Refugees Welcome'. *Games and Transgressive Aesthetics* (blog). 27 October 2017. https://web.archive.org/web/20220128123050/https://gta.w.uib.no/2016/10/27/refugees-welcome/.

Bjørkelo, Kristian A. 2019. '"It Feels Real to Me": Transgressive Realism in This War of Mine'. In *Transgression in Games and Play*, edited by Kristine Jørgensen and Faltin Karlsen. Cambridge, Massachusetts: The MIT Press. https://doi.org/10.7551/mitpress/11550.003.0015.

Bjørkelo, Kristian A. 2022. 'Playing with Boundaries: Empirical Studies of Transgressions and Gaming Culture'. Doctoral thesis, Bergen, Norway: The University of Bergen. https://bora.uib.no/bora-xmlui/handle/11250/3026904.

Bjørkelo, Kristian A. Forthcoming. 'What Is Indie in Indie'. In *Essays on Indie Tabletop Roleplaying Games*, edited by Stephanie Hedge. McFarland.

Bjørkelo, Kristian A., and Kristine Jørgensen. 2018. 'The Asylum Seekers Larp: The Positive Discomfort of Transgressive Realism'. In *Proceedings of Nordic DiGRA 2018*, 12. Bergen, Norway.

Bowman, Sarah Lynne. 2014. 'Educational Live Action Role-Playing Games: A Secondary Literature Review'. In *The Wyrd Con Companion Book 2014*, edited by Sarah Lynne Bowman, 112–31. Los Angeles, CA: TheWyrd Con.

Bowman, Sarah Lynne. 2015. 'Bleed: The Spillover between Player and Character'. *Nordic Larp* (blog). 2 March 2015. https://nordiclarp.org/2015/03/02/bleed-the-spillover-between-player-and-character/.

Bowman, Sarah Lynne, and Kjell Hedgard Hugaas. 2021. 'Magic Is Real: How Role-Playing Can Transform Our Identities, Our Communities, and Our Lives'. In *Book of Magic: Vibrant Fragments of Larp Practices*, edited by Kari Djukastein, Marcus Irgens, Nadja Lipsyc, and Lars Kristian Løveng Sunde. Oslo: Knutepunkt. https://urn.kb.se/resolve?urn=urn:nbn:se:uu:diva-462545.

Bowman, Sarah Lynne, and Josefin Westborg. 2024. 'Cheat Sheet : What We Can Learn from Edu-Larp and Other(Non-TT) RPGs'. In System Matters Verlag. https://urn.kb.se/resolve?urn=urn:nbn:se:uu:diva-516611.

Chalk, Alex. 2023. 'Mapping an Online Production Network: The Field of "Actual Play" Media'. *Convergence* 29 (2): 449–466. https://doi.org/10.1177/13548565221103987.

Consalvo, Mia. 2009. 'There Is No Magic Circle'. *Games and Culture* 4 (4): 408–417. https://doi.org/10.1177/1555412009343575.

Dalstål, Elin, Sage LaTorra, Elena Melega, Jason Morningstar, and Gregor Vuga. 2013. *Sagas of the Icelanders*. Self-published.

Daniau, Stéphane. 2016. 'The Transformative Potential of Role-Playing Games: From Play Skills to Human Skills'. *Simulation & Gaming* 47 (4): 423–444. https://doi.org/10.1177/1046878116650765.

Deterding, Sebastian. 2018. 'Alibis for Adult Play: A Goffmanian Account of Escaping Embarrassment in Adult Play'. *Games and Culture* 13 (3): 260–279. https://doi.org/10.1177/1555412017721086.

Elliott, Kathleen. 2018. 'Challenging Toxic Masculinity in Schools and Society'. *On the Horizon* 26 (1): 17–22. https://doi.org/10.1108/OTH-11-2017-0088.

Fine, Gary Alan. 1981. 'Fantasy Games and Social Worlds: Simulation as Leisure'. *Simulation & Games* 12 (3): 251–279. https://doi.org/10.1177/104687818101200301.

Goffman, Erving. 1974. *Frame Analysis: An Essay on the Organization of Experience*. Cambridge, Massachusetts: Harvard University Press.

Harrington, Carol. 2021. 'What Is "Toxic Masculinity" and Why Does It Matter?' *Men and Masculinities* 24 (2): 345–352. https://doi.org/10.1177/1097184X20943254.

Hopeametsä, Heidi. 2008. '24 Hours in a Bomb Shelter'. In *Playground Worlds*, edited by Jaakko Stenros and Markus Montola. Helsinki: Ropecon.

Jørgensen, Kristine. 2014. 'Devil's Plaything: On the Boundary between Playful and Serious'. *DiGRA Nordic '14: Proceedings of the 2014 International DiGRA Nordic Conference* 11:11. Gotland, Sweden.

Kristoffersen, Karl Otto. 2023. *Kvad*. Oslo: Game Forlag.

Kupers, Terry A. 2005. 'Toxic Masculinity as a Barrier to Mental Health Treatment in Prison'. *Journal of Clinical Psychology* 61 (6): 713–724. https://doi.org/10.1002/jclp.20105.

Lasausse, Lysiane. 2024. 'Vikings and Gaming: Cultural Representations of the North in Video Games'. In *Viking Heritage and History in Europe*, edited by Nilsson, Sara Elisson and Nyzell, Stefan. Abingdon, Oxon: Routledge.

Malmberg, Alf Peter, and Amos Johan Persson. 2021. *Blood Feud*. Bläckfisk Forlag.

Mayer, Lauryn. 2019. 'Mythogyny: Popular Medievalism and Toxic Masculinity'. In *Studies in Medievalism XXVIII: Medievalism and Discrimination*, edited by Karl Fugelso, Aida Audeh, Angus J Kennedy, Carla A. Arnell, Christopher Caldiero, Helen Young, Jennifer FitzGerald, et al., 21–32. Boydell and Brewer. https://www.degruyterbrill.com/document/doi/10.1515/9781787444713-006/pdf?licenseType=restricted.

Mochocka, Aleksandra, Piotr Milewski, Michał Mochocki, and Bartosz Adamiak. 2018. 'Larp Typology'. DIGRA 2018. Torino.

Montola, Markus. 2010. 'The Positive Negative Experience in Extreme Role-Playing'. *DiGRA Nordic '10*, 8.

Mortensen, Torill Elvira, and Kristine Jørgensen. 2020. *The Paradox of Transgression in Games*. 1st edition. New York: Routledge.

Ninja Theory. 2017. 'Hellblade: Senua's Sacrifice'. Windows PC, Xbox One, Xbox Series X/S, Nintendo Swithch, PS4. Unreal Engine 4. Hellblade. Ninja Theory.

Paul, Christopher A. 2018. *The Toxic Meritocracy of Video Games: Why Gaming Culture Is the Worst*. 1st edition. Minneapolis: University of Minnesota Press.

Pearson, Elizabeth. 2019. 'Extremism and Toxic Masculinity: The Man Question Re-Posed'. *International Affairs* 95 (6): 1251–1270. https://doi.org/10.1093/ia/iiz177.

Plass, Jan L., Bruce D. Homer, and Charles K. Kinzer. 2015. 'Foundations of Game-Based Learning'. *Educational Psychologist* 50 (4): 258–283. https://doi.org/10.1080/00461520.2015.1122533.

Pötzsch, Holger. 2017. 'Selective Realism: Filtering Experiences of War and Violence in First- and Third-Person Shooters'. *Games and Culture* 12 (2): 156–178. https://doi.org/10.1177/1555412015587802.

Pötzsch, Holger. 2019. 'Forms and Practices of Transgressivity in Videogames: Aesthetics, Play, and Politics'. In *Transgression in Games and Play*, edited by Kristine Jørgensen and Faltin Karlsen. Cambridge, Massachusetts: The MIT Press. https://doi.org/10.7551/mitpress/11550.003.0006.

Prewitt, Ryan. 2021. 'Bronze Age Pervert, Narrative, and the Digital Fascist Project'. M.A., Missouri: Saint Louis University. https://www.proquest.com/docview/2558505310/abstract/CDD3F63FF353428CPQ/1.

Raffield, Ben. 2019. 'Playing Vikings: Militarism, Hegemonic Masculinities, and Childhood Enculturation in Viking Age Scandinavia'. *Current Anthropology* 60 (6): 813–835. https://doi.org/10.1086/706608.

Sandquist, Siri. 2012. 'Making of a Man - the Hegemonic Masculinity of the Viking Age'. Master Thesis, Glasgow: University of Glasgow. https://www.academia.edu/2427334/Making_of_a_Man_the_hegemonic_masculinity_of_the_Viking_age.

Santa Monica Studio. 2022. 'God of War Ragnarök'. PS4, PS5. God of War. Sony Interactive Entertainment.

Skogstrand, Lisbeth. 2016. *Warriors and Other Men: Notions of Masculinity from the Late Bronze Age to the Early Iron Age in Scandinavia*. Oxford: Archaeopress Publishing Ltd.

Stenros, Jaakko. 2012. 'In Defence of a Magic Circle: The Social and Mental Boundaries of Play'. *DiGRA Nordic '12: Proceedings of 2012 International DiGRA Nordic Conference* 10:19. Tampere.

Stenros, Jaakko. 2014. 'What Does 'Nordic Larp' Mean?' In J. Back (Ed.), *The Cutting Edge of Nordic Larp* (pp. 147–156). Gøteborg: Knutpunkt.

Stenros, Jaakko, and Markus Montola, eds. 2010. *Nordic Larp*. 1st print. Stockholm: Fea Livia.

Švelch, Jan. 2022. 'Mediatization of Tabletop Role-Playing: The Intertwined Cases of Critical Role and D&D Beyond'. *Convergence*, June. https://doi.org/10.1177/13548565221111680.

Torner, Evan. 2021. 'Actual Play Reports'. In *Watch Us Roll: Essays on Actual Play and Performance in Tabletop Role-Playing Games*, edited by Shelley Jones, 20. McFarland: Studies in Gaming.

Trammell, Aaron. 2023. *Repairing Play: A Black Phenomenology*. Cambridge, Massachusetts: The MIT Press. https://doi.org/10.7551/mitpress/14656.001.0001.

Ubisoft Montreal. 2020. 'Assassin's Creed: Valhalla'. Windows PC, Xbox One, Xbox Series X/S, PS4, PS5. Assassin's Creed. Ubisoft.

Vandiver, Josh. 2021. 'Metapolitics, Masculinity, and Technology in the Rise of "Bronze Age Pervert"'. In *Contemporary Far-Right Thinkers and the Future of Liberal Democracy,* edited by McAdams, A. James and Castrillo, Alejandro. London: Routledge, Taylor & Francis Group.

Waern, Annika. 2011. '"I'm in Love with Someone That Doesn't Exist!!" Bleed in the Context of a Computer Game'. *Journal of Gaming & Virtual Worlds* 3 (September): 239–257. https://doi.org/10.1386/jgvw.3.3.239_1.

Waling, Andrea. 2019. 'Problematising "Toxic" and "Healthy" Masculinity for Addressing Gender Inequalities'. *Australian Feminist Studies* 34 (101): 362–375. https://doi.org/10.1080/08164649.2019.1679021.

White, William J. 2020a. *Tabletop RPG Design in Theory and Practice at the Forge, 2001–2012: Designs and Discussions*. 1st ed. Cham, Switzerland: Palgrave Macmillan.

White, William J. 2020b. 'The Discourse of Player Safety in the Forge Diaspora, 2003–2013'. *RPG学研究* 1 (September): 35–47. https://doi.org/10.14989/jarps_1_35.

Zabala, Jailyn, Josie Zvelebilova, and Alexandra To. 2024. 'Queer TTRPGs' Visibility, Safety, and Allegory as Resistance'. In *Proceedings of the 19th International Conference on the Foundations of Digital Games*, 1–10. FDG '24. New York: Association for Computing Machinery. https://doi.org/10.1145/3649921.3650022.

Index

For Product Safety Concerns and Information please contact our EU representative GPSR@taylorandfrancis.com
Taylor & Francis Verlag GmbH, Kaufingerstraße 24, 80331 München, Germany

www.ingramcontent.com/pod-product-compliance
Ingram Content Group UK Ltd.
Pitfield, Milton Keynes, MK11 3LW, UK
UKHW022118190926
475702UK00013B/1514
* 9 7 8 1 0 4 1 0 7 6 1 4 8 *